ArtScroll Series®

Rabbi Nosson Scherman / Rabbi Meir Zlotowitz

General Editors

THE GIFT OF LIFE

WITH HEARTS

Published by

Mesorah Publications, ltd

ספר מתנת חיים

FULL OF LOVE

ON SAFEGUARDING THE MESORAH FROM GENERATION TO GENERATION

Based on a series of talks on chinuch by
RABBI MATTISYAHU SALOMON

ADAPTED FOR PRINT BY RABBI YAAKOV YOSEF REINMAN

FIRST EDITION
First Impression … February 2009
Second Impression … May 2009
Third Impression … July 2009

Published and Distributed by
MESORAH PUBLICATIONS, LTD.
4401 Second Avenue / Brooklyn, N.Y 11232

Distributed in Europe by
LEHMANNS
Unit E, Viking Business Park
Rolling Mill Road
Jarow, Tyne & Wear, NE32 3DP
England

Distributed in Australia and New Zealand
by **GOLDS WORLDS OF JUDAICA**
3-13 William Street
Balaclava, Melbourne 3183
Victoria, Australia

Distributed in Israel by
SIFRIATI / A. GITLER — BOOKS
6 Hayarkon Street
Bnei Brak 51127

Distributed in South Africa by
KOLLEL BOOKSHOP
Ivy Common
105 William Road
Norwood 2192, Johannesburg, South Africa

Typography by CompuScribe at ArtScroll Studios, Ltd.

Printed in the United States of America by Noble Book Press Corp.
Bound by Sefercraft, Quality Bookbinders, Ltd., Brooklyn N.Y. 11232

TABLE OF CONTENTS

Part 4: On Chinuch in Midos

Part 5: On Chinuch in Activities

Part 6: On Reaching for a Higher Chinuch

Appendices

FOREWORD

Over seven years have passed since the publication of *With Hearts Full of Faith* by Harav Mattisyahu Salomon *shlita*, Mashgiach of the Lakewood Yeshivah. It was a great honor for me to write the book based on his *schmuessen* and *derashos*. The book was enthusiastically received, and the Mashgiach and I discussed doing other books in the same format.

The Mashgiach is a prolific thinker and speaker, and he has amassed a voluminous body of his life's work, which exists in the form of hundreds of audio recordings, several volumes of *maamarim* in Lashon Kodesh and massive binders full of closely written notes. It is a treasure trove of insightful and inspiring material that can yield numerous books on a wide range of topics. However, the potential book the Mashgiach mentioned most often was a book on *chinuch*, on bringing up Jewish children in accordance with the guidelines of the Torah and passing on our hallowed *mesorah* intact from generation to generation.

The Mashgiach smiled when he spoke about the idea of the new book. He often expresses his disapproval of parenting books, so how could he justify writing his own? But the truth is that this new book, *With Hearts Full of Love*, is not really a parenting book in the conventional sense of the term. It is a book about the *mitzvah* of *chinuch* and all the obligations that it entails. And it is as much about how parents should be *mechanech* themselves as it is about how they should be *mechanech* their children.

The Yiddish word *shteig* is commonly used word in our circles to indicate growth or progress. The precise translation of the word, however, is "to climb." When a person *shteigs*, he climbs. Life is like a mountain, the Mashgiach said to me as we were reviewing the manuscript. A person spends all his years climbing up the mountainside trying to reach the highest levels of existence. Even those who are content to remain on the same level must still do some climbing, some upward striving, because if they stand still they stagnate and gravity pulls them down. Parents have to be aware that they are on the mountainside of life and that their children are tied to them with ropes of dependency. Wherever the parents are on the mountainside will determine where the children will be.

This book is based on a series of *vaadim* that the Mashgiach gave in his house to a small group of young *kollel* men in the Lakewood Yeshivah over a period of a year and a half. It is an intensely Torah-centered approach firmly founded on the teachings of Chazal and the classic *sefarim* of the Rishonim and Acharonim. It is augmented and enriched by the Mashgiach's own numerous discussions with *gedolei Yisrael* of the past fifty years and the advice he received from them regarding *chinuch* and the obligation to pass on the *mesorah* to the next generation in the best possible form.

The material came to me in hundreds of audio tracks arranged in chronological order of delivery. Some of the tracks featured prepared remarks, while numerous others featured question-and-answer sessions. The discussions were wide-ranging and not necessarily organized in any particular order. Some *vaadim* were inspired by written questions submitted to the Mashgiach. Others related to the particular time of the year during which they took place. Many themes came up again and again at various times without substantial differences or additions.

Putting this book together, therefore, was an exceedingly difficult task. I had to eliminate the duplications and organize the material into a series of chapters that followed a more formal pattern; some repetitions do remain, however, because the Mashgiach tends to revisit some of his favorite themes in different contexts. In addition, I had to write the book in a homogenous style that captures the voice the Mashgiach uses when he speaks in more intimate settings, rather than the one he uses when he delivers the soaring oratories for which he is so deservedly famous.

Finally, I had to adapt the material for a much broader audience than the small groups that attended the *vaadim* in his house. These *kollel* men had very ambitious spiritual goals and aspirations for themselves. They wanted very much to *shteig* to the greatest extent possible, and they wanted advice and direction on how to awaken in their children higher aspirations, a deep yearning to live on a higher level and even to become big *tzaddikim* and *gedolei Yisrael*.

The answers the Mashgiach gave were, therefore, not always the same as those he would have given most people who sought his advice. So I had to sift through the final manuscript carefully to ensure that it contained what the Mashgiach would want to say to a general readership. I also took some chapters that were directed more to this audience than to a general readership and grouped them together in the last part of the book, entitled "On Reaching for a Higher Chinuch." After I completed the manuscript, the

Mashgiach reviewed it in its entirety, and everything that appears in the book is there with his approval.

Nonetheless, it is possible that certain nuances particular to the original audience remain. Readers should, therefore, take into consideration the context in which these remarks were originally made and that just as there is no one-size-fits-all in the *chinuch* needs of children there is no one-size-fits-all in *chinuch* guidelines for different communities. Readers are advised to use this book as a general guide and to seek specific advice from their own *rabbanim* and *mechanchim*.

Writing this book was a real challenge, but it was also a great honor and privilege for me to perform this service for the Mashgiach with whom I have been learning *b'chavrusa* for ten years and with whom I enjoy a very close and warm relationship.

◄§ A Clash of Blessings

With the Mashgiach's permission, I would like to present some ideas from my *Sefer Abir Yosef al Hatorah* that are relevant to the subject of *chinuch* and to this book in particular.

In Parashas Chukas, as the Jewish people are emerging from the wilderness and seeking to enter the Land of Canaan, they arrive at the border of the land of Edom, the ancestral home of Eisav's descendants. The most direct route into Canaan is through the land of Edom, but they must first ask permission to pass. Moshe sends messengers to the king of Edom assuring him that the Jewish people do not pose a threat to him and promising that they will stay on the king's road until they pass completely through to Canaan.

The message begins with a reminder that it was the descendants of Yaakov rather than the descendants of Eisav who bore the cruel yoke of bondage in Egypt and that it would only be fair for the Edomites to show them some consideration by letting them pass through.

And then Moshe says (Bamidbar 20:16), "And we cried out to Hashem, and He heard our voices, and he sent a messenger to take us out of Egypt." Rashi adds, "And He heard our voices through the blessing we received from our ancestor, '*Hakol kol Yaakov*, the voice is the voice of Yaakov' (Bereishis 27:22), that we cry out and we are answered."

The king of Edom responds by mobilizing his forces, and he sends back a message (Bamidbar 20:18), "You shall not pass." Rashi elaborates, "You pride yourselves on the *kol*, the voice, that your ancestor bequeathed to you, as you say, 'And we cried out to Hashem, and He heard our voices,' but I come out against you with what my ancestor bequeathed to me (Bereishis 27:40), '*Al charbecha tichye*, you shall live by your sword.'"

So we see a clash of blessings in the wilderness on the border of Edom. The Jewish people come with the blessing of *hakol kol Yaakov*, the power of *tefilah*, and the Edomites come with the blessing of *al charbecha tichye*, the power of armed force.

The phrase *hakol kol Yaakov*, the voice is the voice of Yaakov, is one of the more readily recognized phrases in the Torah. The moment we hear these words, the setting in which they were spoken immediately comes to mind. Yitzchak is old and blind, and he wants to give a *berachah* to Eisav before he dies. He sends Eisav out into the fields to hunt for fresh game, which he will eat and then deliver the *berachah*. But Yaakov, following his mother's advice, disguises himself as the hairy-armed Eisav and comes for the *berachah* before Eisav returns from the field.

Being blind, Yitzchak does not see who has come into the room. Is it indeed Eisav or is it someone else masquerading as Eisav? Yitzchak is puzzled, and he says, "The voice is the voice of Yaakov, but the hands are the hands of Eisav." Finally, he inhales the scent of the garments Yaakov is wearing and is convinced that it is Eisav.

Is there anything in this story to suggest that *hakol kol Yaakov* was a blessing? If anything, it appears to be a bit of detective work. Who, Yitzchak wondered, can this person be? The voice is Yaakov's voice, which would seem to indicate that this person is not Eisav. But wait. The hands are Eisav's hands, which would seem to indicate that it is indeed Eisav. So who is this person after all, Eisav or Yaakov? Very puzzling. A mystery.

Where did Rashi see in these words, *hakol kol Yaakov*, that Yitzchak gave Yaakov the power of *tefilah*?

Perhaps these words were a blessing in an unconventional sense.

A young person may sometimes have certain qualities and tendencies that manifest themselves naturally. A person with an especially kind heart may find himself being helpful to other people very often, and he will do it as a matter of course. It is not part of his self-image. It is not how he identifies himself or views himself. He doesn't even give it much thought. It is just something he does naturally, almost reflexively.

And then one day, a parent or a *rebbe* or someone else says to this young person, "You know something, you are a real *baal chessed*." And from that moment on, a deep change occurs in him. His natural tendencies have crystallized into an identity. He is not just someone who does kind things when the occasion arises. He is a *baal chessed*, a person whose life rests on the pillar of *chessed*, who draws his identity and personality from the Ribono Shel Olam's *midah* of *chessed*, who suddenly has goals and ambitions of great accomplishments in the world of *chessed*. And so these few words have transformed a kind young person into a *baal chessed* simply by helping him form an identity and a self-image.

Or imagine a talented *bachur* in *yeshivah* who has a naturally creative mind. The *rebbe* asks questions in *shiur* and the *bachur* is consistently one of those who offer answers. He is just doing what comes naturally to him. And then one day, he gives a very insightful answer to one of the *rebbe's* questions, and the *rebbe* gives him a sharp look. The *rebbe* points at the *bachur* and says, "You are a *lamdan!*"

At that moment, the *bachur* is transformed from a good *yeshivah* boy into a young *lamdan*. He had always done well in *shiur* and on his tests just because it came naturally to him, but his eyes were suddenly opened. He has a new identity and self-image. He is a budding young *lamdan*, someone who will join the ranks of the *talmidei chachamim* of the ages. Suddenly, the Torah is at the very center of his life, and he is a different person. From that moment on, his learning is different, his *tefilah* is different, his outlook on life is utterly and profoundly different. And all because of a few words spoken by the *rebbe*. Maybe he knew the effect his words would have, maybe he didn't. It doesn't really matter. The *bachur* heard them, and they penetrated his heart and made him a different person.

It is true that Yitzchak said the words *hakol kol Yaakov* in an effort to identify the person standing in front of him. But what did he hear that sounded like Yaakov? It wasn't the timbre of the voice. Rashi says it was the way Yaakov spoke, with *tachnunim*, entreaties. That was Yaakov's natural manner of speaking. Conciliatory. Pleading. Ingratiating. He was not aggressive, not demanding. He pleaded with humility and self-effacement. This was what Yitzchak heard. Here stands a person who says "please" and "if you would be so kind" all the time. This is the voice of Yaakov.

These words transformed Yaakov. Until then, he had spoken in this manner because it came naturally to him, because he was a gentle, unassuming person, but now he realized that it was a voice, an identity. In his mind, it became crystallized that he was a pleader, a supplicant. It wasn't just something that he did. It was who he was. It was who he had become. And if a genuine supplicant of the highest order stands before the Ribono Shel Olam and *davens*, he has an excellent chance of his *tefilah* being answered.

In effect, then, when Yitzchak said that this was the voice of Yaakov, he empowered Yaakov to be successful in his *tefilah*. This power that Yaakov acquired through Yitzchak's words was the blessing that he bequeathed to his descendants for all generations.

⇜§ Certificates of Parenting

I truly believe that the Mashgiach's book will be a blessing to all its readers in the same way. The Mashgiach begins his first *vaad* on *chinuch* by asking a question. Why is there no requirement for couples about to get married to earn a certificate of parenting? Since bringing up children properly is such a difficult and complex task, why aren't all prospective parents required to take courses and be certified before they are allowed under the *chupah*?

The Mashgiach answers that all well-meaning Jewish men and women have within them the inborn skills needed to bring up children according to the requirements of the *mitzvah* of *chinuch*. There is no need to learn special techniques or strategies. The home is not a laboratory. All that is needed is a conscientious devotion to the Torah and to the future of the children and a few basic guidelines. The rest will come naturally.

It is only normal for new parents to be apprehensive about the enormous task that faces them, and the apprehension itself can be damaging to the *chinuch* of the children by sapping the confidence of the parents. The Mashgiach's book assures them that they have all the abilities they need to be successful parents. This assurance itself will help them see themselves as good parents and actually become good parents.

⇜§ The Four Sons of the Haggadah

I would like to express one more thought, also from *Abir Yosef al Hatorah*, that relates to this book.

There is a famous question that the commentators raise regarding an apparent contradiction between a *passuk* in the Torah and the Haggadah. The Torah says (Shemos 12:26-27), "And it will be when your children say to you, '*Mah ha'avodah hazos lachem? What is this service that you have?*' *Va'amartem zevach pesach hu Lashem*. And you shall say to them, 'It is a *pesach* sacrifice for Hashem ...' And the people bowed down and prostrated themselves."

In the Haggadah, we speak about the Four Sons, the wise son, the wicked son, the simple son and the speechless son. The wicked son is the one who asks, "*Mah ha'avodah hazos lachem?*" And the response is a harsh rebuke that bears no resemblance to the gentle answer prescribed in the Torah, "*Va'amartem zevach pesach hu Lashem*." Why, ask the commentators, does the Haggadah give an answer to the wicked son's question different from the one we find in the Torah?

A number of other questions can be raised regarding this *passuk*. When the Torah mentions the questions of the other three sons — the wise son (Devarim 6:20), the simple son (Shemos 13:14) and the speechless son (ibid.13:8) — it always speaks about *bincha*, your son, in the singular. Yet in the aforementioned *passuk*, which presents the wicked son's question, the Torah speaks about *bneichem*, your children, in the plural. How do we account for this difference?

The *passuk* concludes with the statement, "And the people bowed down and prostrated themselves." Rashi explains that they did so in gratitude for the good tidings they had just received — that they would be redeemed, that they would come to Eretz Yisrael and that they would have children. But why were these good tidings if the children they were promised would ask, "*Mah ha'avodah hazos lachem?*" What is so wonderful about having wicked children who ask wicked questions?

There is a *passuk* that states (Bereishis 8:21), "The inclination of a person's heart is evil from his youth." A person is born with a *yetzer hara*, and his natural inclination is not toward the good. It is the function of *chinuch*, therefore, to mold and educate children so that they will learn to recognize and follow the good rather than to follow their natural inclinations in the opposite direction.

That is what the Torah is saying, "And it will be when your children say to you, '*Mah ha'avodah hazos lachem?*'" All your children — *bneichem*, in the plural — will ask this wicked question in the beginning, because that is the question that comes naturally to all children. And that is all right. That is to be expected.

So what are you supposed to do when your children ask you this wicked question? How are you supposed to respond? The Torah tells you how to respond, "*Va'amartem zevach pesach hu Lashem.* And you shall say to them, 'It is a *pesach* sacrifice for Hashem.'" You have to be *mechanech* your children. You have to explain to them what you're doing. You have to give them an appreciation for the *mitzvah* and a love for it.

There is nothing improper or alarming when your children ask this wicked question at first. This does not mean that they are not fine children, and you certainly have to be grateful to the Ribono Shel Olam for them. But you have a responsibility to be *mechanech* them, to guide them in the right direction.

The Four Sons of the Haggadah only part ways after this *chinuch* of *va'amartem zevach pesach hu Lashem*. Once you've taught your children about the *mitzvah*, once you were *mechanech* them, the paths of the Four Sons diverge. The wicked son continues to ask his wicked question, and you have to respond to him with the harsh rebuke that is found in the Haggadah.

The idea that children cannot be expected to start out on a high level of observance is a recurring theme in the Mashgiach's book. He consistently advises parents to guide their children in the right direction with gentleness, patience and an abundance of love and not to press them to do more than they are inclined to do. The *va'amartem zevach pesach hu Lashem* does not always take five minutes. It is a work of years, and it starts from the very earliest age.

❦❦❦

A few final remarks. The ideas about *chinuch* presented here sometimes relate to both sons and daughters, and sometimes only to the one or the other. In the old conventions of the English language, the third person singular masculine pronoun could also be used as a generic pronoun. In more contemporary usage, however, "he or she" or "he/she" has become fashionable. In general, I've followed the old conventions, although from time to time I've used plurals, which circumvent the issue entirely. Sometimes, however, such as when the book speaks about the *mitzvah* of learning Torah, the word "he" does refer specifically to sons. The reader can easily differentiate between the specific "he" and the generic "he" based on the context of the material.

Unlike the Mashgiach's previous book, *With Hearts Full of Faith*, this book makes much greater use of transliterated Hebrew words. An extensive glossary has been provided for readers unfamiliar with any of the terms and phrases.

I would like to take this opportunity to offer my thanks to Rabbi Sadya Grama for providing me with the relevant audio recordings of the Mashgiach's talks and to Mrs. Miriam Hirsch for her expert transcription of difficult material that was delivered in a blend of English and Yiddish. I would also like to express my gratitude to Mrs. Judi Dick at Mesorah Publications for her expert reading of the manuscript and her numerous comments and suggestions. They were very helpful.

In closing, I would like to express my gratitude to the Ribono Shel Olam for giving me this opportunity to participate in a work of true *harbatzas Torah*, which will bring honor to His holy Name and everlasting benefit to His people.

Yaakov Yosef Reinman

Lakewood, New Jersey
Tu b'Shvat 5769 (2009)

PART ONE

On Being Good Parents

CHAPTER ONE

Tehillim and Tears

Every parent wants to know the key to success in *chinuch*. How do you mold a small baby, over a period of years, into a fine, decent and productive man or woman who will bring honor to the family, to Klal Yisrael and, above all, to the Ribono Shel Olam?

There is a famous saying by the Brisker Rav that the only way to do this with any reasonable expectation of success is with "Tehillim and *treren*," by making an investment of Tehillim and tears. We cannot expect to succeed in bringing up our children properly without the constant help of the Ribono Shel Olam. The key to success in *chinuch*, therefore, is *tefilah*.

It goes without saying, of course, that there is one underlying element upon which the success of the *chinuch* depends, and that is love. Tehillim and tears rest on a foundation of love. If parents treat their children with common sense and a pure love focused on the needs of the child, and if they *daven* constantly to the Ribono Shel Olam to give them the wisdom, patience and forbearance they need to bring up their children, they have an excellent chance of achieving the success they desire.

In our times, we have witnessed an avalanche of books on *chinuch*, and it seems to be an expanding industry. Bringing up children has come to be viewed as an esoteric science understood only by highly-trained experts who offer parents rules and formulas, based on their own perceptions, analyses and experiences, that must be studied, absorbed and followed meticulously. I suspect, however, that many of these books are themselves a cause of the widespread confusion among well-meaning parents seeking guidance in *chinuch*. I also contend that no rules or formulas can be applied to all children. The *passuk* states (Mishlei 22:6), "*Chanoch lanaar al pi darko.* Raise the child according to his way." Every child is different.

Now, I'm not saying there's nothing of value in these books. Some of them may have good suggestions. But you cannot put your faith in books that generalize and are based on trial and error. How do you know what will work for your particular child? How do you know what will work in the particular environment and circumstances of your home? These books will do more to confuse you than to help you.

So what should you do if you want to be successful in the *chinuch* of your children?

✿ A Certificate of Approval

I want to begin by asking a simple question.

If someone wants to become a *shochet*, there is a process to be followed. He has to go through a period of study and training. Then he has to receive a *kabalah*, a certificate of authorization, from an established *rav*, someone known to be an authority on matters of practical Halachah, or from a leading *shochet* with many years of experience and a reputation for high expertise. Before receiving this *kabalah*, the aspiring *shochet* must take a test to demonstrate a solid knowledge of the laws of *shechitah*. He must also show that he knows how to prepare a slaughtering knife and that he has the physical dexterity to slaughter an animal quickly and cleanly. If he does not receive a *kabalah*, he is not allowed to slaughter animals, because providing kosher meat for the community is a very serious responsibility.

Bringing up a Jewish child is certainly no less serious a responsibility. The entire future of Klal Yisrael depends on the proper molding of our young children. In our community, having children and raising families are a primary purpose of getting married. Every *chassan* and every *kallah* who stand under the *chupah* know and understand this and take upon themselves the responsibilities of *chinuch*. Nonetheless, when two young people marry, no serious consideration is given at that time to their potential capabilities as parents and molders of young children. I have never heard a *rav* standing under the *chupah* declare, "I refuse to officiate at this wedding unless I am shown a *kabalah* that attests to the competence of these two young people to serve as practitioners in the field of *chinuch*."

Why should this be? Why should a *shochet* need a *kabalah* but not a parent? True, providing kosher meat for Jewish people is extremely important. But raising Jewish children and ensuring the future of Klal Yisrael should be at least of equal importance. How can we entrust young people with the awesome responsibility of raising children and building the future generations of Klal Yisrael without special training and preparation? Shouldn't we be concerned that they might be like loose cannonballs that will wreak destruction and havoc?

Klal Yisrael has always paid meticulous attention to factors that can influence the welfare of our communities, and yet we find no record of training programs for prospective parents. How can this be? Why is there no *takanah* enacted by Chazal or some time-honored tradition that forbids a marriage unless the couple has been trained to raise children properly?

The answer to this question leads us to one of the most fundamental principles of *chinuch*.

It appears to me that every well-meaning father and mother who want to build a good Jewish home will find within themselves the knowledge and the skills to be *mechanech* their own children properly. I don't know if they would have the ability to offer advice to other people on matters of *chinuch*, but for their own children, the Ribono Shel Olam has instilled in each and every man and woman the inherent ability to bring them up properly. He has given all of us the skills and the wisdom and the talent to understand our own children and give them what they need. We do not need special training for this. We do not need certificates of authorization. We don't need special books or classes. The specific answers that apply to our own children are implanted in our own hearts and minds.

Now, it's not my intention here to dismiss the usefulness of experts in child psychology. Sometimes, problems arise with children despite our best efforts to avoid them. Many different factors can affect a child's state of mind. Children are inevitably exposed to experiences in school, with friends and all kinds of other situations, and coupled with their own psychological makeup, they may go off track to some degree. In those cases, it's a good idea to seek expert assistance according to the recommendation and guidance of a *rav* or *rosh yeshivah*. But when parents are starting out with a newborn child with no discernible problems, it can be safely assumed that they will know what to do and how to do it for their own children.

Moreover, specific outside advice, in the form of books or courses, which is not tailored to their children may do more harm than good. It can confuse and bewilder parents and lead them to disregard their own natural instincts and talents and try to bring up their own children according to the advice of people who do not know them and their situations.

Readers should be forewarned that this book as well is only meant to be used for general guidelines and that they should seek specific guidance from their own *rabbanim* and mentors.

◈§ Well-meaning Parents

As I said before, all well-meaning parents are endowed with the natural ability to bring up their own children properly. But how do we define well-meaning parents? We certainly cannot say that all people, regardless of their behavior and attitudes, are equipped to bring up Jewish children and build the future of Klal Yisrael. There must be a baseline, certain qualifications without which we cannot assume that a person is capable of bringing up a Jewish child in the proper manner. What are these qualifications?

The first qualification, it would seem to me, is that the father and mother have a firm grounding in Torah values and are engaged in the continuous process of being *mechanech* themselves. Well-meaning parents are those that work hard at improving and perfecting themselves, at controlling and overcoming their character flaws and developing their better qualities. They face the challenges life presents to them with a resolve to succeed in the best possible way.

Who is the well-meaning parent who has the natural ability to bring up a child? Someone who takes responsibility for himself and works on his own growth. This is the kind of person in whom the Ribono Shel Olam implants the wisdom and skills to bring up a child as well. If he is sincere and dedicated to his own growth and his thoughts and aspirations are pointed in that direction, then he can also be entrusted with the responsibility of guiding the growth of a child.

The most important qualification of a parent is *ehrlichkeit,* approaching all aspects of life with honesty and integrity and the will to do the right thing. Such a person can reasonably aspire to *siyata dishmaya,* the help of the Ribono Shel Olam, at every step of his life in all the issues that confront him. And if he approaches his responsibilities in bringing up his children in the same *ehrliche* way, we can assume that the Ribono Shel Olam has given him the skills he will need in order to be successful.

If so, there is no need for certificates, and tests and examinations will do no good, because if he is an *ehrliche* person with the right outlook on life, he will undoubtedly have the ability and insight he will need to bring up his own children properly. But if he approaches his responsibilities with the wrong outlook and bad *midos,* certificates and examinations won't help. Some parents look to the upbringing of their children as another avenue of competition with their friends, neighbors and family. They want to show off their cleverness and child-rearing skills. They want to show that they can mold their children into intelligent and accomplished youngsters, that they can steer them to the point where they become the best in the class. If parents look to their children as a source of reflected glory and pride, their *chinuch* will not be successful, and all the certificates and high scores on parenting tests will not make any difference at all. They will derail the development of their children, and then they will have to seek the assistance of outside experts to help get them back on track.

All well-meaning, *ehrliche* people, however, have the innate ability to bring up their children successfully, even simple, unlearned people. As long as a parent tries to bring up his children in a way that fulfills the will of the Ribono Shel Olam, he will not need outside assistance. As long as his motives and intentions are pure, he will be able to tap into his own reservoir of skills and talents. But if his intentions are otherwise, he is headed for trouble no matter how many parenting books he reads and classes he attends.

This is the deeper meaning of the Brisker Rav's statement that the key to *chinuch* is "Tehillim and tears." Only by putting your primary focus on doing the right thing according to the will of the Ribono Shel Olam can you hope to be successful in *chinuch*.

✥ An Investment of Serious *Tefilah*

The Mishnah Berurah writes (47:10), "The *tefilos* of the father and the mother should always be fluent in their mouths, *davening* that their children should learn Torah, that they should be *tzaddikim* and have good *midos*. They should concentrate particularly during the *berachah* of 'Ahavah Rabbah' and in Birchas Hatorah when they say, 'May we and our descendants learn Torah,' and also during 'Uva Letzion' when they say, 'In order that we should not toil in vain nor give birth to confusion.'"

Parents have to become accustomed to *davening* for good children until these *tefilos* stream from their mouths with great fluency; Chazal inserted these pleas in different parts of the *tefilos* so that we come back to them again and again.

This is at the heart of success in *chinuch*. *Tefilah*! A faithful Jew knows that everything is in the hands of the Ribono Shel Olam. A faithful Jew rejects the idea of *kochi ve'otzem yadi*, that his own power and strength alone can bring the desired results. If you think your wisdom and cleverness will guarantee you success in raising your children, you are as guilty of *kochi ve'otzem yadi* as if you thought that making millions in business is entirely within your own grasp. But if you understand that there is no *kochi ve'otzem yadi* here, if you understand that you have to *daven* for the success of your children — "always," as the Mishnah Berurah writes — then you have a chance to be a successful parent. If you approach your *tefilos* with the proper gravity and appreciation of their critical importance, then you have a reasonable expectation of bringing up fine and worthy children. All the parenting techniques cannot compare to a single heartfelt *tefilah*.

It is like everything else in life. We have to make a normal *hishtadlus*, a normal effort toward achieving our goals, but we have to realize that the actual achievement of those goals is entirely in the hands of the Ribono Shel Olam. Without *tefilah* it will not work, and the more intense and sincere the *tefilah* the better your prospects for success will be.

The Chazon Ish writes that it is well understood that our efforts in business are no more than *hishtadlus* and that we do not deserve any credit for our success. It is the same in spiritual matters as well. Whatever we may accomplish is all from the Ribono Shel Olam, and what we do is no more than *hishtadlus*. When we make the effort and demonstrate that this is what we want, the Ribono Shel Olam has mercy on us and makes it happen. In effect, our *hishtadlus* is like a *tefilah*. That is how it works. It follows, therefore, that if *hishtadlus* is effective because it resembles *tefilah*, actual explicit *tefilah* should be even more effective.

That's how it is in *chinuch* as well. If parents are successful, it's not because they were so wise and so clever. It's because the Ribono Shel Olam gave them the gift of success. And if they fail, it's not because they didn't read enough books or attend enough classes. It's because the Ribono Shel Olam withheld from them the gift of success. If you want success, you have to ask for it. That is the most effective thing you can do. You have to *daven* with all your heart. Then the Ribono Shel Olam will send you success along many different avenues. He may arrange the circumstances of your child's life to be influential in a very positive way. He may lead you to the right methods and strategies that are perfectly suited to your child. There is no limit to the number of ways He can send you success, as long as you do the right *hishtadlus* and, even more important, as long as you *daven* for it.

Listen to the words of the Mishnah Berurah's *tefilah*, and you will understand the kind of feelings that need to be invested into our aspirations for our children. As the Mishnah Berurah writes, we have to *daven* that our children will learn Torah, that they will be *tzaddikim* and that they will have good *midos*. And one of these *tefilos* is "in order that we should not toil in vain nor give birth to confusion." We have to feel that if our children do not reach those basic levels of achievement — if they do not learn Torah, if they are not *tzaddikim*, if they do not have good *midos* — then we will have toiled in vain and given birth to confusion. If we do feel this way and we beg the Ribono Shel Olam not to allow our lives to go to waste by giving us anything less, then we have an excellent chance of succeeding in bringing up our children properly. The Ribono Shel Olam will give us the skills and the insight we will need, and most likely, we will not encounter any significant problems.

This is what the Brisker Rav meant by Tehillim and tears.

✑ You Have To Be Specific

In the collected letters of the Chazon Ish, there is a brief *tefilah* that he once gave to a mother to say for her children in the *berachah* of Shema Koleinu; it appears in some Siddurim as a mother's *tefilah* for her child. It reads as follows, "*Yehi ratzon milefanecha Hashem Elokeinu v'Elokei avoseinu sheterachem al bni vetahapoch es levavo l'ahavah ul'yirah es shemecha v'lishkod besorashech hakedoshah.* May it be Your will, Hashem our Lord, the Lord of our fathers, that You have mercy on my child (the name of the child and the mother's name should be mentioned here) and persuade his heart to love and fear Your Name and to work diligently in Your holy Torah."

This is how the *tefilah* begins, and then it gets specific. This is the part which is, I believe, very instructive. He writes, "*Vetasir milefanav kol hasibos hamon'os oso mishkidas torasecha hakedoshah vetachin es kol hasibos hameivios lesorasecha hakedoshah ...* And You should remove from before him all factors that prevent him from diligence in Your holy Torah and You should prepare for him all factors that lead to Your holy Torah ...."

It seems that the focus of the *tefilah* is on protecting the child from bad influences. It is not enough to *daven* that the child should become a *talmid chacham* and a *tzaddik*. We have to be more specific, and the main thing we need to ask for is that the child be sheltered and safe. In our own times, we can understand this perfectly well. So much can happen on the way to and from the *yeshivah*. Whom will he see? With whom will he have a conversation? What kind of graffiti will he see painted on the walls? So much can happen that can have a negative effect on a child.

We don't really know the story behind the letter that the Chazon Ish wrote to that particular mother. Perhaps she was a widow whose child was running wild. Perhaps that was why the Chazon Ish put the focus on this matter. Perhaps it does not apply to every child in every situation. But this much I do know. We see from the words of the Chazon Ish that it is important to be specific. And it is the responsibility of parents to be specific in their *tefilah* in those areas that are most applicable to their own children.

That is where the expertise in *chinuch* comes into play. The parents have to identify what the child needs and from what he needs to be protected and *daven* for it. They should recognize and understand what the child needs, even though they may not know exactly how to give the child what he needs. For that they will need a great deal of *siyata dishmaya*.

There is a clever saying from Rav Chaim Shmulevitz. He asked a question. What is the meaning of the expression a *dor yasom*, an orphaned generation? In what way is our generation compared to a *yasom*? Some would say it means there is no one to worry about our needs just as there is no one to worry about the needs of a *yasom*. But in our times especially, this is not true. There are plenty of people who worry about a *yasom*. There are many organizations and individuals dedicated to providing the *yasom* with all his needs so that he lacks for nothing.

No, says Rav Chaim Shmulevitz, a *yasom* is not someone about whom no one worries. A *yasom* is someone whose worries no one knows. Of course, there are people who are ready to come forward to provide for a *yasom*. They will give the *yasom* clothing and food and whatever other basic needs he requires. But who knows what goes on in his mind and heart? Who knows the exact nature of his emotional needs? Who can really know a child other than his father and mother? And if he has no parents, there is no one else who really knows the worries that occupy his mind. There are plenty of people who are ready to help him, but if they do not know what he needs, they may actually be hurting him more than they're helping him. Our generation, he concludes, is compared to a *dor yasom* in the sense that there are too few leaders who are fully attuned to the worries and concerns of the people they're leading.

This is where the responsibility of the parent lies. We cannot expect parents to know what to do in every situation, but we can expect parents to be attentive to their children and to know their worries and their needs. After that, all depends on *tefilah* and *siyata dishmaya*.

And it is not enough to say to the Ribono Shel Olam, "Please make my child great." It is as if someone were to plant a field and *daven* that the plants grow tall. But what good does it do for the plants to grow tall if they're not protected from the insects and weeds that can choke the life out of them? What's the good of being large and tall, if there is no protection?

So when we begin our *tefilah* by asking the Ribono Shel Olam that our children should "love and fear Your Name and to work diligently in Your holy Torah," we are actually asking Him to make our children into big people. But that is not enough. We have to know the vulnerabilities of our children and we have to speak about these in our *tefilah*, as the Chazon Ish's *tefilah* concludes, "And You should remove from before him all factors that prevent him from diligence in Your holy Torah and You should prepare for him all factors that lead to Your holy Torah."

The parents have to beseech the Ribono Shel Olam that the child should not be exposed to bad influences or fall into bad company, and they also have to ask for the positive, that he should have the patience to study the Torah diligently. We have to be specific.

This is the first and most crucial and fundamental factor in *chinuch*. Of course, there is also a place for ideas and strategies. But it all begins with *tefilah*, a sincere and heartfelt *tefilah*.

A Feeling of Responsibility

Actually, in the broader perspective, the obligation to focus on *tefilah* applies not only to parents seeking to be successful in *chinuch* but to any person who bears a responsibility on his shoulders. The first thing he must do is turn to *tefilah*.

The Torah tells us (Bamidbar 35:25) that the *rotzeiach beshogeg*, inadvertent murderer, must remain confined to an Ir Miklat, a City of Refuge, until the Kohein Gadol passes away. What is the connection between the two? Rashi explains that the Kohein Gadol bears some of the responsibility for the actions of the murderer, because he should have *davened* that such a calamity should not happen during his lifetime.

It is not enough for the Kohein Gadol to *daven* that the Ribono Shel Olam should find his *avodah* in the Beis Hamikdash pleasing. The Kohein Gadol is responsible for the spiritual standards of the people, and it is incumbent on him to *daven* for all their needs. One of these needs is that people should not do *aveiros*. Therefore, if someone kills inadvertently through negligence, part of the responsibility devolves on the Kohein Gadol who should have *davened* that these things should not happen. If he was not specific in his *tefilah* on behalf of the people, if he did not feel the responsibility for the specific needs of the people, then he bears part of the guilt.

Parents also bear a responsibility to *daven* for their children that they develop properly and that they be protected from negative influences. Being successful in *chinuch* is not a matter of choice.

It is not optional. And it all begins with *tefilah*. Parents cannot excuse their failures in *chinuch* by saying, "We tried this and we tried that, and we spent so much money." What is the difference how much money they spent if they didn't *daven* for their children? How much Tehillim did they say and how many tears did they shed for their children? That is the pertinent question. It is the responsibility of parents to *daven*, and if they don't do so properly, they are being negligent.

❧ A Living Part of *Chinuch*

It is also worthwhile that children should know that their parents are *davening* for them, that whenever an issue arises the first thing their parents do is take out the Tehillim and pour out their hearts and their tears to the Ribono Shel Olam and beg Him for guidance. This itself is excellent *chinuch*, because it makes a tremendous impression on the children. If a child misbehaves and he sees his mother respond by taking out her Tehillim, he will think twice about what he has done. The very idea of *tefilah* must become an active, living part of *chinuch*.

I once heard a story about the Siddur of the Chafetz Chaim's mother. The Chafetz Chaim lost his mother when he was a young child. Many years later, someone brought the Chafetz Chaim the Siddur from which his mother had *davened*. The Chafetz Chaim took the Siddur in his trembling hands and kissed it and shed tears over it. "Can you imagine how many *tefilos* my mother *davened* and how many tears she shed," he remarked, "so that her young Yisrael Meir should grow ...."

The mother's Siddur, that is the key to *chinuch*, that is the fundamental component of the entire field of parenting. As we go on, we'll discuss many ideas and how to deal with specific situations. But it all begins with *tefilah*. In that sense, this first chapter is much more than an opening statement. It is the foundation of *chinuch*. Everything that follows, although important and illuminating, is only incidental to the centrality of *tefilah* in *chinuch*. It all begins with Tehillim and tears.

CHAPTER TWO

Love Comes First

Once we've spoken about *tefilah* as the foundation of *chinuch* as well as all other endeavors in life, we can turn our attention to the practical aspects of bringing up children. There are numerous points that are significant, and it would be difficult to establish a precise hierarchy of what follows what in importance. But it appears to me that the second critical element in *chinuch* immediately after *tefilah* is love. In fact, in a certain sense, it can be considered the first, because it is our love for our children that inspires us to *daven* for them.

In the development of our relationship with the Ribono Shel Olam, we know that *yirah*, fear, comes before *ahavah*, love. First, we must train ourselves to have the proper fear of the Ribono Shel Olam, to stand in awe of His great majesty, and only then can we progress to the level of loving Him. That is because to stand in awe of Him is much more attainable for most people, while loving Him requires a higher degree of sophistication.

In *chinuch*, however, it is important to know that the reverse holds true. Before we can train our children to fear their parents, they must feel our undying and unconditional love. If the main thrust of our *chinuch* is through fear and intimidation, there is the danger that, Heaven forbid, the child will be broken. Such an approach will only promote distortions in the child's personality and character. It is doomed to failure.

One of the great principles in life our Sages have taught us appears in the Gemara (Gittin 6b), "A person should never introduce excessive intimidation into his home. We find that the husband of the concubine of Givah was excessively intimidating to her, and as a result, tens of thousand of Jews fell in battle." Intimidation is a poor basis for a healthy relationship. It can only lead to disaster in one form or another. The Gemara speaks with regard to the relationship between husband and wife, but the phrase "into his home" clearly encompasses all familial relationships.

Excessive intimidation will only condition a child to inappropriate behavior. It will bring out the worst in him. When a child lives in fear of his parents, when he feels unsafe, insecure and constantly on the defensive, when his main concern is to protect himself from punishment, he will lie, he will steal, he will be *mechalel Shabbos*. He will do anything and everything he needs to do in order to protect his safety. Instead of producing a fine Jewish child, *chinuch* by intimidation will produce the exact opposite. And in the worst-case scenario, intimidation can cause serious psychological damage to the child. This is not *chinuch*. It is child abuse.

It is true that the Torah demands that everyone (Vayikra 19:3) "fear his mother and father." But that only applies when the child is already secure in the knowledge that his parents love him. If the child does not have that sense of security, there is no point in training him to fear the parents. On the contrary, such training is likely to damage or even break him. And besides, the fear we must have for our parents does not mean that we should be afraid they will hurt us but rather that we should respect them and stand in awe of them.

Everything starts with love. The parents must first show the child that they have boundless love for him. Of course, they must insist that the child behave with proper respect, but the focus of their upbringing should be through love. Only later can they begin to guide the child toward the fear of parents that the *mitzvah* of the Torah demands.

✌§ If You Knew How Much I Love You

Many years ago, when I was learning in the *yeshivah* in Kfar Chassidim under Rav Eliahu Lopian *zatzal*, I was privileged to witness an incredible story that left a lasting impression on me.

In those days, the *yeshivah* was housed in a small, simple, wooden structure. The *beis midrash*, which barely had room for about sixty or seventy *bachurim*, was used for *shiurim* and for the *tefilos*. Behind the *beis midrash*, there was a library and a room for *vaadim*, which were reached through the *beis midrash*. The door leading into the *beis midrash* provided the only access to the entire building. It opened onto a veranda that ran across the front of the building.

Every once in a while, Rav Elya, who was already over ninety years of age, would go on a campaign to get the *bachurim* to come to Shacharis on time. Wearing his *tallis* and *tefillin*, he would walk through the dormitory saying Ashrei out loud. If he noticed a *bachur* still sleeping in his bed, he would take his *tzitzis* and tickle the *bachur's* ear until the *bachur* awoke.

By the time he got back to the *beis midrash*, they were usually up to Vayevarech David. Rav Elya would take up a position near the door, the only means of entry into the *beis midrash*, and he would take note of the *bachurim* who came late. He didn't say anything to the latecomers, but they knew that their lateness had been noticed. Rather than bring their lateness to Rav Elya's attention, the *bachurim* made extra efforts to be on time. That was the plan.

One clever *bachur* decided to beat the system. Although he woke up late, he was determined to get into the *beis midrash* without Rav Elya becoming aware of his late arrival. Since there was only one door and since Rav Elya was standing directly inside the door, this *bachur* climbed through a window into one of the rooms behind the *beis midrash*, walked into the *beis midrash* and went to his seat.

Toward the end of Shacharis, Rav Elya looked around the *beis midrash* and noticed that the *bachur* had suddenly appeared in his seat.

After Shacharis, he went over to the *bachur* and asked, "When did you come to the *beis midrash*?"

"Before Ashrei," the *bachur* replied deceptively, referring to the second Ashrei rather than the first.

Rav Elya became very angry. "How did you get in?" he wanted to know. "I've been standing by the door, and I didn't see you come in. How did you get in? Tell me!"

"I came in through the window," the *bachur* confessed.

Rav Elya began to seethe. I saw it myself. His face became red, and his hands trembled. I was frightened for him; an old man so upset, who knew what could happen?

"Through the window!" he cried out. "That's trickery. It is crooked. If you do such things, you will become a crooked person." He took a deep breath. "I want you to know ... if you only knew how much I loved you, I would give you a slap right here and now."

And that's the end of the story.

Rav Elya's last words stunned me. I felt as if I had discovered a diamond, a gift of wisdom that I would treasure my whole life through.

What an incredible rule! You can only slap a child if the child knows how much you love him. Otherwise, what's the point of striking him? Will he become better because you slapped him? Will he feel anything other than resentment? But if he knows how much you love him, and he understands that despite this vast love you still felt that you had to give him a slap or discipline him in some other way, it will lead him to stop and think. He will realize how deeply he had upset you and how wrong his actions had been. It will enter his thoughts and his heart, and he will have learned an important lesson. The slap itself will become an expression of love if the child knows how much love there is behind it.

But if he is not secure in the love of his parents, intimidating and disciplining him will not accomplish anything. The fear of immediate consequences may stop him for the moment, but no *chinuch* value will result from it, only damage. It is even possible that the parent has so antagonized the child that he has become the enemy of his parent.

And who can blame him? All he knows is that his parents are persecuting him and forcing him to do things he doesn't want to do. Let us even concede that the parents are acting out of their perception that this is what their *yiras shamayim*, their fear of Heaven, demands of them. But the child knows nothing about this. All he knows is that he is a *nirdaf*, that he is being persecuted by his parents.

The Torah tells us (Devarim 8:5), "And you will know in your heart that just as a man disciplines his son so does the Lord discipline you." What does this mean? It certainly doesn't mean the way some fathers discipline their children, with anger, negativity, vengefulness. We would be in deep trouble if that's what it meant.

No, the Ribono Shel Olam disciplines us as a loving father disciplines his child.

A father who loves his child and treats him with love would never dream of doing something painful to the child if there was an alternative. If there is no alternative, and the father must punish the child, it literally hurts him more than it hurts the child, because he loves the child so much. And the child knows how much his father loves him. He feels it. If he knows that nothing will make the father happier than the success of his child, then he will be receptive to the discipline of the parents, even if it sometimes comes with a loud rebuke or even a rare slap. He will not resent it if it is given in a spirit of love. On the contrary, he will take it seriously.

These are the conditions under which a father has the right to discipline his child, because it causes only good and no harm. The discipline has to be entirely an act of love with no other emotions involved, no resentment, no anger, no vengeance. This is how the Ribono Shel Olam disciplines us, and this is how we should discipline our children.

I'm not sure that the analogy holds up in our high stress times when so many parents have lost sight of the critical importance of showing love to their children and treating them with understanding and patience. The analogy rather refers to parents of an earlier, calmer time, when parents showed more love to their children than they do today.

A loving atmosphere in the house is the best catalyst for *chinuch*. The parents have to show their love for their children by their deeds and also by expressing their feelings in no uncertain terms. The parents cannot rely on the child to infer that they love him from their actions toward him. They have to tell him that they love him and show that they mean it by the way they behave toward him.

✒ A Mother's Love

While we're on the subject of the balance between fear and love, I'd like to digress a little and discuss the role of the mother in this context. The father and the mother are partners in the enterprise of bringing up their children, but we have to define their roles.

As we mentioned before, the Torah tells us that everyone must fear "his mother and his father." When it comes to honoring parents, the Torah mentions the father first, but when it comes to fearing them, the Torah mentions the mother first. Why is this so?

Rashi explains that a person is more likely to fear his father than his mother. Therefore, the Torah has to impress on us that we have to have an equal measure of fear for our mothers as we have for our fathers. We can derive an important principle from this *mitzvah*. Apparently, that is the natural state of affairs in a normal home. The father is the disciplinarian, and the mother is the safe haven, the Ir Miklat, so to speak.

These days, however, the roles are often reversed. Many mothers are schoolteachers, and after they finish their school day, they make their homes extensions of the classroom. They are the strict ones. They are the ones who discipline the children, while the fathers often don't know how to deal with it. This is a recipe for trouble. Children need a loving, nurturing mother to be their place of refuge. They need to hold onto their mother's apron strings when their father has disciplined them. But when the mother is also a disciplinarian, to whom can the children turn for solace?

Another part of the problem in our times is that many women are well-educated and view themselves as intellectuals, which they may very well be. The problem, however, is that some of them feel that it is beneath them to be sentimental, emotional and warm. They feel they must approach issues and situations with cool and precise logic. They don't realize that by doing so they're depriving their young children of what they need most from their mothers, a warm embrace, a kind word, the safety of unquestioning love.

Rav Shmuel Rozovsky speaks about the two Jewish midwives who rescued numerous Jewish infant boys from the death decree in Egypt. One of them was named Shifrah, and the other was named Puah.

Who were these women?

Chazal tell us that Shifrah was actually Yocheved, the mother of Moshe, and Puah was actually Miriam, his sister. Yocheved was called Shifrah, because she was *meshaperes es havlad*; she cleaned, beautified and swaddled the infant after birth. Miriam was called Puah, because she was *po'ah umedaberes vehogah lavlad*; she cooed, murmured and whispered comfortingly to the newborn infant.

These two women had the gift of *nevuah*; they were prophetesses. In order to attain prophecy, a person has to be on the highest intellectual and spiritual level. He has to possess great wisdom and wide knowledge, and he must never entertain any thoughts about insignificant matters. So it follows that Yocheved and Miriam were among the intellectual elite of the Jewish people. Furthermore, they must have had very strong personalities if they were able to defy the explicit orders of the fearsome Pharaoh. And yet, the Torah identifies these strong, cerebral, intellectual women as Shifrah and Puah. The Jewish people knew them as Shifrah and Puah, women who tend to and comfort little infants, as women who take care of babies.

This, explains Rav Shmuel Rozovsky, is the primary and most natural role of the woman, to take care of the young, to protect them and nurture them and mold them into the people the Ribono Shel Olam intended them to be. A woman is all emotion, compassion and love. This is her essence, and this is where she finds her greatest fulfillment. More than all her intellectual achievements and accumulated knowledge, it is the soothing of an anxious child that gives her the greatest satisfaction and fulfillment. A woman is a mother, and that is what her role in the home should be.

We have to ask a question. From where did a Moshe Rabbeinu grow up? How did he become such an incredibly empathetic person? From where did he get his extreme sensitivity to every slightest cry and groan of his Jewish brothers and sisters? From where did Aharon emerge? From did he become such a lover of peace and brotherhood?

The Torah doesn't tell us anything about Amram, the father of Moshe and Aharon. We have no description of his *midos*, his character, his personality. But we do know about their mother and older sister. We know who they are. We know about their strength of character, their love, their devotion, their compassion. We know that they were Shifrah and Puah, and that accounts for the greatness of Moshe and Aharon.

Incidentally, speaking about Puah who comforted and calmed the weeping infants, today it has become fashionable in parenting wisdom to let a child cry until he realizes that it won't do him any good and he'll stop. But who says he is meant to find crying futile? Maybe Jewish sensitivity and compassion demands that an infant crying should elicit a response. Maybe he needs the comfort and reassurance of his mother's love. Who knows what damage can be caused by letting a child cry for a very long time? Who can say that it doesn't engender feelings of anger in him that will stay with him all his life?

All I know is that the Torah seems to say that what Puah did was a good thing then and it is a good thing now.

The mother should be the Puah of her home. She should be the one who embraces her children and envelops them in her overflowing love. There must certainly be boundaries and rules, but the child has to know that his mother's love flows freely through his home. When the father disciplines him he has to know that he can run to his mother for comfort. This does not mean that she should contradict her husband or counteract anything he has done. This does not mean that she should spoil the child. On the contrary, she should be firm and reinforce the father's lessons even while she is calming her child. The father and the mother must work together as partners, each one contributing that which he does best, and from the balance of the two, the good child will emerge.

This then is the second principle in *chinuch*. It begins with *tefilah*, and it is followed by love. Love from the father, love from the mother. A warm, embracing, unconditional, boundless love that manifests itself not only through emotional expressions but also through an abiding concern for what is best for the welfare and the growth of the child.

CHAPTER THREE

For the Benefit of the Child

Unlike in our relationship with the Ribono Shel Olam, our efforts in *chinuch* have no value without the proper motives and intentions. The Gemara states (Pesachim 50b), "*Leolam yaasok adam b'Torah uvemitzvos afilu shelo lishmah shemitoch shelo lishmah ba lishmah*. A person should always be involved with Torah and *mitzvos* even if it is not for their own sake, because doing something not for its own sake eventually leads to doing it for its own sake." Doing something not for its own sake, *shelo lishmah*, has a value in *avodas Hashem*.

But *shelo lishmah* has no value in *chinuch*. In fact, it is destructive.

When a parent demands certain behavior from his child as part of his *chinuch* not because it serves the interest of the child but because it serves the parent's own interest, that is not *chinuch*. It will not succeed. Moreover, it is quite likely to elicit strong resentment in the child against the parent. When a child senses that his parent is demanding something of him because it suits the parent, he may very well feel used and exploited, and he will be upset and angry.

The Ribono Shel Olam is content to have people serve Him even *shelo lishmah* because it will eventually lead to *lishmah*, but a child who feels exploited is not so patient. The child has to feel that what he is being asked to do and how he is being asked to live his life is all for his own good and for no other purpose. He is not interested in what the future will bring, only the here and now. If he feels the parent is acting *lishmah*, in his best interests, then he is fine with it. If he feels the parent's intentions are *shelo lishmah*, he will find it unacceptable.

We see this all the time. People ask their children to show off in front of friends and family. Show them how much Mishnayos you've learned, they tell the child. Show them how well you read. And so forth. What's the parent's motive? The child recognizes right away that the parent is doing it for his own glory. The parent, of course, may tell himself that he is doing it for *chinuch*. He may tell himself that he wants his child to have a strong love for the Torah, that he wants him to know a lot, that he wants him to be diligent, that he wants him to be the best in his class, that it's all for his own good. But more often than not, he is only showing off his child because it brings him reflected glory. All the frustrated goals and ambitions that he himself failed to achieve he is now trying to achieve vicariously through his child. He may not know it, but his child does, and he is not happy about how he is being used.

So this is the next important principle after love. It is not enough to love your child. You also have to act entirely for his benefit and leave your own needs out of it. Otherwise, you risk abject failure. You have to do only that which makes your child better, stronger, more secure.

To put it in more spiritual terms, you have to do only those things that will improve your child's prospects in Olam Haba. If you focus on the sublime spiritual goal of Olam Haba, you will see more clearly what is for his own good and what is for yours. The primary purpose of having children is not to have *nachas* from them but rather to help them lead the kind of life that will culminate in their holy *neshamos* entering Olam Haba. That is the goal that should define the tone of our *chinuch*. The *chinuch* of a child is not an investment that is supposed to bear fruit for the parent. There is no question of "What's in it for me?" That is not the purpose of having children.

◦§ An Extreme Case

Sometimes, parents use their children to compensate for their own shortcomings, and this usually expresses itself in contradictory behavior. They may not see the contradiction themselves, but the child will see the contradiction clearly.

There is one extreme case that I witnessed myself. A father came to *shul* with his little boy. He gave the boy a Siddur, opened it for him and told him to begin *davening*. Then he turned to his friends seated nearby and started to chat with them. The *tefilah* is moving along, the people are *davening* and this father is still talking to his friends. Then he notices that his little boy has looked up from the Siddur and is gazing around the shul. "Keep your eyes in the Siddur," he says and gives the boy a slap. Not a very hard slap, I admit, but a slap nonetheless, a clear reproof for his laxity.

So what did this father accomplish? Was this slap an act of *chinuch*? Was he teaching his child how to *daven* properly when he himself was chatting with his friends instead of *davening*?

How do you train a child to *daven* properly? Not by sitting him down at a table with a Siddur and telling him, "Keep your eyes glued to that Siddur or else." Not by slapping him if he looks out of his Siddur. The correct and only way to be *mechanech* a child to *tefilah* is to bring him to *shul* and let him observe how his father *davens*. Let him sit nearby and watch and learn from the example of his father. Eventually, he will get a feel for the process of *tefilah* and an appreciation for it. Then he will begin to *daven* with passion and conviction.

But if the father stands around chatting with his friends and slaps his child for looking out of the Siddur, is that a *chinuch* in *tefilah*? The child may have seen something remotely resembling *chinuch*, but he certainly hasn't seen *tefilah*.

In this case and in similar cases, the father is probably aware of his own shortcomings in *tefilah*. He knows that his behavior in *shul* is improper, but he finds it too hard to change. He is not ready to give up the stimulating conversation he enjoys while most other people are *davening*. But he doesn't want his son to fall into the same bad habits. So while he chats, he insists that his son *daven* without interruption, even though he's only a little boy. Somehow, his guilty conscience is appeased because even though he himself is talking during the *tefilah* he is making sure that his son is *davening* properly. In his own mind, he may be rationalizing. The child, however, sees the contradictions in his father's behavior, and he understands that he is paying the price for them.

This is, of course, an extreme case, although you would be surprised at how frequently it occurs. More subtle variations of this scenario are even more common, and they are almost invariably destructive to the progress and development of the child. They are the opposite of *chinuch*.

The only *chinuch* that has a reasonable chance of being successful is *chinuch* that is entirely focused on the needs and the benefits of the child, *chinuch* that bears no benefits or satisfactions for the parent other than the satisfaction of seeing the child he loves grow and blossom as a person and as a servant of the Ribono Shel Olam.

CHAPTER FOUR

Honor and Respect

W e've already discussed the primacy of warm and genuine expressions of love in the relationship between parent and child. These are the most important lines of communication with the child. They condition him to be receptive to the discipline, the training and the teaching of the parents, because he knows that it is for his own good and benefit. Therefore, even if the process of *chinuch* is sometimes less than comfortable, the child is willing to accept it.

Before we go on to speak about the actual process of *chinuch*, there is another fundamental principle that must be established, another prerequisite for a meaningful and successful process of *chinuch*. This is the concept of *kavod*, honor, and *morah*, fear.

There are two *mitzvos* in the Torah regarding the relationship between a parent and child. One is the *mitzvah* of *kibud av va'eim*, respecting and honoring parents (Shemos 20:12), and the other is *ish imo ve'aviv tira'u*, fearing parents (Vayikra 19:3). The Torah commands that we honor and fear our parents. A number of laws are derived from these *mitzvos*. We have to stand up when a parent walks into the room. We may not contradict what they say. We may not sit in their places. And many others.

The Torah gave us these *mitzvos* for a reason, but some parents, whether out of a feeling of humility or perhaps out of a misguided concept of modern parenting, choose to forfeit their prerogatives as parents. They don't insist that their children stand up for them. They don't insist that their children speak to them with the utmost respect and reverence. They aspire to be friends and buddies with their children, and the strict rules of respect and honor don't exactly fit into their scheme of things.

This is a serious mistake. We all know that the purpose of the *mitzvos* of honoring and fearing parents is to teach us *hakaras hatov*, appreciation and gratitude. But there is also another purpose, a very important purpose. It is a critical element in the *chinuch* of children.

◢§ Respect and Influence

What is the concept of *kavod* in the Torah? Why must we show respect and deference to certain things and certain people? What do they gain by receiving our respect? Why do they need it?

The answer is that they really do not need it. No one needs *kavod* in a real, substantial sense. People that hunger after *kavod* are only chasing an illusion. So why are we meant to give *kavod* to parents and rabbis and older people if they have no need for it?

It is because we need it. We need to give *kavod* to others for our own benefit.

There is a direct correlation between *kavod* and *hashpaah*. The more we honor and respect the people from whom we need to learn and derive inspiration the more we will be receptive to what they have to give us. We need to respect the Torah, because we need it to exert its influence over our lives. We need to respect the Beis Hamikdash, because we need it to inspire us with its holiness. We need to respect our rabbis, because we need to be guided by their leadership. We need to respect our parents, because we need to be molded by their loving and devoted *chinuch*.

It is foolishness, therefore, for parents to forfeit their right to be treated with honor and respect by their children. True, parents have the right to be *mocheil*, to forfeit their rights and privileges, but they should think long and hard before they do. Is the price they will pay in forfeited influence over their children worth it? Sometimes, we find among very great people that they forfeit their rights to honor and respect. But those are exceptional cases. Usually, those people are so great that by their very forfeiture they gain so much respect that their influence is expanded rather than diminished. But for most people it is simply not so. If you allow yourself to be treated with less than full respect, your influence will inevitably shrink. Is that what you want for your children?

This does not mean, of course, that parents should go to the other extreme. They should not institute draconian measures in their homes. In England, there used to be something called a Victorian discipline. It was named after the old Queen Victoria who ruled for more than sixty years with an iron hand. During the Victorian period, children were not allowed to open their mouths to speak at the table. They were required to say please and thank you a thousand times. They were required to follow innumerable rules of strict etiquette. In brief, children were oppressed and suppressed.

This is not what we want to accomplish with the *mitzvah* of *kibud av va'eim*. This is making the child a virtual prisoner. But there is a point where demanding respect in moderation will benefit the child without crushing him. At the very least, he should stand up for his parents when they come to the Shabbos table or the first time they walk into the room but not every subsequent time. The outward expressions of respect for the parent will eventually engender a genuine respect in the heart of the child and make him receptive to the parent's *chinuch*.

In our generation, many people are actually proud that they do not insist on the *kavod* to which they are entitled. They see themselves as enlightened and progressive. But did the Torah give us these *mitzvos* for no reason? Were they only meant for backward, unenlightened people? Certainly not. They were given for the benefit of the child. They are an essential component in his personal growth, and if we forfeit our rights to *kavod*, we may pat ourselves on the back, but our children will suffer the consequences.

⋖§ Domestic Harmony

So how do we teach our children to have *kavod* for their parents? We can't just sit them down and read them the *passuk* in the Torah and tell them that they must obey this commandment. It is not enough to simply lay down the law for them. Teaching children to have *kavod* for their parents is in itself a very important act of *chinuch*. There is a process that must be followed, steps that the parents must take.

It all begins with *shalom bayis*, domestic harmony, between husband and wife. There cannot be a proper *kavod* for parents if there is no *shalom bayis*. When a child sees a beautiful relationship between his parents, when he sees the love between them, when he sees how they come to a meeting of the minds when they are confronted with problems and issues, when he sees how they speak to each other with kindness and respect, when this is the example that is set before him then he will naturally respect his parents as well. But if he sees discord in the home, if he sees resentment and antipathy, if he sees dissension, if he sees that his parents do not speak nicely to each other and perhaps do not speak nicely about each other, then how can you expect him to have *kavod*? How can you expect him to respect his parents when they don't respect and honor each other?

Without *shalom bayis*, the very foundations of the home are shattered and destroyed. Without *shalom bayis* there cannot be *kavod* for parents, and without *kavod* there cannot be any *chinuch*. In fact, it occurs to me that the whole *mitzvah* of *shanah rishonah*, giving special attention to the wife during the first year of married life, was given for the very purpose of establishing a solid *shalom bayis* before the children arrive in the world. If there is an atmosphere of *kavod* in the home, a child can have *kavod* for his parents.

The Chasam Sofer offers an interesting thought on this issue. The Torah speaks (Devarim 21:18) about the punishment that is administered to a *ben sorer umoreh*, a rebellious son. The Gemara says (Sanhedrin 71a) that this law only applies when the mother and father have the same voice. We assume that this means their physical voices have an identical sound, either she has a masculine-sounding voice or he has a feminine-sounding one. But the Chasam Sofer has a different interpretation. He understands the "same voice" to mean that they are both on the same page. They speak the same language to their children. They have the same views and the same outlook. They have the same opinions, and even if they sometimes disagree they find common ground on which they can both stand. They present a united front to their children, with no discord and no dissension. They speak with one voice. But if they do not, the rebellious son cannot be held responsible for his rebelliousness, because he was denied a proper *chinuch*.

◆§ The Chain of Tradition

The Torah tells us (Vayikra 19:3), "A man should fear his mother and father, and you should safeguard my Shabbos." What is the connection between these two parts of the *passuk*? So the Gemara explains (Yevamos 5b) that I might think you have to obey your father if he orders you to violate the laws of Shabbos. That is why the Torah has to tell you that you may not.

The Meshech Chachmah finds this very puzzling. Why in the world would it occur to anyone that you have to listen to your father if he tells you to commit a terrible *aveirah*? We have a rule of *divrei harav vedivrei hatalmid divrei mi shom'im*, if there is a conflict between the words of the teacher and the words of the student, whom do we obey? Why would I think that with regards to the *mitzvah* of *kibud av va'eim* the rules are different?

The answer, he explains, lies in a deeper appreciation of the *mitzvah* of *kibud av va'eim*. We know that the Asseres Hadibros, the Ten Commandments, are divided into two groups of five. The first group, which appears on the right side of the Tablets, applies to the *mitzvos bein adam la'Makom*, the *mitzvos* that apply to our relationship with the Ribono Shel Olam. The second group of five, which appears on the left side of the Tablets, applies to the *mitzvos bein adam lechaveiro*, the *mitzvos* that govern our relationships with other people. The *mitzvah* of *kibud av va'eim* is the fifth *mitzvah* in the first group. If its purpose was only to express our gratitude and appreciation to our parents then it would not really belong in this category. Clearly, there is another aspect to the *mitzvah*.

The role of parents, the Meshech Chachmah continues, is to serve as conduits for the transmission of the *mesorah*, the unbroken chain of Jewish tradition, from the earlier generation to the next generation. Every aspect of Jewish life comes down to us through the transmission of our parents. They teach us from earliest childhood what is right and what is wrong, what attitudes are proper, what customs we must hold dear and the innumerable other teachings that make up the rich fabric of our lives.

In order for their work to be effective, however, we must honor them, because if we don't, their influence on us will be diminished. Consequently, concludes the Meshech Chachmah, we might think that no matter what we have to obey our parents regardless of what they tell us to do, even if it involves an occasional violation of the Shabbos. Because to allow us to disobey our parents even occasionally would undermine their ability to transmit the *mesorah* to us, and that would be devastating. Therefore, the Torah has to inform us that if a parent tells us to violate the laws of Shabbos we should not obey.

Apparently, for children to honor their parents is so critically important that we might have thought that it better to violate the laws of Shabbos than to show a lack of respect to parents. How then can we think that there is something commendable about lowering ourselves to the level of our children and forfeiting the respect due to us as parents? If we don't demand respect from our children, they will not listen to what we have to tell them. They will not respect authority. And we will not be able to fulfill our critical role as custodians of the *mesorah*.

❧ A Spirit of Respect

It is not enough for parents to demand that their children respect them. There must be a spirit of respect in the home. The father should consistently speak to the children about all the wonderful things that the mother does for the family. He should encourage them to express their appreciation to her by giving her a kiss and by telling her how special she is. And the mother should tell the children what a good father they have, and she should set an example for them by standing up for him when he walks into the room. This is good *chinuch*. The Chazon Ish writes that children learn much more from the examples set for them by action than by lessons and mere words. Respect has to be a natural outgrowth of the spirit and dynamics of the home.

Rav Elya Lopian once gave an interesting illustration. What if a boy gets up one day and says, "Why should I respect my father? How do I know he's my father? Just because he says so? Maybe he's not my father."

So he goes to his rabbi, and the rabbi points out a Gemara that says (Chullin 11a) we can assume the man married to our mother is our father due to the rule of probabilities.

The boy accepts the rabbi's ruling and says, "All right, I'll respect him based on the rule of probabilities."

Is this respect or is this perhaps the opposite?

A person must respect his father because it is the most natural thing in the world for him to do so, because that is how he was brought up, because that is in the very air of the home in which he lives.

So these are the fundamental principles. First, there must be *shalom bayis* between husband and wife. The children have to see that their parents love and respect each other. Then they will feel that respect themselves. And they will open to what their parents have to give them, whether it is instruction, advice or even rebuke.

That is the foundation of a good Jewish home.

CHAPTER FIVE

An Image of Dignity

I was once giving a talk to group of young men, and one of them said that he had never seen his father when he wasn't wearing a shirt. The other young men seemed to take this as high praise. As for me, I was shocked and appalled. The reaction of the young men indicated that they saw this as something truly remarkable and extraordinary and that it was a common occurrence for children to see their fathers in various stages of undress. I found this incredible. This was the praise of a father? That he had the dignity not to walk around the house without his shirt on?

The Gemara tells us (Sotah 36b) that when Yosef was on the verge of doing a terrible *aveirah*, when he was about to give in to his overwhelming desire, the *dmus diukno shel aviv*, the image of his father's face, appeared before his eyes, and he was able to overcome his desires. The image of his father's face, which he had not seen for twenty-two years, enabled him to resist the urge to do the *aveirah*.

In *sefarim* we find that this is a *segulah* that can be used by all people. If someone should find himself in a situation where his desires are awakened and he is in danger of doing an *aveirah*, he should keep before his eyes the image of his father, and that will help him overcome the urge to do *aveiros*. When a person sees the *dmus diukno* of his father, he can overcome the *yetzer hara*.

Rav Shamshon Raphael Hirsch makes a remarkable observation. He says that this places a tremendous responsibility of *chinuch* on every father. It demands of every father that he behave in such a way that his *dmus diukno*, the image of his face, will make a lasting impression on his children. Should they ever be on the verge of doing an *aveirah* the image of their father's face should stop them in their tracks. They should be filled with shame in front of their father who would never do such a thing and who would be mortified if he knew his children were doing such a thing. The image of their father should be like a shock treatment that will drive the *yetzer hara* out of their hearts.

It follows, therefore, that the image of the father requires that the children always see him with full dignity. Even though he is in the intimate setting of his family, he cannot allow the children to see him in a way that is at all undignified. Walking around the house without a shirt is certainly undignified. It certainly diminishes the effectiveness of the *dmus diukno shel aviv*, and it reduces the influence of the father over the child.

Today, there is a spirit of egalitarianism in society, and this extends into the home. Children tend to look at their parents as first among equals. They concede a certain degree of authority to their parents, but they do not tend to look up to them with awe and reverence. So how can the parents exercise real influence over the children? It is very difficult.

But that is not our way. We place our parents on a pedestal. We honor them, and we revere them. We invest parents with the responsibility of *chinuch*. We expect them to exert a powerful influence over their children, to give them values, to initiate them into learning Torah and doing *mitzvos*. And they cannot be effective if the children do not look up to them with absolute reverence. The children shouldn't see their parents in less than dignified attire. The bedroom of the parents should be off limits to the children. They should not be allowed to open the door unless they knock and are given permission to enter, and if the parents are away, they should not step over the threshold. That will go a long way toward preserving the *dmus diukno shel aviv*.

As we've discussed earlier, the purpose of *kavod* is to promote influence, because we are influenced by those we respect. In today's world, where respectability is not respected, where casualness is the ideal, how can we expect the leaders and elders to exert a positive influence on the younger generation? We have to resist this spirit of looseness and irresponsibility. We have to bring up our children to respect parents and elders, and if parents want the respect of their children they have to present themselves with respectability at all times.

◄§ Respectful Thoughts

The Chayei Adam writes (67:3) that respect for parents needs to be in thoughts, deeds and speech. We understand that we have to respect our parents in deeds and speech. That is obvious. We have to treat them with respect, and we have to speak to them with respect. But the Chayei Adam adds another facet to the *mitzvah* that is perhaps not so obvious. He says we have to respect them with our thoughts. If a child does everything required of him in deed and speech but in his mind he thinks that his father is a fool, he has not fulfilled the *mitzvah* properly.

This is an illuminating insight into the *mitzvah*. But if we think into it, this is how it has to be. If a child doesn't respect his parents in his thoughts, then all the respect he shows through his deeds and speech is really nothing but a sham.

The Ribono Shel Olam laments (Yeshayahu 29:13), "Because this nation came close to me with its mouth and its lips, but in its heart it was far away from Me." If there is no heart in the outward expressions of closeness, then it is not very meaningful.

Imagine a king who enjoys when his subjects show him respect even though he knows that while they're bowing down they're thinking about how they would love to stab the king to death. Can a king really take pleasure in such respect?

So when the Ribono Shel Olam tells us to honor our parents, is it possible that He means only through deeds and speech? When we think into it, we realize that the fundamental respect demanded of us is in our thoughts and that all other forms of respect flow from what we feel in our hearts and think in our minds.

The Chayei Adam goes on to write that the primary respect for parents is in our thoughts. We have to think of them as "the greatest and most respected people in the land even though other people do not hold them in such high esteem."

A child has to think that his father is a special person, a great person, someone worthy of widespread esteem. If he sees that others don't have the same high opinion of his father, he understands that it is only because they do not really know him, because he does not show off all his qualities, because he is a more private person. But the child knows the father. The child sees him at home. He sees how his father conducts himself. He sees how his father knows how to treat his wife with honor and respect. He sees how his father brings up his children with sensitivity and wisdom. He sees his father's kindness and goodness, and he believes with all his heart that his father is as worthy as any other man, even if he does not get public recognition for his virtues and qualities.

Yes, every child can respect his father in his thoughts and consider him to be, as the Chayei Adam writes, among "the greatest and most respected people in the land." But what if the father doesn't behave like "the most respected people in the land" at home?

So the burden falls on the father. If the child sees the proper *dmus diukno* of the father in the home, if his father's dedication to Torah and *mitzvos* is genuine, if his father's *midos* are admirable, if his father's deeds and relationships are exemplary, if his father's respectability is impeccable, then the child can respect him not only by deed and speech but in his thoughts as well.

It is up to the father to earn the respect of his children. Of course, the obligation of the children to treat their father with honor and respect does not depend on their father earning it. But if the father wants his children to have a genuine and deep respect for him in their hearts, he has to work at it. He should not be a tyrant at home and demand respect as his right. He doesn't have to be a star in the outside world, but he has to be the star of his home. And as long as he is sincere, conscientious and focused on the needs of his family, the Torah gives him all the support to enable him to attain that status. The Torah demands that children treat their father with utmost respect so that the *dmus diukno* of their father will be reinforced. Children are naturally and instinctively prepared to look up to their father, but what they see is up to the father.

⊷§ A Higher Standard

The Tanna Devei Eliahu writes (Ch. 21), "A person should not see his parents speaking improperly, and [if he does] he should voice his objections. If he fails to do so, he and they will not live out their lives, Heaven forbid."

If a person sees his parents saying things they shouldn't be saying, even if it is only vulgar language, he has an obligation to rebuke them. Although they are his parents, he has a *mitzvah* of *tochachah*, giving rebuke, but of course, he must do so without overstepping the bounds of *kibud av va'eim*. His rebuke must be respectful and indirect. And if he fails to give them *tochachah*, both he and his parents are at risk of a premature death.

But what does this mean? Since when is vulgar language punishable by death? Clearly, it is not the vulgar language itself that creates the problem. It is the outrage of speaking in this way in front of the children. Young children are impressionable, and if they hear their parents speaking improperly, even if it is just with a lack of refinement, how can such parents still exert a positive influence over their children?

If a person sometimes succumbs to the *yetzer hara* and steps over the line, it may be forgivable, as long as he has only himself to worry about. But if he holds the future of his young children in his hands and still allows himself to step over the line, it is unpardonable.

Parenthood is an awesome responsibility. Not only do you hold your child's entire future in your hands, you also have to be doubly concerned about your own deeds and behavior. Everything you do is magnified in the context of the children who look to you for *chinuch*.

A parent has to be a paragon of virtue in the eyes of his children. They have to see him as a prince, a person of the highest caliber who would never do something forbidden or even unrefined. If a parent doesn't care about his own dignity, how can he expect his children to respect him, to look up to him as a role model and to take instruction and advice from him? Even if his children continue to treat him according to the established rules of *kibud av va'eim*, you can be sure that they no longer respect him in their hearts.

And if a parent disregards the welfare of his children and allows himself to lose their respect, there is something seriously wrong with him, and he deserves to be punished. It is not the *aveirah* itself that is being punished but rather the cavalier disregard for the *chinuch* of his children. And if there is an older child present, a child who is capable of speaking to the parent properly, and he fails to do so, then he shares their guilt and its consequences.

A child hungers for the guidance of his parents. He loves his parents and looks up to them and wants to please them and be like them, the boys like their father and the girls like their mother. That is the nature of a child. If you watch children playing father and mother, you can actually discover what goes on in their homes, and you can see the image of the parent and how the child wants to fit into that image himself.

This places a heavy burden of responsibility on parents. Regardless of how they are themselves in their natural state, they have to rise to a higher standard in front of the children. They have to be extremely careful even when they speak on the telephone if the children are anywhere within earshot. The children hear everything and learn from everything, and the parents always have to be aware that the children are evaluating everything they do and forging paths for their own lives based on these evaluations.

Parents must protect their dignity, because without dignity, the father figure and mother figure dissipate, and they lose all their influence. You should not lower yourselves to the level of your children and try to be their friends. Your children don't need you to be their friends. They can find plenty of friends. But they only have one father and one mother. You have to be that father or mother with the full dignity and refinement and scrupulous behavior that the role requires.

✌ Setting an Example

The *Sefer Hachinuch* states that the *mitzvah* of *kibud av va'eim* is designed to bring a person closer to the Ribono Shel Olam. The father and mother serve as a physical paradigm for our Father in

Heaven. By honoring and respecting our parents we express our *hakaras hatov*, our gratitude for all the good things they always do for us from earliest infancy when we could nothing for ourselves through all the years of our growth into independent adults. Above all, we are grateful to them for giving us life.

It follows that he will make the connection and realize that he is certainly obligated to be thankful and express his gratitude to the Ribono Shel Olam Who created the entire world and sent his *neshamah* down into it to be exalted through Torah and *mitzvos*. That is the thought process that is expected of a person, to make the connection between his earthly father and his Father in Heaven.

So how do children relate to their Father in Heaven? How do they feel about the Ribono Shel Olam? When their parents told them that the Ribono Shel Olam is our Father in Heaven, what did this mean to them? What kinds of images were formed in their minds? Do they think of the Ribono Shel Olam as someone who comes into the house and screams at everyone and terrifies everyone?

How can you expect your children to have a positive conception of their Father in Heaven if you didn't set a good example for them?

This then is the responsibility of a parent. If he doesn't live up to what is expected of him, even if he uses unrefined language on the telephone, the damage he can cause to his children is far-reaching, and we can understand why his punishment is severe.

CHAPTER SIX

Attention and Love

Why are there more problems with children in our times than there generally were in earlier times? It's not a simple question, and the answers are likewise not simple. Life has become increasingly complicated in modern times, and complicated times can cause all sorts of complications. I want to focus on one important factor.

It seems to me that parents no longer have enough time for their children. The pace of modern life is very fast. Everyone is busy today. The father is busy. The mother is busy. And they're busy doing good things. And they simply do not have enough time to give to their children. The children are not getting the normal attention they need, and they feel it. Sometimes, they can actually feel that their parents consider them a hindrance in their lives in a certain sense.

I also have to mention that wonderful invention called the telephone. When the parent finally squeezes out some time for the child and they sit down together, the telephone rings, and for some reason, the person on the telephone seems to take priority over the person in the room. You're in middle of a conversation with someone seated right next to you, and the ringing telephone interrupts your conversation. You pick up the telephone, and you forget about the person in front of you and begin conversing with the person on the telephone. It is incredible. And when the person right next to you is your child, you can imagine the feelings that go through his heart. That's why children very often disturb telephone conversations. They instinctively resent them.

There have to be rules in the house regarding telephone calls during family time. It is better not to pick up the telephone at all, but if you feel you must, tell the person on the line that you can't talk at the moment. Unless it's an emergency, of course. And the definition of an emergency must be very narrow, almost life and death.

A child has to feel that his parents care about him, that they're interested in him, that he is at least as important as some of the other things going on in his parents' life. If he feels he's being allowed to fall by the wayside, a spark of resentment and even hatred will arise in his little heart where it can smolder until it bursts forth and causes untold damage. It can break families apart. And all because there was not enough time for the child.

It is a terrible thing when a child thinks his parents aren't interested in him, when he wants something and they have neither the time nor the patience to listen to him. A child needs special care and special attention. He feels safe and protected if he knows that he's the focus of his parents' world. If he doesn't feel that then he's on his own, and that is a terrifying thought. So when he comes home from school, his mother should stop what she's doing and ask him what he did that day, how he enjoyed it, what she can do for him. Give him the attention he needs.

⇜ The Shabbos Table

You would think that Shabbos is a time for children. The whole family gathers around the Shabbos table. There's a lot of good food, and a festive atmosphere. There are no disturbances or distractions. There should be plenty of time to engage the children in good conversation. You would think this is a wonderful time for the children. But it is not necessarily so.

These days, every child comes from school with a sheaf of papers covered with quizzes and questions. The *rebbe* or the teacher said that the child should be tested on this and tested on that, and the *rebbe* or the teacher said that the father should review this and that with the child. And all of a sudden, the Shabbos table has become an extension of the classroom. And not just the classroom but one big examination board.

Not only has the opportunity for some warm family time been lost, but it can also lead to some quite unpleasant results. One child may be crying because he didn't know the answer, and another child may be screaming that he doesn't want to do it, and you have your hands full. And at the same time, another is standing there with six papers, and he's disappointed that you can't ask him all the questions on them. It can become quite harrowing. Heaven forbid that a child should be reduced to tears at the Shabbos table because he fails to remember the answer to a question.

What is going on here? Is this what a Shabbos table is meant to be? Is it meant to be one big competition? Is this a good *chinuch* for the children?

A Shabbos table is supposed to be a special time for the family, a time to bask in the warmth and unquestioning love of the family. It is a time to sing together and say *divrei Torah* and tell stories and have conversations in which everyone participates in some form or another. A family is not a classroom.

I recognize that it would be hard to change the educational system in this respect once the Board of Education has gained control of the Shabbos table. So until the system changes, I'd recommend that you do not allow the extended classroom to take over your Shabbos table. Just do a little bit to get by. Ask a few questions of those who want to be asked, glance at the sheets, and move on. The Shabbos table shouldn't be a place of tension and frustration. It should be a place of warmth, joy and inspiration.

✌§ A Safe Haven

Rabbeinu Yonah, in *Iggeres Hateshuvah*, talks about the Ribono Shel Olam's instructions to Moshe (Shemos 19:3), "So shall you say to the house of Yaakov [the women] and to the sons of Israel [the men]." Why did the Ribono Shel Olam tell Moshe to speak to the women first? Rabbeinu Yonah explains that He wanted Moshe to give the women a synopsis of the Torah before he spoke to the men. Because "they are the ones who send off their children to school and see to it that they learn Torah, and they are merciful (*merachmos aleihem*) when their children come home from school. They give them treats so that they should want to learn Torah, and they watch over them so that they shouldn't forsake the Torah. They teach them when they're still young to be fearful of *aveiros*, as it is written (Mishlei 22:6), 'Raise the child according to his way; even when he is old he will not turn from it.' The modest women," Rabbeinu Yonah concludes, "are the ones who bring about Torah and *yirah*."

It is the women who deserve the most credit for the Torah and *yirah* in Klal Yisrael. They set the child on the path of Torah and *yirah*, and in recognition of their importance, the Giving of the Torah began with them.

But let's take a closer look at a few of these points that Rabbeinu Yonah makes in favor of the women. What does it mean that the mothers "send their children off to school"? Does that make them better than the fathers who pay the tuition? And what does it mean that the mothers "are merciful when their children come home from school"? Why does welcoming a child back from school call for *rachmanus*?

Rabbeinu Yonah is telling us something very important here. When a child comes home from school, he's a *rachmanus* case. He's been battered and bullied all day, and now, he's a candidate for a little mercy. This is such an incredible insight that I would almost say it takes a Rishon with *ruach hakodesh* to reveal this to us. Every single child who comes home from school needs to be greeted with *rachmanus*.

Even if he's a star pupil, even if he loves going to school and can't wait to leave in the morning, the long day in school is still a grueling experience, and when he comes homes, he needs to be greeted with compassion and understanding. It is not an easy thing for any child to sit through hours and hours of classes, restricted to his seat, required to pay attention without wavering or looking out the window and daydreaming. It's a lot to demand from anyone, let alone a young child.

And I'm not saying there's anything wrong with putting him through this process. This is how we have to be *mechanech* children in Torah, as the Gemara says (Bava Basra 21a), "Stuff it into him like an ox." But by the end of the day, he's a *rachmanus* case, and when he comes home, he needs a breather. He needs to get away from the pressure and relax. He needs that his mother greet him with a cup of milk and a cookie, that she ask him if he's all right, if there's anything she can do for him.

Unfortunately, sometimes this young *rachmanus* case is greeted in an entirely different way. Sometimes, his mother puts him through a cross-examination about what he accomplished that day in school. "What did you learn today? What did the teacher say? What happened here and what happened there?"

Sometimes, it even happens that there was a problem in school, maybe he didn't listen so well, and the teacher phoned the mother and told her about it before he came home from school. You can imagine what kind of greeting he'll get on that day.

The mother means well. She is concerned about the progress of her child and she wants to support what the school is doing and make sure her child is successful. But if she really wants him to be successful, she should not worry so much about what went on in school and focus instead on her emotionally bruised and battered child who at this moment needs a strong dose of *rachmanus* from her. She needs to sympathize with him and show him that she understands that he had a hard day. She has to reassure him that he's safe at home and that now he can relax. "Let's sit down. Let's share a cookie. Let's play a little." These are the things he needs to hear. Forget about school for a while. Think about your child. He needs *rachmanus*.

And the way he is sent off to school is just as important. If everything is bedlam, if he is scolded for trying to pour the milk on his cereal and spilling it on the table, if he has one arm in his coat sleeve and the other sleeve is dragging on the floor behind him as he runs out the door, can he come to school in a proper frame of mind? Is it a wonder he ends up hating school? That is not how mothers are meant to "send their children off to school."

The mothers "see to it that they learn Torah," says Rabbeinu Yonah, "and they're merciful (*merachmos aleichem*) when their children come home from school. They give them treats so that they should want to learn Torah." At home, the whole focus has to be about making the experience of learning Torah enjoyable. It's all about awakening a love for Torah in the heart of the child.

How does the mother do this? Not by being the teacher's agent. Not by extending the feeling of persecution from the school into the home. Not by putting him through an interrogation before he has had a chance to breathe. No, it's by giving him the unquestioning respect and affection he has earned by going to school and enduring the ordeal that it inevitably is for all children. It is not an easy thing for anyone to sit through a whole day of school, especially a child, and the mother has to be waiting to shower him with *rachmanus* when he comes home.

And when Rabbeinu Yonah tells us that the mothers "watch over them so that they should not forsake the Torah," it is not a contradiction. How do they watch over them? By making sure that they go on time. By making sure that they're happy. By speaking with admiration and respect about *rebbeim* and teachers. By fortifying the child with love, affection and understanding and making the consummate learning experience sweet for him.

When a child feels an outpouring of love when he comes home, he will respond with love of his own, and that love will be extended to the Torah he is learning He will associate the entire experience with love, and he will love it. By the time he wakes up in the morning, he will have forgotten the hardships he endured, and he will remember only the joy of coming home.

If, however, the home to which he returns is stressful and judgmental, if he goes to sleep with resentment and frustration, in what frame of mind will he go to school the next day? And the entire school experience will become a downward spiral. And his resentments will be directed toward his parents, his brothers and sisters, his *rebbeim* and teachers, the Torah and even the Ribono Shel Olam, Heaven forbid. And then we're surprised when some children become dropouts. I don't call them dropouts. I call them pushouts. How can we blame them when they were pushed out by the way we treated them, albeit without malicious intent?

❧ An Atmosphere of Love

A child has to feel that he is being nurtured in an atmosphere of love. He consistently needs encouragement, a kind word and a warm smile from his parents. And he needs to be given time and attention.

This doesn't mean that you have to give him a large amount of time. You don't have to sit down for an hour with the child every night. More important than the amount of time you give him is the attitude and the spirit with which it is given. You have to sit down with him and give him your undivided attention as if you have all the time in the world, and then you can decide how much time you can actually manage. Don't tell him that you can only give him ten minutes. Don't look at your watch. For whatever amount of time you can give him, make him feel that he is the most important person in the world to you at that moment, and indeed, he should be.

He doesn't need a lot of time from you. He needs your love and attention. If he feels secure in your love, he will be happy. And then, even if he sometimes needs to be punished or disciplined he will not resent it, because he'll know that it's only because he deserves it. He'll understand that it all comes from your love. But if he is insecure in your love, then he'll wonder if he's being punished because he deserves it or because you don't like him.

In an atmosphere of unquestioning love, a child can feel secure and understood. He doesn't have to worry that he's not perfect. He knows that he is loved despite his imperfections. And this applies to older children as well. The parents have to be their place of refuge. If he needs to go on an outing to catch a breather, don't worry about *bittul Torah*. On the contrary, such outings, within reason, are an important part of *chinuch* in Torah, because they'll make him happy about the overall experience and he'll come to love learning Torah.

That is the role of the parents, and especially the mother. Show compassion and mercy to your children. Unless there are special problems, you don't have to worry about the schools. They'll take care of themselves. You have to take care of your children.

CHAPTER SEVEN

Use the Rod Sparingly

I f you witness someone doing something he shouldn't be doing, are you allowed to strike him? Are you allowed to berate and embarrass him? Are you allowed to scream at him? Of course not. The Torah specifically forbids (Devarim 25:3) *chavalah*, hitting, and (Vayikra 25:17) *onaah*, persecution. It is forbidden to cause another person physical or emotional pain or injury. Just because you see someone doing something wrong does not give you the right to humiliate or hit him.

When it comes to *chinuch*, however, we find that these prohibitions are suspended. The Gemara says (Makkos 8a) that not only does a father have the right to strike his son, he actually has an obligation to strike his son. How is this obligation applied? This is a very controversial question.

The *mitzvos bein adam lechaveiro* apply to parents and children as much as they apply to any two other people. Children are entitled to the same protections in the Torah as are other people. Nonetheless, the father is exempted from the prohibition of *chavalah* and *onaah*, because he has an obligation of *chinuch*. The *mitzvah* of *chinuch* overrides the prohibitions of *chavalah* and *onaah*. The Torah says (Mishlei 13:24), "He who spares the rod despises his son." But this does not mean that parents get a free pass to strike and humiliate their children. They still have to honor and respect the protections the Torah extends to their children. But in order to fulfill their obligations of *chinuch* they are permitted to do things that are otherwise prohibited.

So before a parent strikes, humiliates or otherwise persecutes his child, he has to consider if the *mitzvah* of *chinuch* demands that he do so. If not, then it is absolutely, unequivocally forbidden. It is in violation of a *lo saaseh* in the Torah, and is as forbidden as eating meat that is not kosher. A parent has no right to strike or scream at a child out of his own anger and frustration. He has no right to persecute and punish a child to get back at him or to settle a grievance. He has no right to do anything to spite or hurt a child because of resentment he harbors in his heart. To do so is child abuse. Before he dares cause pain and suffering to a child, he has to know without question that he has no other motivations than the *chinuch* of the child. If he has a question, then he must desist, just as he would from a piece of questionable meat.

Besides the prohibitions involved, persecuting a child without justification only causes the child to hate his parents and to hate everything for which they stand. The child feels abused and resentful, and very often, the relationship is ruined for life.

So before a parent resorts to harsh measures, he has to ask himself two questions. One, is this completely for the benefit of the child? Two, is there a gentler way this can be accomplished that will cause less pain to the child? If there is a different way, then you have no right to persecute the child.

✌️ An Undeserved Slap

As we mentioned before, the Gemara says that a father is required to slap his child. The Gemara also says that even if the child is learning well the father should still find a pretext to give him a slap. This is quite an amazing piece of Gemara. Why in the world should a father slap his son if the son has done nothing to deserve it?

The purpose of this slap, says Rabbi Dessler, is not as a punishment for anything the child has done. On the contrary, the child being discussed in the Gemara appears to be a model child who deserves to be rewarded rather than punished. The purpose of this slap is that the child should recognize his father as an unquestioned authority figure. A slap can only be administered by the person in charge, and when a child receives a slap from his father he knows beyond a shadow of a doubt that his father is in charge and that he is a subordinate under his father's jurisdiction. Once this perspective of the father-child relationship is implanted in the mind of the child, he will submit to his father's authority and be entirely receptive to his father's instructions in the future. This is crucial for a successful *chinuch.*

Therefore, the Gemara says that the father should find a way to administer that slap. For instance, it the child is guilty of some minor infraction that the father would normally be inclined to disregard, he should nonetheless use this opportunity to administer the slap that will solidify the image of the father as an authority figure in the child's mind.

That slap should, of course, be administered without the least bit of anger. It should not be violent or abusive. It should deliver a message of authority in a firm but loving manner. You should not slap any child if there is the slightest chance that he will slap back. Nor should you slap the child if you know that the message of the slap will be lost on him or that it will only arouse his anger and resentment.

Most important, the slap that the Gemara advocates should be administered only once or twice during the entire span of the childhood.

CHAPTER EIGHT

Home Is Not School

N o one has ever gone through the sayings of Chazal and made a code for *chinuch* in schools, a *shulchan aruch* of how children should be taught and what the relationship between the school and the home should be. Every school and every *mechanech* has his or her own theories, and very often, what seems like a good idea actually does a lot of damage.

◄§ An Invention Called Homework

First, I would like to make a few remarks about the modern invention called homework. Contrary to what people may think, any more than a limited amount of homework is not necessarily a positive contribution to *chinuch*. The nature of homework we are seeing more and more these days is increasingly complex and elaborate. Most children simply cannot complete such homework assignments without the help of a parent. I recently saw a homework assignment that required the child to find and collect all the mentions of Dassan and Aviram in Chazal. For whom was this assignment meant, the child or the parents? And not every parent at that!

Besides subjecting the children to undue pressure and tension, such homework assignments can be unwelcome intrusions into the world of the home. They may force parents into the role of assistant teachers. How are parents with six children supposed to get anything done at home if they must spend hours and hours every evening doing homework with their children? And what if the parents simply cannot manage it? What happens then? They need to hire tutors to take their places, and the costs can be prohibitive. It is difficult enough for many families to pay their tuition. They do not need this added financial burden.

It might be more helpful if homework, if there is to be any at all, were limited to straightforward review of material the child is assumed to have learned and digested in the classroom, material that will not require the help of a parent. And the homework period might best be kept to a limited amount of time. Schools are pressed to assign so much homework because they've set ambitious goals for how much the children should learn. Perhaps it would be better if children learned a little less and had more time to be children and enjoy their childhood years.

In the traditional system of *chinuch*, the school was the place where the child learned, and the home was the place where the child did other things. It was the place where he played, where he ate, where he slept, where he helped his mother, where he relaxed. If the child was on a level where he could learn by himself beyond what he learned in school, he went to the *beis midrash*.

Demanding that a child do homework is very questionable. As we've mentioned in the name of Rabbeinu Yonah, the home is supposed to be the child's safe haven, the place where he is greeted with love and *rachmanus*. The home is the place where he acquires a love for Torah, because it rounds off his relationship with Torah in a positive way. The school is a place of pressure, and the home is where he is praised and rewarded for having made the effort in the pressured learning environment of the school. But if the pressure continues when the child comes home, if he has to do sit down and do his homework when he really wants to play and relax, he may lose his enthusiasm for learning and become resentful.

With Gemara homework especially, there can be very sensitive issues. If a father learns Gemara with his son, he has to make it an enjoyable experience, because if he doesn't, the damage is far greater than any possible gain. Even if the child eventually knows the Gemara, the price that will have been paid in anger and resentment is way too high. He may have learned this piece of Gemara, but he will not love the Gemara. He will see it as a source of torture and frustration. [See Chapter Eleven: Fathers and Sons.]

If the father can't make learning Gemara with his son an enjoyable experience, if he is not a good teacher, if he is too tired after a long day at work or whatever the reason is, it is better that he should sell the shirt on his back and hire a skilled tutor than to do it himself. Indeed, many fathers are simply incapable of learning with their own sons. The child can be overly anxious that the father will be angry at him if he doesn't know the material. It often happens that a child learning with his father will burst into tears, although that hardly ever happens with a teacher. Learning with a child can become a complicated and emotionally charged situation, and if it does, it is best to avoid it. The *mitzvah* of learning with your son can be fulfilled by hiring someone to do it. In fact, if it doesn't work than I would venture to say that the *mitzvah* is that the father should not learn with his son.

A father once asked Rav Yaakov Kamenetsky for advice. He works very hard, he said, and he has two hours at night when he can learn. Just that and no more. He would like to take a *chavrusa* and learn for these two hours on a high level, as he used to learn when he was still in *yeshivah*. He also has a son who needs help with his learning. He could learn with his son. It would work, but if instead of taking a *chavrusa*, he learns with his son, his learning will be on a much lower level. What should he do?

Rav Yaakov told him to take a *chavrusa* and find a tutor for his son. And then he added a very illuminating comment. "If you take a *chavrusa* and learn with him at home," he said, "and the learning really goes well, with a real *geshmak*, you will be accomplishing a tremendous amount for the *chinuch* of your son. You will be teaching him that a person has to sit and learn, that Torah is what life is all about. But when you learn with your child, you're not teaching him that everyone has to sit and learn. You will only be teaching him that a child has to sit and learn."

When a child sees his father learning after coming home from a hard day's work it makes a deep impression on him, and there is far more *chinuch* value in this than in many hours of homework.

If it were up to me, I would abolish homework or limit it severely unless a child was having a particular problem in school and was in need of remedial help.

◆§ The Shabbos Table

Another modern development is the proliferation of Shabbos sheets. This does not come from traditional *chinuch*. This is not how it was for our grandparents. It's a new phenomenon. The *rebbeim* and *moros* think that by sending home piles of sheets with questions and *divrei Torah* they are enhancing the Shabbos table for the children and their families. And that is a mistake.

What happens at the Shabbos table as a result of this new system? The father sits in his place and tests the children. The children line up, and each one has a turn taking an oral examination. All too often, one of the children will run off in tears because he didn't know the answers well enough. For him, the Shabbos table has turned into a Tishah b'Av table.

It is true that some children take pride in showing off what they've learned, but many do not welcome the pressure and the frustration. They come to the Shabbos table with dread. As for the child that feels proud, it's not so simple that showing off his superiority is good for him. It only encourages him to be a *baal gaavah*. And his success causes the other children to feel jealous and resentful. Where is the gain in this whole mess?

The Shabbos table should be a place of joy and warmth. The children should be happy. The father should say a Torah thought on the *parashah*. They should sing *zemiros*. They should enjoy the good food. It should be a festive time, not a strained and pressurized experience. The home should not be made an extension of the classroom, and certainly the Shabbos table should not be drawn into the equation. If you want to test the children about what they learned in school, it would be best to find another time to do it and to do it in a friendly, nonthreatening manner.

The schools should do all their teaching in school. The home should be a place of refuge for the children, a place to relax and unwind after a long and exhausting day in school. If a father wants to learn with his son, and if it works well for the two of them, and if the son also wants to learn with his father, then they should learn together for as long as they both find it enjoyable. Otherwise, children should be allowed to be children at home. Anything that interferes with this interferes with the chances of their gaining a love for Torah, and that is not *chinuch* at all.

PART TWO

On Chinuch in Mitzvos

CHAPTER NINE

The Joy of Mitzvos

As we've discussed earlier, the Ribono Shel Olam doesn't expect us to do *mitzvos* and learn Torah for their own sake from the beginning. He is patient with us. It's fine if we initially serve Him for the sake of reward, because eventually we will rise to the level where we will have such a profound appreciation for what we do that we will do it for its own sake.

With this in mind, let's look at two *pesukim* (Tehillim 112:1-2), "Fortunate is the man who fears Hashem, who strongly desires His *mitzvos*. His offspring shall be the mighty of the earth, a virtuous generation that shall be blessed." I once heard — I don't recall from whom — an interpretation of these *pesukim* and this Gemara that is very illuminating.

What is meant by a man who desires His *mitzvos*? The Gemara tells us (Avodah Zarah 19a) that it means someone who desires the *mitzvos* themselves rather than the reward of doing the *mitzvos*. He is the one who is considered fortunate.

But why is the one who does *mitzvos* for reward not considered fortunate as well? True, this is not the highest level of serving the Ribono Shel Olam, but it is a perfectly acceptable path to Him. Why is the person who serves for reward excluded from the fortunate?

The answer lies in the second *passuk*. "His offspring shall be the mighty of the earth, a virtuous generation that shall be blessed." For himself, a person can take the long route to the Ribono Shel Olam by serving Him at the outset for the sake of the reward. But if he wants that his children should be "the mighty of the earth," if he wants to raise "a virtuous generation," he has to show them a love for the *mitzvah* itself. When children see their parents perform *mitzvos* with zest and enthusiasm, when they see that their parents talk about *mitzvos* all the time and hold *mitzvos* in the highest esteem, when they see that their home is permeated with the joy of *mitzvos*, they will also be drawn in that direction. When parents genuinely desire *mitzvos*, then their very way of life is an important expression of *chinuch*. In fact, it is the best kind of *chinuch*, because it teaches by example.

But what if a parent speaks to his children about the advantages and rewards of doing *mitzvos* rather than the sheer joy of living with *mitzvos*? What if he says to his children, "Do this *mitzvah*, because if you do it you will get your reward in Olam Haba"? Or better yet, what if he shows his children that he himself is doing this *mitzvah* with real excitement because he will get a share in Olam Haba? It would seem that this is good *chinuch*. After all, he is talking about looking ahead to Olam Haba, which is a very worthy thing.

Nevertheless, if he shows his children that the motivation for doing the *mitzvah* is the reward, it is not good *chinuch*. All he has taught his children is that you should do the *mitzvah* because it is worth your while. The child, however, may think that for his father a reward in Olam Haba makes it worthwhile, but he has other ideas of what makes something worthwhile. If we're talking about reward, it's possible that becoming a doctor is the reward to which he aspires. So, the child may think, let my father go after the reward that interests him and I will go after the reward that interests me. He will have learned from the *chinuch* of his father that *mitzvos* are done for the rewards, and then he can apply his own standards of rewards.

If, however, the child sees the joy that his father experiences when he is doing a *mitzvah*, if that joy is the foundation of the home in which he grows up, then he will inevitably be affected by the spirit and the mood and the atmosphere, and he himself will feel that selfsame joy when he does the *mitzvos*. This kind of *chinuch* will reach into his very soul regardless of his conception of what constitutes a worthwhile reward.

Therefore, even though it is perfectly acceptable for a person to do a *mitzvah* because of ulterior motives, even if he does the *mitzvah* because he wants to receive his reward in Olam Haba, the *chinuch* of his children will suffer. If he wants his children to be "the mighty of the earth" and "a virtuous generation," he has to show them the sheer spiritual joy of doing the *mitzvos*.

✌ A Life of Sacrifice

In the early part of the twentieth century, keeping Shabbos was very difficult for Jews in America. Everyone knows the stories. In most jobs, if you didn't want to work on Shabbos, you were fired on Friday. You found a job on Monday and worked there the whole week. On Friday, the boss told you to come in on Shabbos as well. If you agreed, fine. Otherwise, he paid you your wages and told you not to come back. The next week the process started over again — a new job if you were lucky to find one, a few days of work and back out onto the street. One week after another, this went on for years.

Unfortunately, many people could not withstand the test. They gave in and worked on Shabbos. But many others clung tenaciously to the Torah. Every Friday, they would come home and spend Shabbos with their families, not knowing what the coming week would bring.

Among these people who sacrificed so much for the dedication to Shabbos, we find two groups. One group was tremendously successful with their children. They raised a truly "virtuous generation" of sons and daughters who became the bedrock of a flourishing Torah community. The other group saw their children drift away from the Torah and assimilate into the American melting pot. Why were some people successful with their children and others not? I heard in the name of Rav Moshe Feinstein that the relative attitudes of the fathers at the Shabbos table accounted for this difference.

Some fathers came home on Friday after they were fired and they came to the Shabbos table despondent. "Oh, what a difficult life it is here in America," they would say. "I would, of course, never work on Shabbos, but look at all the hardship I have to endure to safeguard the holy Torah. Look at how much I have to sacrifice for Shabbos. And what's going to be next week? Where I am going to find another job? And if I do, will I be fired again next Friday? It's so hard to be a Jew!"

The children sitting at the table would hear this, and all too often they would think to themselves that, even though their father might be prepared to put himself through such ordeals every week, they were certainly not inclined to do so. Shabbos in their minds became a difficult, unpleasant burden that just brought sorrow and pain with it every week. And as soon as they grew up, they couldn't get away from an observant life fast enough.

Other fathers came home with an entirely different attitude. They came to the Shabbos table with tremendous joy and enthusiasm. They sang *zemiros* and said *divrei Torah* and gave their children an altogether good time. And even when they spoke about what had happened to them at work, they said it in a positive way, "Well, I finished the week and got paid, and of course, the boss told me not to come back if I'm not ready to work on Shabbos. So I told him that Shabbos is such a precious gift, I would never even consider giving it up. In fact, I consider it a privilege to stand up for the honor of Shabbos. There are plenty of other jobs, and my family will be just fine, but we would never, ever give up such a precious thing as Shabbos." And then the father would burst into song, and perhaps he would dance around the table with his children. Children who grew up in such an atmosphere would not be pulled away from Shabbos so easily.

Of course, this was not a hard and fast rule. All kinds of factors often come into play, but as a general rule, this was at the root of the difference between the two groups.

The attitude of the parents to *mitzvos* has the most profound effect on their children. This is what the *passuk* is telling us. If parents "strongly desire His commandments," then their children will be "the mighty of the earth, a virtuous generation that shall be blessed." This is a fundamental principle. If you love *mitzvos*, your children will love them, too.

⚜ The Perils of Coercion

So should a child be forced to do *mitzvos* against his will? It seems to me that he should not. The purpose of *chinuch* in *mitzvos* is to introduce a child to them when he is still young so that when he grows older he will become conditioned to doing *mitzvos* and so that he should perform them with enthusiasm and appreciation. Forcing a child to do *mitzvos*, therefore, can only have the opposite effect. It can be the most counterproductive thing imaginable.

Let us take, for instance, *chinuch* in *tefilah*. Sometimes, a parent attempting to train his child to *daven* properly puts the boy next to him and expects him to say every word from beginning to end and keep his finger on the place all the time. This really doesn't make sense. The boy probably wants to go out and play, and it's hard to keep him tied down to the Siddur for more than ten minutes. And for a child, even ten minutes can seem like a long time. So forcing him to *daven* will not engender a love for *tefilah* in his heart. If anything it will make him look upon *tefilah* as an unpleasant experience.

Moreover, there is a deeper danger in forcing a child to *daven*. The father should ask himself why he is so insistent that the boy stand next to him for such a long time and *daven*. Why isn't it acceptable to me to have my son play more and become accustomed to *tefilah* in small incremental steps according to how much he can tolerate? Why am I reaching for such a high level of *chinuch*? Is it because I think I believe this is the most effective way to guide my son toward *davening* properly when he becomes an adult? Or am I doing it show other people that my son excels at *davening*?

The father should understand that the purpose of *chinuch* is not to create a shop window of his achievements; it is not an opportunity to compete with friends and neighbors. When parents conduct the *chinuch* of their children in order to show off what they've accomplished, the results can be disastrous. The child will know that the parent does not really care about the *mitzvah* he is being asked to do. Instead of the *chinuch* teaching the child the importance of the *mitzvah*, it will teach him that the *mitzvah* itself is not really important but that its main value is as a means of competition.

How does the child know this? He doesn't have to be a master psychologist to figure it out. Every child growing up in the home of his parents is entirely at the mercy of his parents, and this makes him extremely sensitive to every nuance of his parents' words and actions that pertain to him. He knows their motivation, sometimes better than they know it themselves. And out of a natural instinct of self-preservation, he will resist the efforts of the parents to exploit him for their aggrandizement.

On the other hand, if the child senses that the parents' motivation is sincere and for his own good, if he senses that his parents think that this is the best way for him to achieve the goals they have set for him for his own good, he will make the effort to comply. Even in this instance, the parent has to consider how much *davening* time the child can tolerate at his particular age, every child being different.

The underlying principle is that a child should not be in *shul* if he is not *davening*. Therefore, I would say that if the *shul* is far away, the child should not be brought until he is much older and able to sit through the *davening*. Otherwise, he will just be bored and fidgety, and it will not be a positive experience. But if the *shul* is close by, the child could come to *shul* for the final ten minutes even at an earlier age. He can hear the last Kaddish and answer a few Ameins. As he gets older, you can perhaps bring him for Kedushah, and so on and so on until he is trained to come and *daven* and to enjoy his *davening*.

But to bring him when he does not have the patience and concentration to sit in *shul* and to force him to *daven* is not good *chinuch*. It has nothing to do with *davening*. It has to do with regimentation. All it will accomplish is to engender bad *midos* in the child, and even if he gives in now, he will rebel against *tefilah* when he gets older. In his mind, he will associate *tefilah* with bad experiences, even though the bad experiences he endured had nothing to do with *tefilah* itself.

I recall a story that happened with Rav Elya when he came to Gateshead for an extended visit. The family made a separate *minyan* for him for his convenience. Almost everyone who came to this *minyan* was a member of his family. I was the only one there who was not a relative.

One of Rav Elya's grandsons, a young boy about nine or ten years old, planted himself near Rav Elya during *davening*. While he was *davening*, the boy shuckled back and forth with great energy. He knew his grandfather was a great *tzaddik*, so he wanted to show that he was also a *tzaddik*. So he shuckled and shuckled and shuckled.

After *davening*, Rav Elya called over the boy's father.

"You have to tell him to stop shuckling," said Rav Elya.

"I understand that his shuckling is just to put on a bit of a show," said the boy's father, "but what's the harm in it?"

Rav Elya shook his head. "It's not good. If he shuckles so much when he *davens*, he'll become exhausted. Then he will come to think that *davening* is exhausting, and he'll get negative feelings about it. But the truth is that *davening* is not exhausting. It's shuckling that's exhausting."

An interesting insight and an excellent guideline for *chinuch*. If the child finds the *davening* experience unpleasant he will not want to *daven*, even though the unpleasantness had nothing to do with the *davening* itself.

◆§ *Segulos* Are Not *Chinuch*

There is an exception to these guidelines. There are certain things that we do with our children that are not really *chinuch* but *segulos*. They are not based on logic but on a mysterious effectiveness that we do not really understand. The Chazon Ish mentions three of these *segulos* with regard to children — washing their hands in the morning, putting *tzitzis* on them and placing *yarmulkes* on their heads. All three of these things are *segulos* for *yiras shamayim*. Since they do not relate to understanding and *chinuch*, the Chazon Ish says they should be done at the earliest possible age. The custom is to wash the hands of the child from the very first day, to put *tzitzis* on him when he can keep himself clean and to place a *yarmulke* on his head when he's ready to keep it on his head.

Another *segulah* is brought down in the Rambam (Talmud Torah 1:6), "As soon as a child begins to speak his father should say with him, '*Torah tzivah lanu Moshe.*'" Even though the child does not understand at all what this means, it is a *segulah* that these should be the first words that come out of the child's mouth when he reaches the stage of speaking.

All these *segulos* have nothing to do with *chinuch*, and they should be done as early as possible.

⋘ Making *Berachos*

Let us now take a look at another area of *chinuch* in *mitzvos*, training a child to make *berachos*. It's very natural for parents to insist that a young child make *berachos*, because otherwise, people might think that *berachos* are not important to him. But sometimes a child resists. He simply doesn't want to make a *berachah*. So what are you supposed to do?

The first thing is you have to consider the mentality of the child. Why doesn't he want to make a *berachah*? It's not such a difficult thing to do. So why does he refuse? You have to understand that the child has a strong *yetzer hara* that stands in the way of his making a *berachah*. The desire for food is a powerful force that seeks immediate gratification. The *yetzer* does not want to be held off even for the fifteen seconds or so that it takes to make a *berachah*.

Imagine that the child's father has promised him a candy if he does a certain thing. The child does what is expected of him and earns the candy as his reward. The father then gives him the candy for which he worked so hard and about which he dreamed. And just as he is about to take it into his mouth and enjoy its delicious sweetness, the father stops him and insists that he make a *berachah*. You can well understand why the child resists.

It's not only children who have this problem. Most adults do as well. They take a delectable morsel in their hands and they are about to eat it when they remember they have to make a *berachah*. The *yetzer* to eat it is very strong, but being adults, we have better control of ourselves. We hold back on our desire to eat, and we make the *berachah*. But was that *berachah* made with the full enunciation and concentration that it warrants? Isn't it true that most people do a better job making a *berachah* on a *mitzvah* than on a piece of food? Why? Because we have a strong desire for the food, so we race through the *berachah* as quickly as we can so that we can get to the food. But there is no physical desire pushing us to do a *mitzvah*, so we have the patience to make a proper *berachah* with full concentration.

When we teach a child to make *berachos*, we have to do it wisely. There is no question that there comes a time when every *berachah* the child makes is important. But we usually have our children making *berachos* at a very young age, well before it is required, and when they skip a *berachah* we become upset. So we're back to the same problem. The child develops a resistance to making *berachos*. Even if he complies and makes the *berachah*, either because he wants to please his parents or because he is afraid of punishment, he certainly has not been taught to enjoy making a *berachah*, to like making a *berachah*, to appreciate the importance of making a *berachah*, and that is not good *chinuch*.

Of course, you can't say that *chinuch* is impossible before the child has an appreciation for a *mitzvah*. Because where does it start? How can we expect a *mitzvah* to be a pleasant experience before the *chinuch*? That is obvious. But when we begin the *chinuch* we cannot and should not expect the child to have the feelings and appreciation that will be engendered by the *chinuch* itself.

So what do we do? First, we have to set a good example, as we said before. This will not be threatening to the child because it does not demand anything of him. It just teaches by example. Then when we call on him to do something we have be resourceful and think of ways to make doing the *mitzvah* and saying the *berachah* into pleasant experiences. We have to make it a joyous experience rather than a time of tension and pressure, and rewards certainly go a long way to capturing the heart of a child.

The Gemara says (Pesachim 108b) that on the Seder night we give different kinds of treats to the children so that they will stay awake. Chazal provided ways to draw children into the *mitzvos* in a pleasant and enjoyable way. It is not enough to get the children to perform the mechanics of the *mitzvos*. They have to be introduced to the *neshamah* of the *mitzvos*, the inner beauty that they will come to appreciate more and more as they grow older. But if they're simply pushed into doing *mitzvos* even though they don't enjoy them, they'll never enjoy them, even when they are older.

✑§ Speaking to the Air

Before we can think about *chinuch* in *berachos*, we have to ask ourselves, What is a *berachah* and when is the proper time to introduce a child to *berachos*? The Gemara tells us (Arachin 3a) that *chinuch* in *berachos* begins when the child understands to Whom the *berachah* is addressed. The child has to know that there is a Creator Whom we are acknowledging with our *berachos*. If the child cannot grasp this concept there is no point in teaching him to make *berachos*. If a child does not understand what is happening when he makes a *berachah*, it is no better than winding him up like a doll and applauding when he is done. And then when his uncle and aunt come to visit he's prodded to make a repeat performance. It's all a game and a show, and it has no real meaning.

The first step, therefore, in *chinuch* in *berachos* is telling the child that there is a Ribono Shel Olam in the world and that what we are eating is something that He has provided and that we have to thank Him for it. Without this knowledge, there is no *berachah* at all.

But even before this first step, the child must be introduced to the idea of *berachos* by watching his father and mother make *berachos*. They have to see that when the parents make a *berachah* they are not just speaking to the air but that they are speaking to Someone. The child may not understand to Whom the parents are speaking, but the child sees that something holy is happening. The parents are not just mumbling a few words into the air and then popping the food into their mouths. No, they close their eyes and say each word with feeling and concentration. The child sees that making a *berachah* is something meaningful and important. When he gets a little older and is introduced to *berachos*, he is already prepared and eager to follow their lead.

There are some people, however, who out of a sense of modesty feel uncomfortable being so demonstrative about *berachos*. They make their berachos quietly and unobtrusively even though inside they have the complete concentration that more demonstrative people do. This is a commendable *midah* indeed, and it is to be encouraged. But when it comes to *chinuch* of their children this kind of modest comportment is a mistake. In front of his children, he should make a point of saying the *berachos* aloud word by word with conspicuous concentration. Otherwise, how will the children learn about the great value of *berachos*?

When the child sees his parents making meaningful *berachos*, when he sees them doing something that is obviously holy rather than just speaking to the air, he will be ready for *chinuch* in *berachos*. We have to begin with basic *chinuch* in *emunah*. We should not be afraid to speak about these things. We don't have to get into lengthy discussions. In fact, it is better not to get into long discussions. But a short sentence or two can work wonders. Once he absorbs this concept, we can move on to *chinuch* in *berachos*.

The main thing we have to remember is that *chinuch* is not disciplining a child to do things that he find difficult and distasteful. It is opening up a wonderful and exciting world to the child, a world of joy and fulfillment that will enrich his life in this world and the next.

CHAPTER TEN

The Other Mitzvos

When we think about *chinuch* in *mitzvos*, we are accustomed to thinking about the *mitzvos asei*, the positive commandments. We think about *lulav, sukkah, tzitzis, tefilah, berachos* and the like. But the *mitzvos lo saaseh*, the prohibitions, are equally *mitzvos* in the Torah, and there is an equal requirement to include them in the *chinuch* of our children.

Let us take for example the prohibition of *lo signov*, you shall not steal. Just about all parents teach their children that it is wrong to take something that belongs to someone else. But how many do so as part of their general *chinuch* in *mitzvos*? It is not enough to tell the child that stealing is wrong, that is not a nice thing to do, that you wouldn't want someone stealing your things so don't steal other people's things, that it is unacceptable. You have to tell the child that the Ribono Shel Olam forbids stealing, that it is an *aveirah* in the Torah. You have to teach him not to steal as part of his *chinuch* in *mitzvos* and *yiras shamayim*. If the only reason not to steal is because it goes against social values and mores, then there may come a time when he will establish different values for himself.

Furthermore, if the prohibition against stealing is not spelled out for a child, he may misinterpret what his parents are telling him. He may think that it not really fundamentally wrong to take something that belongs to someone else. He may just see it as something that is not so nice, something that displeases his parents because of their own sensibilities even though it not really of such critical importance. He may have noticed that his parents are particular about behavior at the Shabbos table; they may even demand that the children sit respectfully while the adults converse. He knows that this is not a *mitzvah* in the Torah but simply a preference of his parents, and he may think that the same applies to their aversion to his touching other people's things.

This is a serious mistake in *chinuch*. The children must be told that there is a *mitzvah* in the Torah that forbids stealing; the Ribono Shel Olam forbids taking something that belongs to someone else. Otherwise, we cannot be sure that they'll take it seriously.

The Rambam writes (Geneivah 1:10), "It is proper for the *beis din* to spank minors, to the limit of their endurance (*kefi kocham*), for stealing, so that they should not become accustomed to doing it. The same applies if they cause other forms of damage." The Maggid Mishneh on the spot comments that he finds no source for this statement but that it appears to be obvious. True, there is an opinion that *beis din* is not required to stop a child from eating non-kosher food. But that applies only to *mitzvos bein adam la'Makom*, commandments that govern our relationship with the Ribono Shel Olam. When it comes to *mitzvos bein adam lechaveiro*, *mitzvos* that govern our relationships with other people, however, *beis din* is required to ensure that minors cause no damage to others.

When young boys are taught *mesechtos* such as Bava Kama and Bava Metzia that deal with damages, we have to ensure that we are not teaching them intellectual abstractions. We have to impress upon them that these are issues that relate to their own lives in a very real way. These relevant issues concern *mitzvos* in the Torah that forbid encroachment on other people's rights and properties. The child has to learn that the Ribono Shel Olam forbids him to damage chairs or doors or other people's toys. He has to learn that the Ribono Shel Olam forbids him to take someone else's property without permission, that if he does so he violates the very serious prohibition of *lo signov*.

This is not a trivial matter. We see that *beis din* can properly spank the child *kefi kocham*, to the limit of his endurance. We, of course, are not *beis din*, and we are certainly not permitted to spank the child to the limit of his endurance. But we can at least infer from the Rambam's statement the gravity of preventing theft and destructive behavior in our children.

In the general *chinuch* of *mitzvos*, we don't find that the child should be spanked if he does not comply. On the contrary, spanking is not a simple matter, and it can often be counterproductive. But when it comes to theft and causing damage, *beis din* spanks the errant child. Moreover, the spanking that *beis din* administers is not a simple slap on the wrist. It is to the limit of his endurance, a spanking he will never forget. We see clearly the extreme gravity of such behavior, and the same applies to lying.

When a parent sees a child behaving in this way, he should tremble with worry and concern. He should realize that if his child becomes accustomed to destructive behavior it can be extremely damaging to the very foundations of his being. He has to rebuke and discipline his child with great seriousness. This should be accomplished without anger or any other bad *midos*, of course, but with the full gravity that the matter deserves. Theft and lying must be completely uprooted, because they can lead to dire consequences, even to an erosion of *yiras shamayim*. And it must be done in the context of the prohibitions in the Torah and the violation of the commandments of the Ribono Shel Olam.

⋖§ The Meaning of the Word *Chinuch*

When Lot was captured by the Babylonian kings and Avraham came to his rescue, the Torah tells us (Bereishis 14:14) that he mobilized *chanichav*, those people he had influenced by his *chinuch* to follow the Torah, specifically Eliezer, as Rashi explains (ibid.; Nedarim 32a). What is the precise meaning of the word *chinuch*? Rashi provides an interesting dictionary definition. It means "the first introduction of a person or an item to the function that he or it will ultimately serve." That is why the word applies to the *chinuch* of people and also to the *chanukah* of the *mizbeyach* or the Beis Hamikdash.

The word *chinuch*, therefore, means the establishment of a person on a solid footing to enable him to assume the role he is destined to assume. We have to make an assessment of the role toward which he is headed, and we have to prepare him for it. If what we have to do will take a long time, then we have to begin earlier. And we have to do those things that will have a lasting effect.

When it comes to teaching a child that theft is wrong, we have to recognize what a terrible effect stealing will have on the child in the long run. We have to recognize that it will corrode his *neshamah*, undermine his *yiras shamayim* and prevent him from becoming what he is meant to be. The goal of the *chinuch* is to avoid these consequences. Telling the child that theft is not nice or that it's not acceptable may be effective for the short term, but the only way to avoid long-term damage is by impressing on the child that theft is a serious *aveirah*, that the Ribono Shel Olam forbids it.

There is another side of this understanding of *chinuch* as focused on the future of the child rather than the present.

I once heard a story about Rav Yaakov Kamenetsky that took place when his children were still young. Rav Yaakov and a guest were sitting at the dining-room table and talking. In the meantime, one of Rav Yaakov's little children came into the dining room, climbed onto the table and started to dance. He was literally dancing on the table. Rav Yaakov was sitting there and talking to his guest without batting an eyelash. After a few minutes, the guest could no longer contain himself.

"With all due respect," he said, "why is this child being allowed to dance on the table? Is this a way to be *mechanech* him?"

"What is *chinuch*?" said Rav Yaakov. "Why do we impose all these restrictions on a child? The child doesn't enjoy it. Sometimes, we are actually harassing him. So why do we do it? Why not let the child run free? Do you know why? Because if you let him run free when he is young he will also run free when he is older, and then he will end up doing things that he should not be doing. Do you agree?"

"Yes, of course," said the guest.

"Well," said Rav Yaakov, "when this child grows up I assure you that he will not dance on tables, so what's the point of stopping him now? If you stop him from dancing on the table, it is not *chinuch*. It is only because you are bothered by the child dancing on the table. But it has nothing to do with *chinuch*."

This is an interesting story, and an important insight into *chinuch*. If you demand something from the child because of your own comfort rather than his *chinuch* you have a whole different set of considerations. Should you impose your will on the child? After all, there is a real issue of *bein adam lechaveiro* with a child as well. It is not allowed to persecute a child without very good reason. So when it comes to *chinuch* you have to do what you have to do as long as it is not counterproductive, but if it's not *chinuch*, you really have to think long and hard about what you demand from a child.

ᴥ The Inclination to Theft

It is not uncommon for children to have an inclination to theft. A child may like money or nice things, and if he sees them, he takes them even if they do not belong to him. This can make the parents very nervous, and they don't always know how to react. Some parents react by depriving the child of material things. They think that if they do not let him have material things he will be cured of his temptations. Often, however, doing this will have the opposite effect.

Let's take a look at a piece of Gemara (Bava Basra 11a). The Gemara addresses a story in Tanach (Shoftim 18:3-45). It is the story of a Levi by the name of Yehonasan ben Gershom who served as a priest in a temple of *avodah zarah*. A Jewish fellow, a descendant of Moshe Rabbeinu, and he was a temple priest for *avodah zarah*. The Navi's account of the story is terse, but the Gemara elaborates.

The people asked the priest, "How can it be that a descendant of Moshe Rabbeinu could do such a thing?"

"I have a tradition from the house of my grandfather," he replied, "that it is better to hire yourself out to *avodah zarah* than to be dependent on other people."

The grandfather to whom he was referring was Moshe himself. Yehonasan had financial problems. He couldn't earn enough money to support himself. And according to his understanding, Moshe had believed that it was better to earn a living as a priest in a temple of *avodah zarah* than to rely on other people for handouts.

Rashi explains that Yehonasan did not really think that Moshe had endorsed *avodah zarah*. He thought that Moshe had considered it better to serve in a temple of *avodah zarah* without accepting the religion of the *avodah zarah* than to accept handouts. You could work in the temple, ring the bells and take care of the building, as long as you didn't actually worship the idols. That's what Yehonasan thought.

But, says the Gemara, that was not what Moshe had actually said. Moshe had said it was better to hire yourself out to do an *avodah* that is *zarah* to you, work to which is alien to you, before you accept handouts from other people. As Rav said to Rav Kahana, "Sell animal carcasses in the marketplace, but don't take handouts from people."

In any case, it was a disgrace that Moshe's descendant was working in a temple of *avodah zarah*. What did they do? So the Gemara says that David did an incredibly clever thing. Recognizing that Yehonasan cared so much about money, David appointed him to be the superintendent of his treasuries.

Listen to this. Here was a man who cared so much about money that he was willing to work in a temple of *avodah zarah* as long as the pay was good enough. So you would think that such a man could not be trusted with money. You certainly wouldn't want to let him anywhere near the royal treasuries. But what did David do? The exact opposite. He appointed him the superintendent of the royal treasuries. Instead of keeping him away from the royal treasuries he put him in charge of them. Amazing.

And what was the result of this bold move? The Gemara says that he did complete *teshuvah*. That he returned to the Ribono Shel Olam with all his heart.

Clearly, sometimes the antidote to a strong *yetzer hara* is not to deprive the person of his desire but to give him what he desires in a permissible form. Of course, this is not always an advisable route. You have to really understand the person and the situation. But David understood that in this case deprivation might not be the best option. Instead, he chose to put him right next to pots and pots of money. And that turned out to be the cure to his money hunger. He returned to the Ribono Shel Olam with all his heart.

In *chinuch*, we have to consider the same principle when a child has a strong lust for material things to the point where he takes other people's things without permission. The parents should consider whether it is better to deal with this by depriving him of material things or whether it is better perhaps to give him what he desires. Perhaps it would be more helpful to wean him away from this *yetzer hara* by removing his need. Of course, we should not deal with a child's *yetzer hara* by giving him something that is forbidden. But when it comes to greed, it may be better to give him what he needs so that his greed should be stilled. Then, hopefully, he will grow out of it as he grows older.

The Torah tells us (Bereishis 32:23) that when Yaakov returned to Canaan with his family he anticipated a confrontation with his estranged brother Eisav. So in the middle of the night he moved his wives and his eleven children across a river to safety. Rashi takes note of the mention of eleven children and wonders where his daughter Dinah was. He answers that Yaakov had secreted Dinah in a box so that Eisav wouldn't see her. And because of this, he was punished by suffering through the incident of Dinah's abduction. Had he not hidden her away and had Eisav married her, Eisav might have repented and changed his ways.

All the commentators immediately ask the same question regarding this statement of Rashi. Did Yaakov do anything wrong by hiding his daughter? Let's consider what lessons we're supposed to take away from this statement. A person has a daughter and there's a *rasha* who wants to marry her. Let's say this daughter has a talent for *kiruv* work and there's a possibility that she may get this *rasha* to do *teshuvah*. So the father goes to ask his rabbi what he should do. Should he continue looking among the best *bachurim* in the *yeshivah*? Or should he marry her off to this *rasha*?

There is, of course, no question. He should do what is best for his daughter. So what was wrong with what Yaakov did by hiding Dinah from Eisav's lecherous eyes? Why did he deserve to be punished?

Rav Elya answered these questions based on a Zohar.

How would Dinah have brought Eisav to *teshuvah*? Would she have argued philosophy and ideology with him? Let's not forget that Eisav grew up in Yitzchak's house. He sat on the same *cheder* bench with Yaakov until his bar mitzvah. There was nothing Dinah could have told him that he didn't already know himself.

So how could she have made an impact on him? Because we learned in Rashi (Bereishis 26:34) that Eisav was a man of great lust, and according to the Zohar, Dinah was the most beautiful woman in the world since the earliest times of antiquity. Eisav was who he was because of his tremendous libidinous desires. His *yetzer hara* was overwhelming. But if he could have married Dinah his *yetzer* would have been stilled and all the great qualities he possessed as the son of Yitzchak and Rivkah would have come to the fore and he would have become a great man. If he could have fulfilled his greatest desires in a permissible way, his *yetzer* would have been stilled.

This is the same principle based on which David appointed a former priest of *avodah zarah* to be the superintendent of his royal treasuries.

When we're talking about the *chinuch* of a child, we're not talking about an Eisav or any other *rasha*. We're talking about a pure, innocent child who exhibits certain material desires. So we have to be clever and wise. Is it better to deprive him of his desires or perhaps it is better to give him what he wants so that his desires do not play such a big role in his thoughts? If he wants cookies, should you put the cookie jar higher up or you should perhaps let him have a few extra cookies? You can always give him a cookie as an easily earned reward. Putting the cookies out of his reach just inflames his desires.

So give him the cookie, but at the same time, teach him the lesson that he needs to absorb for life. Tell him that he should enjoy the cookie because if you gave it to him it is kosher. But emphasize that if he had taken it without permission it would not be kosher. It would be forbidden by the holy Torah. With this kind of *chinuch*, he is more likely to grow up with integrity and the strength to face the ordeals that life will put in his way.

Of course, you shouldn't go to extremes. You have to use common sense. Some things require *yiras shamayim*, and some things require common sense. And I would venture to say that in navigating the shoals of life a person needs as much common sense as *yiras shamayim*, especially when it come to *chinuch*.

CHAPTER ELEVEN

Fathers and Sons

T here is one area of *chinuch* that is reserved for fathers and sons, and that is the *mitzvah* of *talmud Torah*. The mother, of course, likewise bears responsibility in the fulfillment of this *mitzvah* to its fullest, as we have discussed again and again, and in the *zchus* of the Torah of her children. But the direct responsibility to learn with the boys falls directly on the shoulders of the father.

Every father has the *mitzvah* of learning with his sons, every single father, regardless of whether he is a great *talmid chacham* or a simple water carrier. The father always has the obligation to fulfill the *mitzvah* of learning Torah with his sons. If he cannot do it himself, then he has to appoint a *shaliach*, an agent, to do it for him.

The appointment of the *shaliach* does not release him from his obligation. A father cannot send his son off to school and feel that he has discharged his obligation, that now it is the responsibility of the school. If the school fails, the father has failed, because his *shaliach* was not effective. If the school succeeds, it is the father's success for having chosen a good *shaliach*.

So let us begin with a father who learns with his son. He has to view his son not only as his child but also as his *talmid*. In fact, the Torah tells us (Devarim 6:7), "*Veshinantam levanecha*. You shall teach them to your sons." We say the *passuk* every day in Shema. And Rashi explains that the word *levanecha*, to your sons, refers here to your *talmidim*, because we find in other places that *talmidim* are called sons. So every father should also view himself as a *rebbe* and his son as his *talmid*, and in that context, he has to understand his role and to consider what he needs to do to fulfill it successfully.

✑ The Sons of Moshe

The Torah tells us (Bamidbar 3:1-2), "And these are the descendants of Aharon and Moshe on the day Hashem spoke with Moshe at Mount Sinai. And these are the names of the sons of Aharon, the firstborn was Nadav, and Avihu, and Elazar and Isamar. There are the names of the sons of Aharon, the anointed Kohanim, whose hands he filled to serve."

Rashi immediately asks the question that really jumps out at you. The Torah tells that we are about to hear about the descendants of both Aharon and Moshe. But then the Torah only identifies Aharon's children. It does not mention the names of Moshe's children.

So Rashi explains — and it's really a Midrash — that this teaches us that whoever teaches Torah to someone else's child is considered to have fathered him. Moshe taught Torah to Aharon's sons. Therefore, they're considered his sons as well.

But why only Aharon's sons? Moshe learned Torah with all of Klal Yisrael, so by the same token, all of them should be considered his children. Why then does the Torah single out Aharon's sons more than anyone else? The Ohr Hachaim raises this question and offers a different interpretation of the *pesukim*.

There is also another question that arises from these *pesukim*. The Torah tells us that these are the descendants of Aharon and Moshe "on the day Hashem spoke with Moshe at Mount Sinai." Why does the *passuk* mention the giving of the Torah on Mount Sinai? At this point, we are nearly two years past Mount Sinai. So why when speaking about the descendants of Moshe and Aharon does the Torah suddenly hark back to Mount Sinai?

Rashi answers this question as well. The sons of Aharon, he explains, became like the sons of Moshe on the day he received the Torah on Mount Sinai, because he taught them what he learned from the Ribono Shel Olam.

Now, Moshe didn't teach the sons of Aharon, or anyone else for that matter, until after he came down from Mount Sinai. It was a long process that took months and years. And yet, the Torah tells us that Aharon's sons were considered like Moshe's sons retroactively from the day he learned the Torah from the Ribono Shel Olam on Mount Sinai. Once he learned with them, they retroactively became like his sons from the first day the Torah was given. An amazing thought. What is the Torah telling us here? What does this mean for all of us?

Before we attempt to explain Rashi's approach, we have to ask ourselves another question. What is the significance of Aharon's sons being considered like Moshe's sons? What is the difference if they are considered like his sons or not? What if they were only considered his *talmidim*? How would that be any different?

The Gemara discusses (Bava Metzia 33a) a person who sees two lost objects lying in the street. He recognizes one as belonging to his father and the other as belonging to his *rebbe*, and he only has the opportunity to salvage one. Which one should he retrieve and return, the one belonging to his father or to his *rebbe*? The Gemara says he should return the one belonging to his *rebbe*. Why? Because his father brings him into Olam Hazeh, while his *rebbe* brings him into Olam Haba.

We see from this Gemara that a *rebbe* shapes his *talmid* in much the same way as a father shapes his son. The difference is that the father shapes him physically so that he can exist in this world while the *rebbe* shapes him spiritually so that he can enter the Next World.

When a person passes away and leaves behind children, his place in Olam Haba is not yet determined. After all his deeds and accomplishments are evaluated and he is assigned a place in Olam Haba, there is no end to his opportunities for advancement. All the *mitzvos* and *zechuyos* of his children and grandchildren and great-grandchildren for all future generations are considered to his eternal credit, because he brought them into this world and set them on their paths of accomplishment.

It is the same with a *rebbe*. If he teaches Torah to someone else's son, it is considered as if he shaped him, and everything good that ever comes out of him and his descendants is considered to the eternal credit of the *rebbe* in Olam Haba. This is what the Torah tells us about Aharon's sons. Moshe taught them Torah so they were considered like his own children, and everything they did was to his credit.

The Midrash asks (Bamidbar 2:22) why "the descendants of Moshe" are mentioned in this *passuk* when only Aharon's sons are actually mentioned. And the Midrash answers that the Torah does not want to diminish Moshe's honor. That's the Midrash. So how would Moshe's honor be diminished if he wasn't mentioned in the *passuk*? And how is it spared by mentioning Moshe's descendants but not naming them?

Obviously, this Midrash also understands that Aharon's sons are considered like Moshe's sons. And the Torah is making an important point here. In the grand scheme of things, Aharon's family has a greater role than Moshe's family. Aharon's family are the Kohanim, the ones that serve in the Beis Hamikdash, the spiritual leaders of Klal Yisrael, while Moshe's family are the Leviim who have a lesser role. In this sense, Moshe's honor is diminished.

So the Torah tells us right here that Aharon's sons are also considered Moshe's sons because he taught them Torah. Therefore, no less than Aharon, Moshe's children and grandchildren and great-grandchildren will be the Kohanim of Klal Yisrael. Everything they do and accomplish will go to Moshe's credit, because he will have shaped them. All of Klal Yisrael are also his children, of course, because he taught them Torah. But Aharon's sons deserve special mention, because through them Moshe gained an eternal share in the Kehunah.

When did Aharon's sons become like Moshe's sons? As we saw, it was not from the time that he taught them, but rather retroactively from the time he received the Torah on Mount Sinai. Why is that so? This brings us into the very heart of the *mitzvah* of learning Torah.

◆§ Learn and Teach

Every day, we say in Ahavah Rabbah, the *berachah* of Torah, "Our Father ... be merciful with us and give understanding into our hearts to understand, to comprehend, to hear, to learn, to teach, to safeguard and to do ...." It's one package. We have a mission in life. We have to learn and fulfill what we've learned. We also have to teach others, whether it is our own children or other people. Teaching is not a secondary thing, something that is optional. It is an integral part of the *mitzvah* of *talmud Torah*.

The Mishnah says (Avos 4:5), "If a person learns Torah in order to teach he is given the opportunity to learn and to teach, but if he learns in order to do he is given the opportunity to learn, teach, safeguard and do." The Mishnah makes no mention, however, of someone who learns in order to learn. Why not? Because that is not the end purpose of learning Torah. The Torah was given to learn and to teach. It is meant to be like blood pumped through the arteries of the body, giving life to all of Klal Yisrael. That is what the Ribono Shel Olam wants.

So the teaching starts with learning in order to teach. And if you learn Torah for yourself with no intent to teach it, and afterward you decide that you want to teach *talmidim*, it is too late. Certainly, you can teach what you know and it will be a valuable contribution, but it will be much more difficult for the people you teach to become the *talmidim* who are like your own children. It will be much more difficult for you to shape them as if you had given birth to them.

When does a person gain the *zchus* of having *talmidim* in the fullest sense of the word? When he's thirty or older and looks for a teaching position? By then it is too late. He earns that great *zchus* during all the years he was sitting and learning with the intent of passing on the Torah he has learned to others. First of all, a person who knows he'll be teaching learns with a higher dedication and seeks a greater clarity. But it is more than that. The Torah that is learned with the intent to teach is a different Torah. It is not a selfish Torah. It is not a restricted Torah. It is a Torah that bursts forth with a dynamic holiness, a Torah that can illuminate the world. That is the kind of Torah that transforms *talmidim* to the point that they are considered like the sons of the *rebbe*, as if he has fathered them.

Aharon's sons were considered like Moshe's sons, because Moshe learned Torah with the intent to teach it to Klal Yisrael. Therefore, when he stood on top of Mount Sinai and received the Torah from the Ribono Shel Olam, the process of transforming his *talmidim* into his very own children had already begun. That is when Aharon's sons became his sons, "on the day Hashem spoke with Moshe on Mount Sinai."

A Father's Torah

Let us now consider what all this means to a father and his sons. He has to understand that his *mitzvah* to teach Torah to his son is the most profound of *mitzvos*. When a father teaches Torah to his son, the father-son relationship is extended beyond Olam Hazeh into Olam Haba. The bond is much deeper, and the rewards are endlessly multiplied. It is the obligation to teach his son Torah to the extent that he himself is able to do so. And beyond that, he has to appoint a *shaliach* to represent him.

But as we saw, the *rebbe–talmid* relationship does not begin when they sit down to learn together. It begins when the *rebbe* is learning Torah by himself with the intent of someday teaching the Torah he learns to others. Therefore, a father's role as the *rebbe* of his sons does not begin when the sons reach the age when they can learn and understand. It begins when the father himself is still a young *bachur*, when he is learning in *yeshivah* and acquiring his knowledge of the Torah.

He may not think at the time that he will someday say a *shiur* in a *yeshivah* or in a *beis midrash*. He may have a different future charted out for himself, perhaps in business or in a *chessed* organization or something else. But he surely intends to get married and have children. He knows that someday he will have the obligation to learn with his sons. And even before they are born, he has to learn Torah with that intent in mind. Then his Torah will be on the exalted standard of "learned in order to teach," and when he teaches it to his sons, they will become his sons in the fullest and broadest sense of the word, not only with regard to Olam Hazeh but also with regard to Olam Haba.

The *Sefer Hachinuch*

What is a father supposed to learn with his sons? If they need help with their homework, he should certainly help them, but I don't know if that is enough to bring the father–son relationship to the highest level. The school is his *shaliach*, but what should he himself learn with his sons?

The *Sefer Hachinuch* would be an excellent choice.

The author of the *Sefer Hachinuch* was a Rishon, most probably the R'ah. As he explains in his Introduction, he wrote it for his young son and his friends so that their minds would be absorbed by keeping count of the *mitzvos* in each *parashah* and by their discovery of the roots and *taamim* of the *mitzvos*. Normally, you would translate *taam* as a reason or rationale, but in this case, it would be too narrow a translation. We cannot narrow a *mitzvah* down to a specific reason. The word *taam* with regard to *mitzvos* should be translated as a taste, a hint of what the *mitzvah* represents.

He called it *Sefer Hachinuch*, because it was meant as a tool for the *chinuch* of the young; it would draw them into the incredible world of the *mitzvos*. Even if they didn't understand the *mitzvos* in their fullest depth, he added, they could expand on their knowledge as they grew older.

The *chinuch* of children in *mitzvos*, he insisted, could not be limited to giving them a list of things they should and shouldn't do. It had to bring the children into the spirit of the *mitzvah* so that they would see the greatness of the Ribono Shel Olam in every single *mitzvah* and appreciate the divine wisdom that went into its formulation.

As long as they could be given a taste of the *mitzvah*, he explains, they would be drawn into the world of *mitzvos*. It is a parent who wants his child to eat a certain fruit because of the vitamins, minerals and other beneficial nutrients it provides. When the child is older, he will understand that the fruit should be eaten for its therapeutic value, but when he is still young, he can be induced to eat it because it is sweet and delicious. In the same way, we have to give the child a taste of the *mitzvos* when he is young so that he will love them and embrace them. An introduction to the roots and the underlying principles of the *mitzvah* will speak to his heart.

I want to give just one example, one among so many, of how the *Sefer Hachinuch* illuminates a *mitzvah*.

The *mitzvah* of *maaser sheni* requires that in specific years of the seven-year Shemitah cycle a portion of the crop must be brought to Yerushalayim where it must be eaten. It may not be eaten outside of Yerushalayim. It can be exchanged for money, but then the money must be brought to Yerushalayim and spent on food to be eaten there. The food is not given to the Kohanim or the Leviim or to poor people. It is eaten by the owners themselves, but instead of eating it in their homes they are required to eat it in Yerushalayim. What is the point of this *mitzvah*?

The *Sefer Hachinuch* explains that the Ribono Shel Olam wanted all of Klal Yisrael to learn Torah and to live on an elevated plane. But people are inclined to focus on the mundane aspects of life. In Yerushalayim, however, the situation is different. Yerushalayim is the center of Torah and *yiras shamayim*. Its streets reverberate with the sound of Torah, and its people are absorbed in its study. The Ribono Shel Olam knew that if a person visited Yerushalayim he could not help being influenced by its holy environment. But a quick visit, such as on a Yom Tov, would not be enough. He might be inspired, but he would not become learned.

Therefore, the Ribono Shel Olam commanded that one tenth of the crop be eaten only in Yerushalayim. This would mandate that either the farmer himself or one of his sons would spend a considerable amount of time in Yerushalayim, since he would have to stay there until all the food is consumed. It could be weeks. It could be months. And what would he do while he stays in Yerushalayim? There was no frivolity in Yerushalayim. It was a place of Torah and holiness, and all the visitors were inevitably drawn into the same pursuits. He would attend *shiurim* and learn Torah until he would reach a level of wisdom.

After the food was consumed, he would return home in a different state, more learned and more inspired than when he had left. As a result, instead of having only one or two learned people in the town, there would be a learned person in just about every home. And all the people — men, women and children — will enjoy the full benefits of their knowledge of the Torah, and the level of the entire nation will be elevated.

That's how you have to learn a *mitzvah* for yourself and with a child. And when you teach a child the *mitzvos* in this way, you are learning Torah with him in a beautiful way.

So this is my recommendation to every father. Teach your child the *mitzvos* using the *Sefer Hachinuch*. By doing so, you'll give him an appreciation for Torah and *mitzvos* in Olam Hazeh and you'll help him earn a share in Olam Haba. You'll be his father in the deepest sense of the word.

CHAPTER TWELVE

Ulterior Motives of Joy

After the eighth plague devastated the land of Egypt, Pharaoh seemed on the verge of relenting. Moshe had demanded from Pharaoh that he let the people go out to the wilderness and bring offerings to the Ribono Shel Olam. With his land in ruins, Pharaoh signaled to Moshe and Aharon that he was ready to give in to their demand. It is worthwhile to pay particular attention to the conversation that followed.

"Go serve Hashem your Lord," Pharaoh said. "Who are the ones that go?"

"We will go with our young and our old," Moshe said, "We will go with our sons and our daughters, our sheep and our cattle, because it is a festival of Hashem for us."

"It is not so," Pharaoh responded. "Let the men go and serve Hashem, because that is what you are requesting."

When we read these lines, we sense an undercurrent in the conversation, a debate about ideological issues. Specifically, the Kli Yakar remarks on the oddity of Pharaoh's question. Who are the ones that go? That is definitely an unusual language. He should have said, Who intends to go? We can also question why he says at the end "let the men go and serve Hashem, because that is what you are requesting." Moshe had requested that everyone go, not only the men.

So the Kli Yakar explains that Pharaoh was asking a general question when he said, "Who are the ones that go?" Pharaoh knew that Moshe wanted to take all the people out of Egypt, claiming that all of them were needed to participate in the service to Hashem. But Pharaoh had no intention of letting them all go. Go and look around the world, he was saying to Moshe, and tell me which are the ones that go to perform the sacrificial service for their gods. Who are the ones that usually go? Do women and children perform the services in the temples of the gods? Do the old people perform the services? No, it is the men who do these things. So you don't really need all the people. I'll let you have the men.

Not so, Moshe replied. We are not like the other nations of the world. Other nations separate themselves from their families and go off to appease their gods. Their service to the gods really has nothing to do with their everyday lives and their families. So who then should go off to this encounter with the gods than the men, who are the strongest and boldest among the people? But that is not how it is with our people. Our service in honor of Hashem is part of the fabric of our lives, and although the actual sacrificial service is performed by the men, the service is a festival for the entire family. Everyone shares in the joy of the service, and in that sense, everyone participates.

But Pharaoh was adamant. He refused to hear about different modes of divine service. Take the men, he said, because that is what you are requesting. You want to serve Hashem? You ask my permission to go out into the wilderness and bring offerings? I'm not interested in your clever fabrications. You have no need for anyone but the men. Take them and go.

Moshe was turned away, but the point he had made to Pharaoh has resonated with us ever since. When a person does *avodah*, it is not enough that he himself is doing it. The completeness of *avodah* requires that the whole family be involved as well. It requires that the *avodah* should also be a *chinuch* for the children and a cause of celebration for everyone. We all have to go, Moshe told Pharaoh, "because it is a festival of Hashem for us."

Even when the children are too young to participate in the *avodah* themselves, a proper *chinuch* demands that they share in the joys of their parents' *avodah*. When they see their parents doing a *mitzvah*, it should be a festival for them, a time of celebration. Then they will always associate doing a *mitzvah* with feelings of joy, and when the time comes they will do them with a great measure of excitement and enthusiasm.

✑ Prizes and Pleasure

The Zohar tells about a man named Yose who came to Rabbi Abba and said he wanted to learn Torah because he wanted to be rich. Apparently, he felt he could achieve his goal of becoming rich by learning Torah. Rabbi Abba was not dismayed. He accepted Yose as a *talmid* and told all the *talmidim* to call him Yose the Wealthy One.

Yose was pleased; he felt he had made the right choice and that this path would bring him the riches he desired. After a while, he saw great success in his learning but there were still no riches. He complained to Rabbi Abba, and Rabbi Abba reassured him he would indeed become rich.

Presently, a simple man came into the *yeshivah* and told Rabbi Abba that his father had died and left him a great amount of *paz*, treasure. The man told Rabbi Abba that he had no need for so much treasure and that he would rather give it to the *talmidim* of the *yeshivah*. Rabbi Abba accepted the treasure and gave it to Yose. Henceforth, he was known as Yose ben Pazi.

Having acquired his riches, Yose ben Pazi continued to learn with great *simchah*, and he discovered the wondrous treasures of the Torah. He now realized that his dreams of riches were nothing but foolishness, and he was very upset. He complained again to Rabbi Abba, but this time his complaint was different.

"Why did you fool me?" he said. "It's as if you took away my very soul. I should be learning Torah for the greatness of the Ribono Shel Olam, not for gold and silver. I don't want any of it."

He returned the treasure and asked that it be distributed among the poor. From then on, he learned Torah for its own sake, and eventually, he became the renowned Rabbi Yose ben Pazi whose name appears often in Shas.

This, concludes the Zohar, is what Chazal said, "A person should always be involved with Torah and *mitzvos* even if it is not for their own sake, *shelo lishmah*, because doing something not for its own sake eventually leads to doing it for its own sake, *lishmah*."

So we see here an illustration of *mitoch shelo lishmah ba lishmah*. In the beginning, Yose was not learning because of his love for the Ribono Shel Olam and his Torah but because he wanted to be rich. And Rabbi Abba understood this and accepted him into the yeshivah anyway, because he knew that the path of *shelo lishmah* eventually leads to *lishmah*.

Why, however, did Rabbi Abba tell the other *talmidim* to call him Yose the Wealthy One as soon as he came into the *yeshivah*? Why didn't he just promise him that he would become rich?

Wouldn't that have motivated the young Yose to dedicate himself to learning Torah? Wasn't the promise of the holy Rabbi Abba enough to convince Yose that he would indeed become rich? And if not, what was to be gained by the other *talmidim* calling him the Wealthy One? Yose wanted money, not a fancy title.

We see here a very important principle in the concept of *mitoch shelo lishmah ba lishmah*. The Torah has to be learned with *simchah*, pure joy, and when we learn Torah joyously, we penetrate into its depths and we gain even greater joy, which leads us even deeper into the Torah. The ideal joy with which we should learn Torah is the joy of learning *lishmah*, for its own sake, for the love of the Ribono Shel Olam and His holy Torah.

But what if a person is not yet on the level of learning Torah *lishmah*? How will he ever penetrate into the Torah to find its deeper *simchah* if he begins to learn without *simchah*? The answer is that he should begin learning *shelo lishmah*. He should create an artificial *simchah* for his learning, a *simchah* that derives from an external source but nonetheless connects to the Torah he is learning. The result is that, in one way or another, he is learning the Torah with *simchah*, and when you learn Torah with *simchah*, it opens up for you, and you discover the genuine and profound *simchah* of the Torah itself. You arrive at the *simchah* of learning *lishmah*.

And it is the same with all the *mitzvos* in the Torah. As long as you do the *mitzvah* with *simchah*, even if it is an artificial, externally applied *simchah*, you will eventually connect with the inner essence of the *mitzvah* and from then on you will no longer need external motivations. The love of the *mitzvah* itself will be your greatest motivation.

Rabbi Abba could have promised Yose that if he learned Torah he would one day become rich, and Yose would have been pleased. But it would not have given him such a great measure of immediate *simchah*. It would not have been enough to infuse his learning with *simchah* and bring him to the next level. So Rabbi

Abba instructed the other *talmidim* to call him Yose the Wealthy One. This made the idea of his future riches more of a reality to him. It raised the level of his *simchah* and thereby also raised the level of his learning.

When Yose grew impatient after a while, Rabbi Abba assured him that the promise would soon be fulfilled, and indeed it was. Yose continued to learn with the great *simchah* of having become rich and that brought him such a high level of Torah that he recognized it as the true source of real *simchah*, and he no longer had any need for the treasures.

This is what you have to do in *chinuch* if you want the *shelo lishmah* lead to *lishmah*. You have to give your child an immediate feeling of *simchah* that he will associate with learning Torah. It can be a simple thing. Give him a candy every time he knows his Chumash, so that learning Chumash becomes for him an occasion of pleasure. And as he learns Chumash with pleasure, he will begin to feel the true spiritual pleasure of learning, and he will come closer to learning *lishmah*.

Promising the child something for knowing is not enough. He will be motivated to do it, but he will not have the *simchah* at the time he is learning, and that will not lead him to *lishmah*. It is only the learning he does after he receives the prize that will lead him to *lishmah*. It is best, therefore, to give him some form of pleasure that he can experience at the time he is learning. It will make his learning sweet, and it will lead him to the next level, until he reaches *lishmah*.

The focus is not meant to be so much on motivating the child. A child is not a horse in front of which you dangle a carrot. The idea of *shelo lishmah* is not to find a way to make him learn even though he doesn't want to do it. It is to make his learning an enjoyable experience right now. If you give him a prize for his learning, then it is the learning he does after he receives the prize that is meaningful rather the learning he does in anticipation of the prize. And the longer he must wait for the prize the less *chinuch* value it has. If you promise him a prize at the end of the school year, all the learning he does during the year will be without that *simchah* and it will not lead him to *lishmah*. But if you give him a prize at the end of every day, then he will experience *simchah* in his learning each day, and he will be well on the path to *lishmah*. That is the concept of *mitoch shelo lishmah ba lishmah*.

✑ Bar Mitzvah Presents

These days, we make a big *seudah* for a bar mitzvah and invite family and friends. The *Yam Shel Shlomo* writes that the bar mitzvah *seudah* is definitely a *seudas mitzvah*, because it celebrates the coming of age of a Jewish child. It is a celebration of his new obligation to do *mitzvos* and all the innumerable *mitzvos* he will be doing in the course of the rest of his life. It is a momentous occasion and a joyous one. There is no greater *simchah shel mitzvah*.

A bar mitzvah *seudah* is, therefore, the highest form of *chinuch*. All his life he has been drawn into the joy of others doing *mitzvos*. But on this day, this young boy is the celebrant, and everyone shares in his joy. This occasion, if properly presented and explained to him, will make the most profound impression on him, an impression that will last his entire life.

Over the years, it has become customary to give the bar mitzvah boy presents. They used to be called *doron derashah*, a present for the speech, a reward for the bar mitzvah *bachur's* efforts in fulfilling the venerable tradition saying a *derashah* at the *seudah*. We don't see a need to reward the bar mitzvah *bachur* for his coming of age, because that happens by itself regardless of any extra effort on his part. But saying a *derashah* requires many hours of study and preparation, and the presents are a form of encouragement.

So how is a boy supposed to relate to all these presents? What should his father tell him to make the presents an effective *chinuch* tool? If his presents are *sefarim*, then it's a little easier, of course. But he usually gets many presents of all kinds. What are those presents supposed to mean to him? Are they just glorified birthday presents without any particular *chinuch* value or are they something more? It all depends on what the father says to him.

If the parents are clever, they can use the presents as a way to give the boy a real feeling of *simchah* over and above the *simchah* of the occasion itself. They can tell him that the reason he has been given all those presents is that people are excited that he will be joining them in doing *mitzvos* on an adult level with a real obligation. Then every present becomes reminder of his honor and status and a source of *simchah* in doing *mitzvos*. As he does his *mitzvos* he will feel proud of what he is doing and gain real satisfaction from it. This kind of *shelo lishmah* will eventually lead him to learning and doing *mitzvos lishmah*.

CHAPTER THIRTEEN

Sources of Pleasure

When do we have to get by with a tiny morsel of food? The answer that immediately comes to mind is during times or situations of depravation and hunger. But when times are good and food is plentiful we can thank the Ribono Shel Olam that we do not have to make do with the barest minimum. But that is not what the Torah seems to tell us.

Rav Moshe Feinstein in a *teshuvah* (Yoreh De'ah 3:71) asks a powerful question. The Ribono Shel Olam assures us (Vayikra 26:3-10) that if we follow the Torah we will enjoy prosperity and crops in such abundance that the granaries will overflow and "you will eat your bread to satisfaction." What does this last phrase mean? Rashi explains that you will eat a tiny morsel and it will be "blessed inside your intestines." In other words, that tiny morsel will provide all the sustenance you need.

Why do we need this last blessing, asks Rav Moshe, if the granaries are overflowing with grain? If a person is hiding in a ghetto or in a forest and all he has is a crust of bread in his pocket, it is certainly a major blessing if a few crumbs will keep him alive. If he doesn't know when and where he will find another crust of bread, it is certainly a major blessing if the bread can go a long way. But in times of peace and plenty, who needs to survive on a tiny morsel?

The answer, says Rav Moshe, is that it is a blessing for an *ehrlicher Yid* if he doesn't have to become too involved with material pleasures. The overflowing granaries provide him with sufficient food to distribute to others and to prepare lavish *seudos* for Shabbos and Yom Tov. They provide him with plenty of surplus grain he can sell and earn money he can use for Torah and *mitzvos*. But for the usual weekday meal, he is far better off when a small meal will provide him with the sustenance he needs.

When the Ribono Shel Olam blesses us with abundance, it doesn't mean that He wants us to become gluttons steeped in worldly pleasures. He wants us to derive pleasure from our blessings but it should be *simchah shel mitzvah*, the pleasure and joy of doing *mitzvos*. We should view prosperity as an opportunity to deepen and expand the *mitzvos* and *maasim tovim* that we do, not as an opportunity to eat, drink and be merry.

We are fortunate to live in countries that are prosperous and even wealthy, and our communities are blessed with almost unprecedented abundance. The Ribono Shel Olam has not given us this abundance to live a life of luxury. He did not give it to us to enable us to indulge all our desires. He gave it to us so that we can do more *mitzvos* and more *chessed*, so that we can support more Torah and learn more Torah ourselves. As for our own material needs, we would do much better to limit the amount of physical pleasure we seek to accumulate in this world.

It is all an illusion anyway. Once the moment of pleasure passes it is completely gone, and all that remains is a desire and a hunger for ever more and ever greater pleasures. But the spiritual pleasures of Torah and *mitzvos* are real and lasting even in this world, and they also bring eternal pleasure in the Next World.

Becoming too deeply involved in worldly pleasures, aside from the utter foolishness of it, invites the risk of a downward spiral. The Torah tells us (Devarim 32:15), "*Vayishman Yisrael vayiv'at. And Yisrael grew fat, and he revolted.*" If we fatten ourselves up on physical pleasures, it can easily lead to rebellion against the Ribono Shel Olam. If we get caught up in the pursuit of good times, who knows where it will lead?

The pursuit of physical pleasures, writes Rav Moshe, is destructive. It conditions a person to indulge his *yetzer hara* with pleasures that are completely unnecessary. And it corrodes his *midos* until he becomes like a hungry, voracious animal rushing from one pleasure to the next. At first, he concentrates on permitted although unnecessary pleasures. But his *yetzer hara* becomes inflamed with desire, and when he gets a whiff of some highly desirable pleasure that is not permitted, he will not be denied.

The next thing he knows he is breaking one barrier after another and doing many *aveiros* in order to satisfy his insatiable *yetzer hara*. But how can he justify to himself that a supposedly religious Jew is behaving in this way? So he has to make a choice, and all too often, the choice is to deny the Ribono Shel Olam and His holy Torah. How else can he go on feeding the hunger of the *yetzer hara*? The Gemara says (Sanhedrin 63b) that the Jewish people worshipped idols only to have access to forbidden relations. That is human nature. Once a person is caught up in his desires and lusts, there are no longer any boundaries.

ᴥ§ The *Chinuch* Implications

The Torah tells us (Devarim 21:18-21) about the *ben sorer umoreh*, the profligate son just past bar mitzvah who deserves to be put to death before his overwhelming lusts lead him to murder people. The Torah considers his *chinuch* a failure and sees no hope for him. Why is his *chinuch* a failure? Because he has allowed his desires and lusts to control him, and his prospects for the future are exceedingly dismal.

The Gemara tells us (Sanhedrin 71a) that because of all the conditions the Torah attaches to the laws of the *ben sorer umoreh* an actual case never occurred, nor can it ever occur. So why is it there? "Study it and be rewarded," says the Gemara.

The reward we can derive from studying this *parashah* is an awareness of the central role in *chinuch* of teaching children to control their physical desires. The word *fresser* is Yiddish for a person who eats like a hungry wolf, without any thought of *eidelkeit*, refinement or moderation, a person whose drive for pleasure turns him into an eating machine. A child cannot be allowed to become a *fresser*.

Children should be taught perspective on pleasures. When you give a child something to eat, it might not be the best idea to say, "Enjoy! This is so delicious." At least not on a regular basis. Perhaps it would be better to say, "Here, eat this. It's good for you. It will make you strong and healthy." You don't want to condition your child to be guided by physical pleasures.

On the contrary, parents should speak to their children often about the greatness of a human being. Animals are driven entirely by their physical needs, but human being should be driven by ideals and aspirations. Everyone knows that a person has free will and that an animal does not have free will. But doesn't an animal also have free will? If it wants to eat, it eats. If it wants to sleep, it sleeps. It does whatever it wants to do. So why isn't that considered free will? The answer is that free will means being able to do what you don't want to do. Animals do exactly what their needs tell them to do. Human beings should be better.

This is what we should instill in our children. We should make them proud of being superior to the lust-driven animals. We should show them how to derive pleasure from doing a *mitzvah*, from learning Torah, from helping another person, from being kind and considerate, and yes, from turning away that second cookie for which there is absolutely no need. If you are *mechanech* your children properly, they will derive more pleasure from turning down the cookie than they would have derived from eating it, and it will also be a pleasure of a higher order.

Let the child see this for himself. When he helps a failing classmate study for a test and because of his help the classmate passes, say to him, "Let's talk about pleasure. Which did you enjoy more, helping your friend pass the test or a bowl of chocolate ice cream?" Ask him to consider why there is no comparison between the two. Help him to see that the *chessed* was a real and profound pleasure on which he will be able to look back with satisfaction even when he is an old man, while the ice cream was a fleeting moment of illusion. Reinforce this lesson again and again, and he will come to see physical pleasure for what it is, a brief casual enjoyment at most, a pleasure for which nothing should be sacrificed.

And when you teach him about learning Torah and doing *mitzvos* and *maasim tovim*, help him to see that these are the sources of the greatest pleasure a human being can experience. We've spoken previously about the *pesukim* (Tehillim 112:1-2), "Fortunate is the man who fears God, who strongly desires His *mitzvos*. His offspring shall be the mighty of the earth, a virtuous generation that shall be blessed." The Gemara comments (Avodah Zarah 19a), "His *mitzvos*, but not the reward of His *mitzvos*." If you tell your children to do *mitzvos* because they will be rewarded, then you're not conditioning to do *mitzvos* but to rather to seek rewards. Show them instead that a *mitzvah* is its own reward, that there is profound pleasure to be derived from drawing closer to the Ribono Shel Olam and emulating His ways.

Teach your children that these are the only true source of real and lasting pleasure for a person in this world. If you share with them your own strong desire for the *mitzvos* themselves, you can rest be assured that your children shall be the mighty of the earth.

PART THREE

On Chinuch
in Emunah

CHAPTER FOURTEEN

The Foundations of Faith

Where does the Torah say that we have to teach our children about *emunah*, faith in the Ribono Shel Olam? There are a number of places where we are told that we have to teach our children Torah, but where does it say that we have to teach them *emunah*?

There is only one place. It's with regard to Yetzias Mitzraim, the exodus of the Jewish people from Egypt, where the Torah tells us (Shemos 13:5), "*Vehigadeta levincha*. You shall tell it to your child." The belief in the story of Yetzias Mitzraim is the foundation of *emunah* and of the concepts of *hashgachah pratis*, divine providence, and *s'char va'onesh*, reward and punishment. The Seder night is the only time when the Torah tells us to sit down with the children and speak to them about our fundamental beliefs.

Unfortunately, that is not what happens at most Seder tables. We say *divrei Torah* and we talk about different aspects of the Yom Tov. We speak about Halachah and Drush. Rarely, however, do we speak about *emunah*. And it's a big mistake.

I'm not saying that we should philosophize about *emunah* at the Seder table. Certainly not. We have to learn how to talk about Yetzias Mitzraim, and if we do it correctly, *emunah* will come out of it naturally.

There is a well-known saying of Rav Elchanan Wasserman regarding *emunah*. Every child, he points out, is obligated to believe in the Ribono Shel Olam. It's the first *mitzvah* in the Torah. And so just about every child, upon reaching bar mitzvah and bas mitzvah, becomes a believer. He believes in the Ribono Shel Olam. He believes in *hashgachah pratis*. He believes in *s'char va'onesh*. Most children do not have problems with *emunah*. Yet we find that Aristotle, who according to the Rambam reached levels of wisdom approaching prophecy, this great Aristotle had problems with *emunah*. Aristotle could not convince himself that there was a Ribono Shel Olam. So if the great Aristotle with all his wisdom couldn't arrive at *emunah* in a conclusive way, how can we expect a bar mitzvah boy or bas mitzvah girl to have *emunah*? This is Rav Elchanan's provocative question.

Rav Elchanan also asks another question. The Torah tells us in the third *parashah* of Krias Shema (Bamidbar 15:39), "You shall not stray after your eye or after your hearts." And the Gemara says (Berachos 12b) that the words "after your hearts" are a prohibition against *minus*, heresy. But heresy is a false ideology. It is an intellectual transgression. Why then does the Torah speak about "after your hearts"? It should rather have said "after your brains" or "after your intellect." What is the connection between heresy and the heart?

Rav Elchanan famously answers that the root of heresy is emotional rather than intellectual. Belief in the Ribono Shel Olam is the most natural thing in the world. It is inconceivable that all of the incredible things in creation came to be without a Creator. A heretic, however, is someone who wants to live his life without anyone telling him what to do. So he construes all kinds of questions and arguments in order to deny the existence of the Ribono Shel Olam. But it is not his intellect that is denying it. It is his character and his emotions. That is why the Torah tells us not to follow our hearts. It is the desires of the heart that lead to heresy.

It is important, therefore, to teach a child about *emunah* at a very young age, because the younger the child the less emotional resistance he will have to belief in the Ribono Shel Olam. The younger he is the more natural this belief will be, and once it is deeply ingrained, it will remain with him for the rest of his life. If you tell him about Yetzias Mitzraim, he will have no problem accepting it, because he is too young to want to cast off the obligation of the human being to his Creator.

The *passuk* says (Yirmiyahu 7:29), "Faith was lost, it was eliminated from their mouths." At first glance, the Navi is saying that because faith was lost no one spoke about it any more. But Rav Simchah Zissel, the Alter of Kelm, says that it means the exact opposite. Faith was lost because it was eliminated from their mouths. If we don't talk about *emunah*, if we don't constantly speak about the Ribono Shel Olam, faith will eventually be lost.

In modern-day society especially, it is not socially acceptable to speak a lot about the Ribono Shel Olam and to say that there is no *kochi ve'otzem yadi* and that everything comes from the Ribono Shel Olam. If someone pulls out a newspaper and tells you about what's happened here and what's happened there and how this person was successful and how this politician did this and that politician did that, try telling him that it is all nonsense, that the Ribono Shel Olam controls the world no matter what any one individual does. The only response you will get is a quizzical look and a shake of the head.

But your young children will not react that way. If you sit down with them and speak to them about Yetzias Mitzraim and the fundamental tenets of our faith, and they see on your face that you are speaking from the heart with full honesty and sincerity, they will accept what you say without question. When something good happens to your family, you should speak about how grateful you are to the Ribono Shel Olam for all the good things He does for us even if we are not always deserving of His bounty. And the more you speak about *emunah* to them the more it will become an integral part of their lives and their way of thinking. You will create an atmosphere of *emunah* in your home, and your children will absorb *emunah* with the very air they breathe.

◆§ When Children Ask Questions

Some children, of course, will ask troubling questions. What is the Ribono Shel Olam? Where is the Ribono Shel Olam? If I take off my yarmulke, what will the Ribono Shel Olam do?

You cannot become flustered when you are faced with such questions. But you have to be prepared for them. For instance, when a child wants to know where the Ribono Shel Olam is, it is not a good idea to say that He is in the heavens. Rav Wolbe says that children should be told He is everywhere, which is the truth. You should tell the child that a person cannot see the Ribono Shel Olam but that He can see you. And you should tell the child that He watches over us and protects us and is always good to us. You won't want the child to be afraid of Him. You want the child to trust in Him and feel safe in His presence. You want him to know that when the light is shut after he's gone to bed the Ribono Shel Olam watches over him in the dark of the night. And you want to speak about *emunah* regularly and in a positive way.

The Torah tells us (Bereishis 39:3) that Potiphera was impressed with his new slave Yosef. He observed that the Ribono Shel Olam was always with Yosef and that the Ribono Shel Olam made sure that everything Yosef did succeeded.

How did Potiphera, a vulgar Egyptian, notice such a thing? What did this idol-worshipping pagan know about the Ribono Shel Olam? How did he come to such a conclusion?

Rashi explains that Yosef consistently spoke about the Ribono Shel Olam. And hearing Yosef speak with confidence and gratitude about the Ribono Shel Olam obviously had a profound effect even on a dyed-in-the-wool idol worshipper like Potiphera until he came to believe in the Ribono Shel Olam himself. If speaking about *emunah* had such a powerful impact on Potiphera, can you imagine what kind of impact it can have on our children?

Later, when Yosef was pulled from the dungeon and brought before Pharaoh to interpret his dream, Pharaoh said to him, "I heard that you can hear dreams and interpret them."

And Yosef replied (ibid. 41:16), "*Bil'adei*! It doesn't come from me. It comes from the Ribono Shel Olam."

Now, you would think that Yosef would have been a little more careful with regard to how he spoke to the fearsome Egyptian king. A fly gets into the bread, and Pharaoh chops off the baker's head. You don't trifle with such a man. So why does Yosef need to correct him as soon as he is brought into his presence?

It was an amazingly audacious thing for Yosef to do. But even more amazing is the effect Yosef's words had on Pharaoh. After Yosef interprets the dream, Pharaoh says (41:39), "Since the Ribono Shel Olam let you know about these things, there is no one wiser or more intelligent than you." Suddenly, Pharaoh is speaking about the Ribono Shel Olam. Suddenly, Pharaoh speaks in the language of *emunah*? How did this come to pass?

The answer is that when a person speaks in a natural way about *emunah*, when he speaks with confidence and conviction, it has an impact on everyone who hears him. When Pharaoh saw how earnest Yosef was, when he saw that Yosef wouldn't take any credit for himself for what the Ribono Shel Olam did, when he heard sincerity and conviction in Yosef's voice, he realized that Yosef was telling the truth, and the spirit of *emunah* entered into him as well.

This is how you impress a child with the truth of *emunah*. The simple straightforward expression of *emunah* by the father is the most powerful tool for instilling *emunah* in a child. There is no need for arguments, proofs and rationalizations. The will be a time for that later, but only if absolutely necessary. If the child persists with questions you will have to give him more substantive answers. If you don't know the answers, ask someone who does. But unless and until that happens, just continue to speak about *emunah* often and as the most natural state of mind. Create an atmosphere of *emunah* in your home, and your children will blossom.

The same approach should be used when teaching your child about *hashgachah pratis*, divine providence. When things happen, speak about how you see the hand of the Ribono Shel Olam directing events, and speak about the kindness He has shown you and your family. Show that you recognize His guidance and that you appreciate His generosity. If something bad happens, you can tell your child that the Ribono Shel Olam always does everything for a good purpose but that our limitations often prevent us from understanding it.

It is even better when husband and wife speak about these things to each other in the presence of the child. When the child hears the parents speaking this way as a matter of course, he will learn that this is the natural way to view the world, and he will do so himself as well.

And finally, the same approach should be used in teaching your child about reward and punishment. The Rambam says that although a person should not do *mitzvos* for reward in this world or the next, children should be taught that they should *mitzvos* for this reason.

People today are reluctant to talk to a child about reward and punishment, especially about punishment, because they don't want to scare the child. Ironically, some of these same people have no reservations about letting their children see all kinds of violent images, but when it comes to speaking about punishment for doing *aveiros*, they draw the line.

But there is really nothing wrong with telling a child with gentleness and sincerity that there is a punishment for doing an *aveirah*. You shouldn't play it up or project vivid images of burning fires. Perhaps it is even better to emphasize the reward for compliance and then to say that obviously you cannot expect the Ribono Shel Olam to reward you if you disobey Him.

You should make clear to the child that reward and punishment applies to adults, but that it is important that children understand the seriousness of doing an *aveirah* and that they become accustomed to doing *mitzvos* rather than *aveiros*.

◄§ Pressure and Discipline

These days, putting pressure on children is considered a major taboo. We don't want to pressure the children, because it will have a damaging effect. But at the same time, allowing a child to do whatever he wants to do is equally damaging. A child has to know that he must live with discipline, because that is what will be demanded of him throughout his life.

Discipline requires that we set firm rules that the children must follow, but we have to exercise good judgment in setting the rules. The child should not have the option of going to shul or not going to shul. If he is not ready for shul, then of course he should not go. Forcing him to do something that is beyond his ability can only lead to trouble. But if you decide he is ready, then there is no choice in the matter. He cannot say yesterday I wanted to go and today I don't. That is not *chinuch*. Once he reaches the stage where he is capable of going to shul, he must go. Maybe he doesn't have to stay all the way through if he isn't ready for that, but he must come. If he doesn't want to get up because he is too tired, then you have to insist that he get up anyway and that he can go to bed earlier that night. He has to understand that he is obligated and that obligations have to be fulfilled.

Discipline, of course, does not mean standing over the child with an angry face and yelling at him. It must be done in a kind and gentle way. You can offer him special rewards if need be. But you must demand compliance with a firmness that sets clear boundaries about what is acceptable and what is not acceptable. The child cannot just do *mitzvos* when it's convenient for him and when he feels the inclination. He has to be taught that once he is capable of doing *mitzvos* he must do them with consistency and regularity.

If you condition a child to live with gentle discipline, he will have no problem doing what is expected of him. Children actually crave discipline, because it makes their lives more predictable; children do not deal well with the unknown. But if you treat a child with laxity, you are inviting problems. Later, when he has no choice but to do what is expected of him, it will still be difficult for him. He will probably find it hard to wake up in the morning even when he is an adult, and he will constantly be hampered by his lack of self-discipline. You're doing him no favor by depriving him of discipline.

Of course, there are exceptions to every rule, and parents have to be discerning enough to recognize when their children need special considerations. But as a general rule, it's good for a child to be brought up with structure and discipline from a young age. This is how we wake up in the morning. This is how we get dressed. This is how we eat breakfast. This is how you make a *berachah*. This is how you *daven*. Today, you don't want to make a *berachah*? There is no such thing. We always make a *berachah*. Kind, gentle, but firm. That is good discipline and good *chinuch*.

When a child is well-conditioned to discipline, when he is the right age and at the right stage, you can begin speaking to him about reward and punishment. He will understand it and accept it. And when he is older, he will be able to graduate smoothly to a higher understanding of the role and the purpose of Torah and *mitzvos*.

CHAPTER FIFTEEN

No One Knows Everything

C hildren ask questions, and the way in which you answer them is sometimes more important than what you actually say. You have to answer clearly and honestly. You don't have to know all the answers, but you have to show the child that you're not avoiding the questions. If the child senses that you are trying to wiggle out of answering, he will assume that you're stumped. This can have a negative effect on him that will last his entire lifetime.

If a child wants to know, for example, who made this table, you should not say that the Ribono Shel Olam made the table.

That would give the impression that there was a piece of wood that was suddenly transformed into a table, and that is simply not true. You should say that a craftsman made the table and that the Ribono Shel Olam gave him the skill and the ideas that went into making the table. And of course, if the Ribono Shel Olam had not allowed him to make the table he could never have done it.

The child may then want to know who made the Ribono Shel Olam and what existed before the world was created. Any child can ask these questions, and many do. You must not tell the child that it is forbidden to ask this question. This will send a message to the child that you are as baffled as he is and that you're trying to avoid revealing your own ignorance. All you will have accomplished is that the child's confidence in you will be undermined, and that is the opposite of *chinuch*. He will no longer fully accept anything you say about any subject.

How do we answer such questions? You must speak with openness and confidence. First, you tell him that it's a good question. Then you look him directly in the eye and tell him that the Ribono Shel Olam was always there. The Ribono Shel Olam created the entire world, and He was always there.

Most children will accept this answer. But what if the child is a little philosopher? What if he asks you how it can be that He was always there?

So then you have to sit him down and say to him, "Look, I'm going to teach you an important principle in life. There are many things in the world that we cannot know and cannot understand. No one knows everything. It's impossible. Some people know about this and some people know about that, but no one knows everything. Now, there are some people in the world who are embarrassed to admit they can't understand everything, but the smarter people recognize that there are many, many things in the world that are simply impossible to understand. The world is made with so much *chachmah* that the human mind simply cannot grasp all of it. So what are we supposed to do? Well, we know that the Ribono Shel Olam gave us the Torah and that everything in it is true. That's why we accept what the Torah says, and what we don't know we don't know."

If a child has an inquiring mind and asks questions of this sort, you need to provide this orientation at the earliest possible age. Of course, your message has to be tailored to his level of understanding, and it has to be clear and unequivocal and delivered with confidence and assurance.

You should not discourage your child from being inquisitive and asking questions. It is important for a person to be a critical thinker. But at the same time, he should know that we are all only human and that there is a limit to how far our intelligence can take us. A child sees his parents as wise and intelligent, and if he sees that his parents have successfully integrated into their lives an awareness of the limitations of their understanding, he will accept it as the truth. The goal of your *chinuch* is to teach him that *emes* is determined by the Torah and not by our limited intelligence. This will serve him well all his life. No matter what he learns from science, if he has a healthy respect for the truth of the Torah, he will only accept as true those concepts that can be reconciled with the Torah.

✑ Look It Up

The Torah tells us (Bereishis 1:26) that the Ribono Shel Olam said, "*Naaseh adam.* Let us make a person." To whom was He speaking? Rashi says that He was consulting with the *malachim*, the angels. Moshe Rabbeinu objected. How could he write something that seemed to imply that there was more than one entity in control of the world and making the decisions? Otherwise, why would you have to consult the *malachim*? The Ribono Shel Olam told him to write it nonetheless and if someone wants to distort the meaning of this statement let him do so.

Why did the Ribono Shel Olam insist that this statement be written in the Torah? Because it carries an important lesson. It is the first *chinuch* that the Ribono Shel Olam gives us regarding how we should conduct our own lives. Even if you are a great person with wisdom and understanding, don't think that there's no need for you to consult with other people. If the Ribono Shel Olam consulted with the *malachim*, you can certainly consult with other people even if they are not as wise as you are.

That is the lesson. A person who has the prideful attitude that he understands everything and never needs to consult with others is at risk of falling into heresy, because when he comes up against something he does not understand he may dismiss it as untrue. Don't be afraid to admit that you don't know something. Don't be afraid to ask. No matter how clever you are, you can always use a little help from other people. This is what the Ribono Shel Olam taught us at the very beginning of the Torah.

This is an important principle in *chinuch*. You have to show humility to your children. You have to show them that you recognize the limitations of your knowledge and understanding. And if your children ask questions to which you don't know the answers, which can often happen, you have to admit that you need to look it up or consult with others before you can give them the answers they seek.

Telling them that the questions are good and that you need to do some research before you can give them the answers will not cause them to lose confidence in you. On the contrary, they will respect you for it.

CHAPTER SIXTEEN

Make the Introduction

If you want to read a description of our times, you will not find a more accurate one than the description that appears in the Mishnah (Sotah 49b). The Mishnah, which was written two thousand years ago, is discussing the time when the footsteps of Mashiach will already tread the earth, the time when the end of history will be imminent. At the time the Mishnah was written, the world was a very different place, and it is amazing how from that distant vantage point Chazal could describe the times in which we live so accurately.

The Mishnah states, "When Mashiach will approach, insolence will reign. Costs will rise. Grapes will be plentiful but wine will still be expensive. The government will turn against religion. No one will rebuke. There will be centers of licentiousness .... The wisdom of scribes will decay. Those who fear sin will be rejected. Truth will be withheld. The young will humiliate the old. Elders will rise before the small. Sons will disgrace their fathers. Daughters will rebel against their mothers and daughters-in-law against their mothers-in-law. A man's enemies will be his own family. The face of the generation will be like the face of a dog. Sons will be shameless before their fathers. And on whom can we rely? On our Father in Heaven."

This is the prophetic vision of Chazal two thousand years ago, and it is eerie how accurately they described today's society. Although the meanings of some of these statements are subject to interpretation, it is safe to say that practically every one of these predictions is manifest in our times.

The Mishnah concludes with a question and an answer. On whom can we rely? On our Father in Heaven.

What is the point of this question and answer? Is the Mishnah just throwing up its hands in defeat? You know, when you ask someone how things are going and he answers, "The Ribono Shel Olam will help," you know that he's in desperate straits. Is this what the Mishnah is saying here? That when we hit rock bottom there will be nothing to do except to rely on our Father in Heaven, that the situation will be hopeless? It seems to me that this could not have been the intent of the Mishnah.

❧ The Missing Factor

How is it possible that the world could come to such a sorry state as the one described by the Mishnah? What has gone wrong that has led the world to its state of moral bankruptcy? People are out of control. They pursue every form of desire and lust with no embarrassment and no shame. There is no respect. Children defy their parents and do whatever they please. They are not interested in the values of their parents.

What is at the root of such a disintegration of the moral fiber of society? How can we pinpoint the one factor that accounts for this wholesale devastation of morality? To say that people have strong desires is not an adequate explanation. People have always had strong desires, and yet they were able to control them to a certain extent. Today, there is no control, no shame. There is no boundary that may not be trespassed. Why?

The change that has brought about the moral collapse of the world at large is the disappearance of *ne'emanus*. This is a word that has many meanings. It means faithfulness. It means trustworthiness. It means reliability. It means loyalty. It means honesty. It means responsibility. It means steadfastness. It means all these things, because they are all come down to basic integrity.

When a person gives his word, it means something. A promise is a promise. A commitment is a commitment. The great praise the prophet lavishes on Avraham is that (Nechemiah 9:8) "You found his heart faithful (*ne'eman*) before You." That is the essence of a human being. A *ne'eman*. But reliable people today are few and far between. It used to be a point of pride to be reliable, but today a person who does exactly what is expected of him without trying to find an angle is considered a bit of a fool.

Promiscuity used to be called infidelity, which means a lack of faithfulness, but the concept has become obsolete. And if there is no faithfulness, no responsibility, no reliability, no accountability, then there are also no boundaries, and morality disintegrates. It used to be that you could rely on authority figures. It used to be that you could rely on people in government. It used to be that you could rely on a policeman. But not any more. Everyone is corrupt. No one assumes responsibility. No one is reliable. And so it is not surprising that all standards of morality and decent human behavior break down.

So the Mishnah tells us that there is a solution. People may have stopped being reliable, but the Ribono Shel Olam is always reliable. On whom can we rely? On our Father in Heaven. We can renew and replenish our relationship with the Ribono Shel Olam and find in Him the reliability and faithfulness that restore the moral fiber of the world. We can teach our children about the Ribono Shel Olam in a meaningful way and bring Him into their lives. Then He can become their bulwark as they work to rebuild a moral world. The Mishnah doesn't conclude with a statement of despair and defeat. It concludes with a statement of encouragement and hope.

◄§ Recognition and Gratitude

It appears to me that the most crucial ingredient missing from our *chinuch* is that we do not teach our children to know the Ribono Shel Olam. When the children are young, they are told that there is a Ribono Shel Olam. But as the child grows older, he still doesn't know what the Ribono Shel Olam is and how exactly the Ribono Shel Olam fits into his life.

He doesn't really develop a genuine *yiras shamayim*, because he doesn't understand the concept of *yiras shamayim*; it was never taught to him. He never heard his parents talk seriously to him about the concepts of reward and punishment and of divine providence. He doesn't really appreciate that the Ribono Shel Olam is the ultimate Benefactor, because he has never heard his parents make more than casual remarks about their gratitude to the Ribono Shel Olam.

He doesn't know the fundamental principles of our *emunah*, because they were never taught to him in a serious way. Chances are that he would not be able to recite the Thirteen Principles, and even if he could, it is still highly unlikely that he understands them in more than the most superficial way.

We have to go back to Avraham's kind of *chinuch*. He taught his family and his disciples all about the *midos* of the Ribono Shel Olam. He declared to the world that there was a Ribono Shel Olam, but he didn't stop right there. He followed through. He opened people's eyes to the endless *chessed* of the Ribono Shel Olam. He educated them about the various divine midos, and he taught people to integrate them into their own lives. He made the Ribono Shel Olam a vital part of their existence.

We don't find many people who speak among themselves about the Ribono Shel Olam. Sure, they say *"baruch Hashem"* and *"im yirtzeh Hashem"* as a matter of rote, a figure of speech, but how often do we hear people say it with feeling? How often do we hear people say it with the same passion and intensity they exhibit when they speak about other people who've helped them through difficult situations?

You often hear someone tell stories about how such and such a person did wonderful favors for them. People gush when they tell these stories, and their faces glow with gratitude. But when was the last time we saw someone gush about what the Ribono Shel Olam did for him? And if the parents don't talk like this among themselves, how is a child supposed to grow up with an appreciation for the role that the Ribono Shel Olam plays in his life?

It is not surprising, then, that some children abandon the Torah. After all, why shouldn't they do forbidden things? Do they really know anything about the Ribono Shel Olam? All they know is that their parents do not want them to do certain things, but that is not going to deter them from satisfying their urges. And so one barrier after another falls. Boundaries dissolve. And all the predictions of Chazal in that Mishnah come to pass.

What is the answer? Introduce the children to their Father in Heaven. Show them that He is the central point of their existence. Let them learn His midos and discover that He is completely reliable and trustworthy. Teach them to live by His rules, and the moral decay will disappear.

◆§ Before He Can Talk

Rav Moshe Feinstein writes in a *teshuvah* (Yoreh De'ah 3:76) that the most important part of *chinuch* is to teach the child *emunah*. He advises the parents to tell him consistently that everything he receives is a gift from the Ribono Shel Olam and that they are only delivering it for Him. When you give the child something good, you should say to the child, "Do you why you're getting this? Because the Ribono Shel Olam gave this to me so that I should give it to you. Say thank you to the Ribono Shel Olam."

If you do this, writes Rav Moshe, the child will develop a natural love for the Ribono Shel Olam and for you as well because you are His messengers. Then his love will inspire him to do whatever the Ribono Shel Olam wants him to do, and you will rarely need to discipline him.

And then Rav Moshe writes something amazing. He says that although Chazal established a proper time for *chinuch* in each particular *mitzvah*, as we've mentioned a number of times, there is no time frame for the *chinuch* in the *mitzvah* of *emunah*. It can start even before the child knows how to speak.

As soon as the child is able to recognize his parents and differentiate between them, you can and should start talking to him about the Ribono Shel Olam. You have to let him know that the Ribono Shel Olam lives in the home with the family although he cannot see Him. You have to tell him that the Ribono Shel Olam is everywhere and that He takes care of the entire world. You have to tell him about the Ribono Shel Olam's goodness and kindness and that everything we have we get from Him. If you start when the child is very young, his knowledge of the Ribono Shel Olam and His *midos* will be as natural to his view of the world as the sun shining in the sky.

When a child is brought up this way then his *chinuch* in *berachos* is really meaningful. There is no rush to teach him to say *berachos*, but when you do, he will understand that he is thanking the Ribono Shel Olam Whom he has known from before his earliest memories. His *emunah* will be implanted deep in his heart, and he will feel as attached to the Ribono Shel Olam as he is to his parents.

CHAPTER SEVENTEEN

The Answer Is Shabbos

I t is not uncommon for young people these days to have serious problems with *emunah*. Sometimes, their own inquisitive minds can lead them to ask questions about the existence of the Ribono Shel Olam, the origins of the Torah and the truth of our faith and our beliefs. Sometimes, they may read or hear something that penetrates into their minds and hearts and gnaws away at their thoughts until their entire *emunah* is undermined.

When this happens, the youngster becomes despondent and depressed. He usually thinks he's the only pebble on the beach, that this doesn't happen to anyone else. Some will confide in their parents, teachers or *rabbanim*. Others are too embarrassed to say anything or to give more than the merest hint about their inner turmoil. Their connection to the Torah becomes weaker and weaker, and when they are old enough, they drift away. It's very sad, but these things happen.

⋖§ Shabbos Cleanses

Parents should be very concerned about their own children, because these problems can and do occur in any family. No one is immune. Parents should look for warning signs and respond with wisdom and sensitivity. If a child has doubts about his *emunah*, there has to be a response that will be effective and satisfying to the child.

So what are parents to do? Should they try to prove the truth of the Torah to their child? Should they debate with him?

Someone asked the Steipler Gaon for his advice on such a situation. It involved a *yeshivah bachur* from a prominent family who was suffering terribly from persistent doubts about the Torah and about reward and punishment. He claimed that he wanted to have complete *emunah*, but that his questions and doubts just made it impossible. His mind was constantly in a state of confusion.

The Steipler replied that he was asked for advice in such cases many times. His general response was to advise the doubter to carry on, because maybe the Torah is true after all. Why turn away from the Torah because it might not be true and take a chance on making a grievous error if it turns out that it is true? This is an answer for the moment. But what about a long-term solution?

There are no rational approaches to dealing with these problems, he goes on to say. The only thing to do falls into the realm of a *segulah*, and it has been proved effective numerous times. The solution is a meticulous observance of the laws of Shabbos. The *bachur* should learn the laws of Shabbos in *Shulchan Aruch* and *Mishnah Berurah* with all their minutest details, and he should practice everything he learns. He should not engage in idle conversations on Shabbos or read newspapers and books. He should either eat, sleep or learn Torah. Should he follow this program, he'll see wondrous results in a relatively short time. His state of confusion will dissipate, even if he still has no rational answers for the questions and doubts that plagued him earlier. They will simply cease to be important to him, and he will recover his peace of mind.

But there is one condition, the Steipler adds. The *bachur* must do this *lesheim shamayim*, for the sake of Heaven. He has to do it because he wants to have a complete *emunah* and fulfill the will of the Ribono Shel Olam. If he does it simply to alleviate the discomfort that his doubts are causing him, it will not be effective. But if he does it genuinely *lesheim shamayim*, he will recover a pure *emunah*. As Chazal say (Shabbos 118b), "If someone keeps Shabbos in accordance with its laws, he is forgiven his sins, even if he worshipped idols."

This is what the Steipler said.

We have to take a close look at this Gemara that the Steipler brings. A person worships idols, a terrible, terrible *aveirah*, but if he keeps Shabbos he is forgiven. The Taz asks how such a thing can be. If an idol worshipper keeps Shabbos he is forgiven? What is the value of his Shabbos if he is an idol worshipper?

So the Taz answers that Chazal are undoubtedly talking about someone who did *teshuvah* for having worshipped idols. But *teshuvah* only removes the *aveirah*. It doesn't automatically cleanse his mind of all the idolatrous concepts and ideologies. The spiritual wounds are not so easily healed. He can do *teshuvah* and still have a mind full of confusion. But if he keeps Shabbos, say Chazal, all the idolatrous impressions will be scrubbed from his mind, and it will once again be pure.

Elsewhere, we find the same idea. The Gemara says (Shabbos 10b), "Whoever gives a gift to someone has to inform him, as it is written (Shemos 31:13), 'To know that I am Hashem Who sanctifies you.' The Holy Blessed One said to Moshe, 'I have a precious gift in my treasure-house called Shabbos. Go, let them know.'"

What is the meaning of "go, let them know"? It cannot mean that he should tell them the laws of Shabbos, because the laws of all other *mitzvos* also have to be told to the people. No, it means go and tell them that Shabbos is a *segulah*, that it has the power to cleanse the soul and the mind of the damage inflicted by *aveiros* and by questions and doubts.

This is what the Steipler was saying. When a person keeps Shabbos properly and with the correct intentions, his mind will be cleansed. It is a tried and true method. He still won't know the answers to all his former questions, but they will no longer bother him. His doubts will evaporate. It is a *segulah*, and it works.

✑§ Preventive Measures

If Shabbos is a *segulah* that removes doubts in *emunah* from the mind of someone who is beset with questions and doubts, it should certainly be effective in establishing the solid foundations of *emunah* in the minds of young children. Especially among young children, meticulous observance of the laws of Shabbos is not so prevalent. People tend to be lenient and do not demand strict compliance from underage children.

But we all know that we live in dangerous times. The influence of the outside world is so pervasive. It tugs at the hearts and minds of our children and undermines their faith in the strongly-held beliefs of our people. The temptations of the world create confusion in their minds and eventually pull some of them away from their people and the Torah.

So how can we prevent these tragedies? Shabbos is the answer. We cannot allow ourselves to be lenient in the observance of Shabbos. By making meticulous Shabbos observance a strong part of our *chinuch*, we can give our children strong foundations of *emunah* that will last them throughout their lives.

It is interesting that nowadays whenever some calamity happens we are quick to lay the blame on our deficiencies in *shemiras halashon*, the avoidance of gossip and slander. This instinctive tendency actually reflects a commendable sensitivity to this important *mitzvah*, a sensitivity that was heightened immeasurably by the efforts of the Chafetz Chaim, personally and through the *sefarim* he wrote.

But if we look into the collected letters of the Chafetz Chaim, we find mention of many calamities that took place. He writes about pogroms, fires, poverty, communism, but he never connects these calamities to *shemiras halashon*. Usually, he lays the blame on the lack of Shabbos observance and *tznius*. Occasionally, he also mentions *bittul Torah* and poor *tefilah*, but never *shemiras halashon*.

When it comes to *chinuch*, therefore, we really cannot know the cause and effect of the different *mitzvos* that we do, which is a *segulah* for this and which is a *segulah* for that. And the truth is, as the Steipler says, a *mitzvah* is only a *segulah* if you do it *lesheim shamayim* and not for the sake of the *segulah*. This puts a difficult burden on someone who comes to use the *segulah*. He is motivated because the confusion in his mind is causing him terrible suffering. But if he does the *mitzvah* in order to alleviate his confusion, it will not be effective. He has no choice but to force himself to put the *segulah* out of his thoughts and do the *mitzvah* completely *lesheim shamayim*. This is a difficult feat to accomplish.

So really the most effective way to gain the *segulah* value of a *mitzvah* is for the parent to incorporate it in his *chinuch*. The parent knows that he is providing the child with a *segulah*, but the child is being trained to do the *mitzvah lesheim shamayim*. The purity of the child's intentions will ensure that Shabbos will be a proper *segulah* for him and protect him from questions and doubts that can disturb his mind.

So when you're dealing with a young child, the first thing you have to do is make the day special for him. A common practice is to have special Shabbos treats so that the child will associate sweetness and pleasure with the holiness of Shabbos. And you have to learn the *halachos*. When he is young, there are *sefarim* and books that are geared for the younger children, and as they get older, they can graduate to the Mishnah Berurah.

Bring a *ruach* of *kedushah* and joy into the house on Shabbos. Make sure, as the Steipler said, that neither you nor your children read newspapers or secular books on Shabbos. Instead, provide them with proper reading and learning material and other activities that will make the day memorable and exciting. The main thing is that no matter what age they are they have to learn to love and honor Shabbos to the best of their abilities.

PART FOUR

On Chinuch
in Midos

CHAPTER EIGHTEEN

Like Planting a Tree

People often make a mistake. They think that the main part of *chinuch* is in *mitzvos* and that *chinuch* in *midos* is secondary, almost an afterthought. But in actuality, the opposite is true. The main focus of *chinuch* has to be in *midos*, because the obstacles to *chinuch* in *mitzvos* are bad *midos*.

Let's take a look at the words of the Shelah Hakadosh (*Shaar Ha'osios* 4 *Derech Eretz* 14-15). I'll summarize a bit.

First, the Shelah gives us an amazing introduction to the entire topic of *chinuch*. The purpose of the *mitzvah* of having children, he writes, is to have children and grandchildren who learn Torah and do *mitzvos* for all eternity. You have to set off a chain reaction of Torah and *mitzvos* that will go on forever and ever, and all of it will be to your credit.

In this sense, the most important responsibility that lies on the shoulders of a person is the *chinuch* of his children. More than anything else he does, the *chinuch* of his children will bring him the largest share in Olam Haba, a share that will grow and grow and grow without limit and without end. Every one of his children, grandchildren and distant descendants who lives a life of Torah and *mitzvos* will bring him more credit and another slice of Olam Haba.

It is not, as people think, that what they do themselves plays the greatest role in determining their share in Olam Haba and the *chinuch* of their children is just one of their side responsibilities. That is not correct. A successful *chinuch* brings greater reward than just about anything else. If a person is *mechanech* his children well, which naturally leads to his children being *mechanech* their children well and so on for all generations, the rewards are virtually limitless. A person has no better place to invest his efforts than in the *chinuch* of his children.

This is the Shelah's preamble to his discussion about *chinuch*. He then goes on to point out that the proper focus of *chinuch* is on *midos*. If we are not successful in *chinuch* in *mitzvos*, it is because our *chinuch* in *midos* was deficient.

◆§ Start at a Young Age

It is well known, he writes, that a person is born wild and that he is saddled with a *yetzer hara* from childhood. Therefore, he has to be trained and conditioned to have good *midos* from the time he utters his first words, as Chazal say (Sukkah 42a), "As soon as a child is able to speak, teach him Shema Yisrael and Torah Tzeevah Lanu Moshe," and the like. And the *passuk* says (Mishlei 22:6), "Raise the child according to his way; even when he is old he will not turn from it." From the time he is young, his father and mother should not deprive him of the benefits of chastisement. Rather, they should add more and more each day to the extent that he is able to tolerate it. Nor should they deprive him of instructive discipline, as it is written (Mishlei 13:24), "He who spares the rod despises his son, but he who loves him is quick to give him instruction."

And then the Shelah becomes specific. People have many bad *midos*, such as swearing, cursing, anger, cruelty, arrogance, impudence, envy, hatred, lust, gossip, mockery, slander, idle talk and thousands upon thousands more. On the other hand, there are thousands upon thousands of good *midos*, such as the opposite of all those mentioned above, as well as shyness, reticence and innumerable others. And above all is the knowledge of the Ribono Shel Olam to the greatest extent possible and constantly speaking about holy matters. In order to become an *adam hashalem*, a complete person, one should shun all the bad *midos* and aspire to all the good *midos*.

It is the responsibility of parents, he continues, to devote themselves to teaching their children to shun bad *midos* and embrace good *midos* until this becomes the very essence of their beings. They should inculcate these midos into their children day after day, even a hundred times a day until it becomes part of them. The parents should give their children explicit guidance in these things at two or three years of age. There are two reasons for this. One, because whatever a child learns at an early age becomes part of his nature. Two, because if a child becomes accustomed to his father as a strong authority figure, he will obey him even as he grows older. If, however, the father dotes on his child and substitutes affection for authority and discipline, the child may obey when he is young, but when he grows older, he will follow his own opinions. A child is like a tree. When you plant a tree, you can form it in any way you wish while it is still a sapling, but when it grows into a sturdy tree it is too late to do any further forming.

This is the gist of what the Shelah writes about *chinuch*. There is more to which we will return shortly.

The work of *chinuch*, of bringing up good *ehrliche* children, begins from when the child is extremely young. You cannot start too early. As soon as he reaches a minimal level of understanding, it is time to start molding his character. You have to train and condition him to have good *midos* and you have to prevent him from picking up bad *midos* from other people or developing them on his own. You have to teach him the lessons again and again, always in a gentle and pleasant way, until the good *midos* become second nature to him. No, perhaps a better way of saying it is that they should become first nature to him.

If you neglect this critical aspect of *chinuch*, the good *midos* that you want to instill in him will not come naturally to him. Even if he reaches the understanding that they are good and that this is the proper way to behave, they will always require a concerted effort from him, and very often, he will simply not have the fortitude to make the effort. Years later, when he goes to *yeshivah* and he sits and learns *mussar sefarim*, he will read about all the good *midos* a person must have. And he will think to himself that these are really wonderful ideals but they are for people on a very high level, for big *tzaddikim*, not for ordinary people. Had you started training him when he was very young, however, all the good *midos* would come naturally to him, and he would understand that this is the way every human being should behave.

From when he is very young, you have to tell the child not to show off because that is *gaavah*, arrogance, a very bad *midah*. It is ugly and repulsive and not something a beautiful child should do. It is forbidden to be a *baal gaavah* just as it is forbidden to eat something that is not kosher.

You have to tell him not to be a glutton, to eat slowly and respectfully, to eat foods that are nutritious. A well-trained child cares about his health. He does not eat only sweets, leaving everything else on his plate.

You have to tell him not to mock people or speak *lashon hara* and *rechilus*, because it is mean and hurtful, because that is not how an *ehrliche* human being behaves. We speak with refined language, we're kind to others, we don't grab anything that does not belong to us — that is how we behave.

This is the work of *chinuch*. You don't yell at the child or hit him or persecute him in any way. Rather, educate him. Teach him. Introduce him to the world in which you expect him to live. Explain what people are all about. Children are curious. They're eager to learn about the world they're discovering. So give them your version of the world before others give them a different version that goes against your beliefs and values. And if you start when the child is very young and you speak about it gently, persuasively and often, the lessons will penetrate, and they will become part of the very nature of the child. When it comes to *chinuch* in *mitzvos*, it won't matter so much if you delay a little and wait until the child is one hundred percent ready. But when it comes to *chinuch* in *midos*, there is no time to waste. If bad *midos* are allowed to take root in a child, it becomes exceedingly difficult to uproot them later.

☙ The Mother's Responsibility

The Shelah goes on (ibid. 17) to make another important point. Mothers, he writes, are just as obligated in the *chinuch* of their children as fathers are. In fact, the obligation of mothers is even greater, because they spend more time in the home. If the father is a *talmid chacham*, then he spends most of his time learning and is not at home enough to supervise the children that closely. If he is a businessman and he has travel, he is likewise away from home much of the time. Therefore, even though women are softer and gentler by nature, a mother has to be determined and persistent in chastising her children, even if they protest loudly, until they turn away from any bad *midos* into which they may have fallen.

That is the way it is. The mother is in the home. She is the authority figure who is present when there are conflicts between brothers and sister or with other children. She is there when bad *midos* threaten to take root. And the responsibility falls squarely on her shoulders. So there is a great need for the mother and the father to talk about *chinuch* and set clear goals and guidelines, to arrive at a joint plan, but the execution of the plan will be primarily by the mother. It is her responsibility and also her *zechus*.

✍ Social Skills

Where do social skills fit into *chinuch*, if at all?

It seems to me that there are two kinds of social skills. One kind is based on interacting well with other people. A child needs to know how to behave around other people, how to talk to other people, when to speak to other people and when to remain silent, how to conduct himself in the street, not to make noise while eating, not to eat with his mouth open. The purpose of all these skills is to avoid offending people, displaying bad character or disturbing conduct, and so they very definitely fall into the category of *midos*. Most social behavior is probably defined by what are considered good and bad *midos*.

But there are also some social skills that have little or nothing to do with *midos*. How you hold your knife and fork has nothing to do with *midos*. Whether or not you place your elbow on the table has nothing to do with *midos*. There are all sorts of mannerisms, conventions and practices that are frowned upon in society that have nothing to do with *midos*. While it is perfectly fine to teach children some of these social skills for practical reasons, they have little more to do with the holy work of *chinuch* than does teaching them to make a double knot in their shoelaces.

~§ Respect and Disrespect

A child has to be taught to have respect for his parents. This is also part of *midos*, as are all other *mitzvos bein adam lechaveiro*, relationships with other people. Here again, it is much easier for a young child to learn respect for parents than for an older child who has already become accustomed to a more causal relationship with his parents. But once again, the conditioning and training must be done with gentle persuasion, love and even bribery if need be; it must be a pleasant experience for the child. Teach him what is right. Get him to want to do it on his own. That is *chinuch*. If the child is forced in his younger years, he will only wait till he gets older and is strong enough to break away. Forcing harms the child. It is the best way to produce a child who doesn't want to listen to his parents. It's not *chinuch*.

If a child is being disrespectful, this behavior cannot be allowed to pass without a firm response from the parents, even when the child is very young. Sometimes, a three-year-old makes a sharp but disrespectful remark, and the parents laugh and enjoy it, thinking he's being cute and clever. But they don't realize that they're making a serious mistake. If the child is allowed to speak that way, speaking with respect will never become his natural way of addressing his parents.

So it has to be stopped. This does not call for a major reaction, a simple statement that "this is not the way we speak to our parents" is usually more than adequate. It is true that the Rambam says that anger may be used as a tool for *chinuch*. But that is only when the anger sends a message about how reprehensible the deed was. The child sees that what he did was so bad that it upset his parents, and he is sorry that he did it. Then it's *chinuch*. But if, instead of sending a message about the deed itself, the anger is used as a weapon in a power struggle, it will not succeed. It may force the child to yield to his parents' superior power temporarily, but it is not *chinuch*. It teaches him nothing.

An angry reaction may also give the child the impression that his parents don't love him, and that is the last thing you want to do. A child needs to be secure in the love of his parents.

It is also important to understand that when anger is used constructively or when you find it necessary to give the child a slap on the wrist, so to speak, he must never get the feeling that you are out of control. If you want to have any control over your child, you've got to be in control of yourself. If you scream and get red in the face, the child will know that you've lost it, and if you've lost it, you've also lost him as well. So even if you feel that a situation calls for a show of anger, you must be sure that it is a calm anger, if we can allow ourselves to coin such a phrase.

What if the child is being stubborn and rebellious? What if he stubbornly refuses to do everything you tell him to do?

This is a difficult problem, and you would be well advised to get some guidance specific to your child, his age, personality and situation. But as a general guideline, let me just say that it would be best to make as few demands on him as possible. You have to become a bit of a politician, maneuvering him into doing what he needs to do without giving him direct orders. You don't want to get into confrontations with him. You want to avoid warfare in the home.

As time goes on, the situation should improve. Stubbornness is a game, and if you challenge him, he will only become increasingly stubborn. But if you do not provoke him by making demands he can stubbornly reject, the force of his resistance will eventually dissipate. And as he grows older and his mind develops, his intelligence will take control of his stubborn tendency and use it for good purposes. He will be tenacious in his learning and in everything else that he undertakes. Then what started out as a bad *midah* might one day be transformed into a good *midah*.

The Brisker Rav said that although honoring parents is a great *mitzvah*, parents should nonetheless give as few orders to the child as feasible. If you only ask for those things that are truly important and only on occasion, there is a much greater probability that the child will obey every order. But if you give many orders, the child may not obey all of them, and he will learn that he doesn't always have to listen. That is not good *chinuch*, no matter how respectful the child may be.

CHAPTER NINETEEN

Building Good Character

The principal problems parents encounter in the realm of *chinuch* relate to molding the characters of their children. How do we teach them to control their flashes of anger? How do we teach them not be jealous? How do we teach them to share? How do we teach them to be kind? How do we teach them to be *mevater*, to back down in situations of potential conflict?

Almost everything we see in Chazal on *chinuch* relates to *chinuch* in *mitzvos*. They give us guidance on how to condition children to do *mitzvos* with regularity and at what ages to begin training them in various *mitzvos*. But they say very little about *chinuch* in *midos*.

The *passuk* says (Mishlei 22:6), "*Chanoch lanaar al pi darko.* Raise the child according to his way." What kind of *chinuch* is the *passuk* discussing, *chinuch* in *mitzvos* or *chinuch* in *midos*? We could say that it is talking about *mitzvos*. The Vilna Gaon, however, understands this *passuk* to be discussing *chinuch* in *midos*, because that is the most problematic area of *chinuch*.

Before a young man marries, there is a custom, especially in *yeshivos*, that an older mentor calls him aside and gives him a little talk to prepare him for married life. The young man is told that he is about to share his life with another person and that he must behave toward her with sensitivity and consideration. He has to be kind, patient, calm and generous. He has to be prepared to forgo his privileges and prerogatives in order to promote domestic harmony. It all sounds good, but in my opinion, these little talks are not worth very much.

Can you really expect a person to change overnight? So he hears what you tell him, and he nods his head and says, "Yes, I will be kind and sensitive and considerate." Do you think he has suddenly been transformed? If his whole life he has reacted to stressful situations with anger, will he suddenly become an island of serenity in his own home? If he never stepped back a single inch from what he felt was coming to him, will he suddenly step aside for his wife? Will he suddenly become an even-tempered and patient person?

I do not believe that a person can change so easily. If a person grew up with bad *midos*, it will take an enormous amount of effort to improve them once he reaches adulthood. If you want to prepare a young man for a healthy marriage, you have to start giving him those little talks when he is five years old or younger. And the same goes for young women.

When a boy grabs something away from his sister who is not as strong as he is, that is the time to step in and talk to him about being *mevater*. Eventually, he will appreciate the importance of being *mevater*, and he will feel good about doing a *chessed*. You may want to reward him and praise when he is *mevater* or when he is not jealous of other people. As time goes on and other opportunities arise, he will become increasingly less reluctant to be *mevater* and more and more likely to do a *chessed* with a genuine smile. And by the time he's ready to get married, he might very well become a good husband.

And as always in *chinuch*, children emulate the behavior of their parents. If the parents were brought up or have trained themselves to have good *midos*, the children will learn from their behavior. But if parents do not speak nicely to each other or to other people, if they scream and shout, if they're quick-tempered and impatient or display any other bad *midos*, we cannot expect their children to behave differently, no matter how much their parents lecture them.

The ideal way to cultivate good *midos* in your children is to set a good example, to be their role models. Of course, that alone is not enough. You have to train them, and you have to do it in a pleasant, natural, enjoyable way. You can play games in which the object is to be kind, thoughtful and considerate. You can make this lesson fun for them. The good *midos* will become part of their character, and they'll grow up to be the kind of people you want them to be.

But if you spoil the child and let him have everything he wants, you're really training him to think only about himself. He'll grow up to be a selfish, insensitive person, and at that point, it will be very hard for him to change, even if he wants to change.

◆§ Games and Toys

Many of the games that children play are grounded in bad *midos*. In fact, the very idea of competition for the sake of competition is not a good thing. Children take these things very seriously, and if they lose, they are ashamed; they lose face. And then on top of everything, the winner gets a prize and the loser is left empty-handed.

Wouldn't it make much more sense to give a prize to the loser? The winner has the satisfaction of winning, and the loser, if he doesn't make a fuss, is rewarded for losing gracefully. Prizes should be given for doing something good and worthy. A child who knows his Mishnayos well deserves a prize. A child who wins a game has really done nothing to deserve a prize. There is no *chinuch* advantage in winning. But a child who loses with grace has shown good *midos*. That is definitely considered doing something worthy.

There are games that teach children to be greedy, to aspire to accumulate lots of money and properties. These promote bad *midos*. Children playing such games become very business-minded long before they need to be business-minded. Outside the world of Torah, such games may be considered quite tame, perhaps even educational. But we should not be interested in introducing our children to greed and the pursuit of profit. There will be plenty of time and opportunity for that later.

And you can't just say that it's only a game. The real and imaginary worlds of a child flow together. If in the imaginary world of games, he makes lucrative deals and becomes wealthy, that will become his self-image. And that is not what he needs at such a young age.

When I was bringing up my own children, I was reluctant to give them toy cars in which to drive around the house. Driving a car is certainly a convenience, but it is much more than that. There's an element of *prikas ol* in driving a car, of breaking away from restraints and heading for the open road. If children develop a desire to be drivers later on, they'll deal with it then. But why stimulate this desire in them while they're still young children? There are plenty of other toys that will make them perfectly happy.

As the child gets fancier and fancier toy cars, what do you think goes on in his mind? He wants a fancy car, with pedals and lights and hooters that hoot. And when this little fellow grows up, he's going to want a real fancy car, even though he really won't have a need for it. That was his *chinuch*, and that's what he'll want.

I mention toy cars from my own experience only as an illustration. Today, of course, things are a little different. Having a car has become like having a refrigerator or a telephone, and a simple toy car would not really present such a problem. But the concept is important. What about guns? Should children be allowed to play with toy guns? Should they be allowed to make believe that they shoot and kill other children? Will that engender good *midos* in them or bad *midos*?

Today we have cars and planes, but a hundred years ago, the primary form of transportation was by horse. You either rode a horse yourself or you hired a horse and wagon and a wagon driver. The wagon driver was called a *baal agalah*. The term *baal agalah* was often used to denote the lowest, most ignorant level of society.

Although it may be somewhat difficult for people living in today's world to relate to the following story, its message is nonetheless instructive.

One time, Rav Chazkel Levenstein came into the house of one of his *talmidim* and saw a child sitting on a rocking horse. In his imagination, the child was riding a horse.

"I don't understand," Rav Chazkel said to the child's father. "You're making a *baal agalah* out of him. You should want him to become a *talmid chacham*, but this is making him a *baal agalah*. He's doing it with such gusto. You can see that in his mind he's already a *baal agalah*. So how is he ever going to become a *talmid chacham*?"

So what do you do if the children of the neighbors have toy cars or their equivalent as the case may be, toys that you've deemed inappropriate for your children? You can't go overboard on this.

If depriving your child of a toy will create serious problems for him, then you really don't have much choice, and you shouldn't make a big fuss about it. I'm not saying that it's forbidden to give your child a toy car or anything of the sort. I'm just giving some examples of how even the choice of toys and games might be significant. As for toys that simulate violence, children should never be given such toys, even if the neighbor's children have them.

◆§ Venting Frustration

There is an old tradition that if a child is frustrated you should let him break dishes. At a very young age, a child does not have many ways to vent his frustration, so we let him break dishes. Young children like to throw things on the floor or to rip paper into little pieces. They do it for the same reason. It gives them an outlet.

As long as a child is very young, you should let him do this. If you try to restrain him, you will make him into an unnatural person, and that is not good. We don't discipline a baby who is crying, because it is natural at that stage of his life. Throwing things down is natural at a further early stage in life. It may call for patience on the part of the parents who have to tidy up after the child, but it is normal behavior. It is a phase, and it will pass.

◆§ A Time to Back Down

One of the *midos* that parents are eager to instill in their children is to be *mevater*. In cases of conflict or potential conflict, they want to teach their children to back down. But the motivation for the emphasis on this *midah* is sometimes misplaced. Why do they want their children to back down? Because it will reduce tensions in the home and make life easier for the parents. It's not easy dealing with young siblings who are at war with each other. If one or both of them back down, there will be peace in the home.

Now, this in itself is not a bad motivation. In fact, it is quite a good one. But it has little to do with *chinuch*. And if being *mevater* is not good for the child, they are buying peace at the expense of the child. Furthermore, do these parents really believe that it is good for a person to be *mevater*? Are they *mevater* when they face comparable adult situations themselves? Or do they stand firm and insist on their rights? I would venture to say that a good percentage of parents who demand that children be *mevater* are not inclined to be *mevater* themselves.

But the truth is that being *mevater* is indeed a very important *midah*, and teaching children to be *mevater* is an important part of *chinuch*.

So first, let's define exactly what being *mevater* means. Being *mevater* means not insisting on your rights.

If a child takes a toy that doesn't belong to him and the other child is screaming in protest, the parent cannot tell the perpetrator to be *mevater* and give the toy back. That is not called being *mevater*. It is called returning stolen property. The parent should say, "Give the toy back to him, because it doesn't belong to you. You have no right to take it without permission."

If a child has a toy and his little brother or sister wants it and is crying, the child will often refuse and say, "No, it's mine." Here again, asking the child to share the toy has nothing to do with being *mevater*. It is a question of doing a *chessed*. If a child has something that really belongs to him and he wants to keep it and he decides to be kind and let someone else have it, that is an act of *chessed*. It is definitely something the parents should encourage, but not as a form of being *mevater*. They should say, "Do him a favor. Do a *chessed*, and I'll be proud of you."

Being *mevater* involves a situation where a child has something to which he is completely entitled and another child grabs it away unjustly. It is not really a *chessed* to let the other child have it, but nevertheless, it is a good *midah* to let the other child have it for a while and get it back later. That is called being *mevater*. The parent tells the child, "It really is yours, and if you want you could take it back, but be *mevater*. You don't really need it right now, and instead of fighting, let him have it for a while. If you do that, I'll give you a candy." That is *chinuch* in being *mevater*. You acknowledge that the child is within his rights, you ask him to forfeit his rights in this situation for the sake of peace, and you reward him.

Now if the second child is this scenario is also your own, your first obligation before you ask him to be *mevater* is to tell the grabber not to take something that doesn't belong to him. But if the grabber is not your child or if he is too young to understand, then it appropriate to ask your child to be *mevater*.

Being *mevater* is a *midah* that will serve your child well throughout his entire life. There will inevitably be times that people will do unjust things to him, and often, the best and wisest response is just to let it go. The cost of reclaiming your rights is often just not worth the effort, and it would be better just to write it off and get on with your life. But if you weren't trained to be *mevater* from early childhood, it may be very difficult to relinquish your rights and not demand that justice be done.

Specifically, the *midah* of being *mevater* plays a very big role in a successful marriage. Situations of potential conflict often arise in a marriage, and the willingness of both partners to step back from what they think are their rights and allow the other to have his way can only promote love and harmony in the home. Sometimes, you can fight for your rights and demand justice, but even if you prevail, you may pay a steep price for your victory. It would be far wiser to be *mevater*. And when children see that their parents are *mevater* to each other, the *chinuch* benefits will serve them well when they grow up and get married and in all situations in life.

⋖§ Inappropriate Language

Children can sometimes pick up *nivul peh*, vulgar language, in the street or in school, and this is certainly a problem. Of course, parents have to make sure that they themselves never use improper or vulgar language, even inadvertently. We are so exposed these days that we sometimes don't realize what penetrates our defenses and creeps into our own way of speaking. So the first thing is to make sure that we are not guilty of using inappropriate language. The language spoken in the home must be clean and pure.

Now, if a child uses inappropriate language at a young age, you can assume that he really doesn't understand what he is saying. He merely heard others using those words and realized that it gives people a rise. Those that hear it laugh or get annoyed, and although the child doesn't understand why those words had that particular effect, he will try to be clever and use them to produce the same effect. So it is basically harmless, but you have to put an end to it right away so that it doesn't develop into a larger problem as he gets older. You have to tell him in no uncertain terms that language of this sort is never spoken in your home. It is unacceptable, and that's that.

But when an older child uses inappropriate language it poses a very serious problem. The first step in addressing it is to understand the extent to which such language is a profound corruption of who we are and what we should be. We need to understand that inappropriate language in its most vulgar and shocking forms is just the extreme manifestation of a deep deficiency. And we have to know what it is before we can attack the problem.

Rabbeinu Yonah writes (3:229) that *nivul peh* comes from *azus panim*, brazenness and impudence. So this is the first point, that *nivul peh* is the product of the *midah* of *azus panim*. A refined and respectful person will not use such language. The Ribono Shel Olam despises *nivul peh* and is disgusted by it, because it is the opposite of refinement and modesty. Furthermore, *nivul peh* defiles and sullies the *klei haseichel*, the instruments of the intelligence, which are our most precious possessions. It takes the most precious component of a person and sullies it. Rabbeinu Yonah uses very strong language in making these points, even stronger language than he uses when speaking about *lashon hara*.

Then Rabbeinu Yonah goes on to explain that it is not enough to avoid *nivul peh*. A person should also strive to speak on a higher, more refined, more sophisticated level. The Gemara says (Pesachim 3a) that a person shouldn't utter unrefined words. In Parashas Noach (Bereishis 7:8), the Torah speaks about "animals that are not clean (*einenah tahorah*)" being brought into the Teivah when it could have said more concisely "unclean (*tamei*) animals." This is meant to teach us that it proper to be a bit wordier and avoid using an unrefined word such as *tamei*.

The question that immediately arises, and which the commentators ask, is that in Parashas Shemini the word *tamei* is used again and again to identify animals that may not be eaten. The Shiltei Giborim answers that in Parashas Shemini the Torah is telling us that these animals are prohibited. Therefore, the Torah uses stronger language. But in Parashas Noach, the Torah is simply relating which animals were brought into the Teivah, and therefore, it uses the more refined forms.

Rabbeinu Yonah has a different explanation. Noach's generation was eventually permitted to eat unclean animals. They were only forbidden to bring unclean animals as offerings to the Ribono Shel Olam. Therefore, the Torah teaches us that we should not use language that disparages the food that we eat. We can use the word *tamei* to describe something that is completely forbidden, but we cannot use it to describe our own food. Why? Because it is demeaning, and our language has to be refined.

I once read a story about the Chazon Ish. Two people came to him for a *din Torah*. In the course of their arguments, one of them said to the other, "You're a liar!" The Chazon Ish opened his eyes wide and said to the man, "You know, you could have said that the same thing in a nicer way. You could have said that it is not true. You didn't have to call it a lie, and you didn't have to call him a liar."

So the *mitzvah* of speaking properly begins with the choice of words, with vocabulary. We have to use measured vocabulary that reflects our own refinement and sophistication and our respect for that most precious of our possessions, our "instruments of intelligence." If this is our fundamental premise when we speak, we will stay far, far away from using vulgarities, profanities, obscenities and other forms of inappropriate language. And we will be on our guard against speaking *lashon hara*.

The Rabbeinu Yonah concludes by saying that it is not enough to avoid inappropriate language, even unrefined language. We also have to see to it that we speak with the proper dignity and to avoid undignified language. If a person has the proper respect for the gift of language, he will make sure to use it with the greatest dignity and sophistication possible. Every word he speaks should reflect the grandeur of the human being in general, and of an *ehrlicher Yid* and a *ben Torah* in particular. The way we present ourselves to the world is a reflection on who we are, on the Torah that we represent and on the honor of the Ribono Shel Olam. Therefore, our speech carries a great responsibility, and we must make sure that the words we speak are clean and pure and completely refined.

So when it comes to our children, as I said, if a young child uses inappropriate language, and he really doesn't know what he is saying, all you have to do is tell him that this is not how we speak in this house. We don't speak Chinese, and we don't use such language. But if the child is older and understands what he is saying, it is important that you explain to him the gravity of what he has done and how damaging it is to speak this way. And then, of course, you have to lay down the law. Not in this house, and not in this family.

≈§ Confidence and Arrogance

While you don't want your child to become a *baal gaavah*, you do want to instill self-confidence in him. So how do you mold him into a secure, self-assured person without allowing him become arrogant?

Actually, self-confidence and *gaavah* are not one and the same. Self-confidence means having a clear understanding of who and what you are, while *gaavah* is having an inflated sense of self. The *baal gaavah* is guilty of *kochi ve'otzem yadi*. He thinks that he alone should get the credit for his accomplishments, and he thinks he is better than other people are. The self-confident person knows the value of his accomplishments, but he also acknowledges that he could not accomplish anything without the help of the Ribono Shel Olam. Therefore, he does not consider himself superior to other people. A self-confident person can easily slip into becoming a *baal gaavah*, but if he has the proper *emunah* and *bitachon*, he can avoid it.

If a child does not have self-confidence, you can help him by assuring him that he can do whatever it is that he is striving to do. And if he makes a mistake, it is also okay. Everyone makes mistakes at one time or another. There is no shame in failure, only in not trying. So tell him that you want him to try and that you believe he can do it. That will not make him into a *baal gaavah*. But when he is successful, you should not go on and on about how clever he is, because that will make him a *baal gaavah*. A simple "well done" will do.

In fact, it is quite possible that people who lack self-confidence actually have a strong streak of *gaavah*. The *baal gaavah* is very worried about his *kavod*, so he is exceedingly afraid of making a mistake. Failure will humiliate him. Therefore, he has no confidence. A person without much *gaavah*, however, is not that concerned with his image. He strives for success, but he will not be devastated by failure. He can concentrate on what he needs to do with a calm determination, and that is self-confidence.

It follows, therefore, that if you want your child to be self-confident, you should work on reducing his *gaavah*, because *gaavah* is a major obstacle to confidence. The best way to do this is to impress on him that we are very limited in what we can do. If we lift our hands, it is only through the *chessed* of the Ribono Shel Olam. Explain to him that *kochi ve'otzem yadi* is a foolish concept.

It is also follows that you should not criticize your child if he fails. Consistent criticism is the surest way to break a child. He becomes frightened to do anything, because he is always afraid that he will invite criticism. And it goes without saying — even though I'm saying it — that you should never ridicule a child. Ridicule is a weapon against which a child has absolutely no defense. If you want to show the child what he did wrong, it would be best to wait until the next opportunity arises and show him how to handle the situation correctly before he makes mistakes.

◆§ Attitudes Toward Non-Jews

As part of our *chinuch*, we teach our children that we are different from the non-Jews. We have a special relationship with the Ribono Shel Olam, we have the Torah, we live according to higher standards and ideals, and we want to keep our children separate and sheltered from the outside world. But in doing so, we run the risk of their becoming arrogant toward non-Jews and disdainful of them. This can easily lead to a terrible *chillul Hashem*, a desecration of the Name of Hashem. Moreover, today that we are living in *galus*, disrespectful behavior toward non-Jews can have serious consequences.

According to the Mishnah (Avos 3:13), every human being was created in the *tzelem Elokim*. The Gemara also says (Megilah 10b) that the *malachim* wanted to say Shirah at Krias Yam Suf, but the Ribono Shel Olam didn't permit it. "The works of My hands," He said, "are drowning in the sea, and you want to say Shirah?"

Moreover, we find references in the Torah, Neviim and Kesuvim too numerous to mention that the Ribono Shel Olam is consistently concerned about the opinions of the non-Jews.

The issues we have with the non-Jews relate to the way so many of them live and behave. We do not have contempt for the non-Jews, only for the bad *midos* that some of them display. And we should also tell the children that there are *chasidei umos haolam*, righteous non-Jews, who have good *midos* and live by higher standards of morality. But regardless of their behavior, we have to show respect to all of them. Indeed, the Gemara says (Gittin 62a) that Amoraim would greet idol worshippers they met in the street. It would be good *chinuch* to teach our children to be polite and respectful to all people.

ৰ্প্থ Other People's Children

If you see someone else's child behaving in an inappropriate manner, you are not obligated to try and modify his behavior. The *mitzvah* of *chinuch* extends only to your own children. You have no obligation in the *chinuch* of other people's children.

It once happened that some boys were being rowdy in the *beis midrash* in Bnei Brak, and the Chazon Ish was there. The boys were jumping around and shoving each other, and one of them pushed the Chazon Ish by mistake. The Chazon Ish was a frail man, and he nearly fell over. A man who witnessed this started yelling at the boys and berating them for their carelessness.

The Chazon Ish turned to the man and said, "Don't you know that the Torah forbids (Vayikra 25:17) harassing other people?"

"But we have to be *mechanech* them," said the man.

The Chazon Ish shook his head. "Only the father and the *rebbe* have an obligation of *chinuch*. Everyone else is forbidden to harass other people. It doesn't matter if they are adults or children. Harassment is forbidden."

CHAPTER TWENTY

Truth and Falsehood

Avraham was a rich man, renowned for his *chessed* and *hachnasas orchim*. His house was open to all directions, and he invited travelers inside to eat and drink and rest their weary legs. He spared no effort and expense in taking care of his guests.

When the *malachim* came to visit him in the guise of dusty travelers, he invited them in and said (Bereishis 18:4-5), "Take a little water, wash your feet and recline under the tree. And I will bring a loaf of bread, and you can satisfy your hunger, then you can go."

That's what he offered them, a little water and a loaf of bread. But then he hurried off to prepare cakes and assorted fine foods and delicacies and he served them in royal fashion. So the Gemara comments (Bava Metzia 87a) that "*tzaddikim* promise a little and do a lot, but *resha'im* promise a lot and do only a little."

It is certainly commendable to "promise a little and do a lot," but in that situation, what is the best course of action? Avraham was the shining example of *chessed* and *hachnasas orchim* in the world. He treated his guests with the highest honor. So how did the guests feel when he offered them a little water and a loaf of bread? Wouldn't they have felt far more honored if Avraham had invited them in and said, "Stay right here, and I will bring each of you an entire fresh tongue"? Shouldn't he have invited them in with a warmth and expansiveness and the assurance that they were about to enjoy a feast they would never forget? Wouldn't that have been *hachnasas orchim* on a much higher order?

The Alter of Kelm explains that Avraham was above all a man of the highest integrity. He would never utter a word that he thought was less than the absolute truth. He never promised to do something he was not absolutely sure that he could deliver. When he offered the *malachim* a little water and a loaf of bread, it was something that he knew he could deliver. But he could not be sure that he could deliver on any other promise. How could he know that everything would work out exactly as he wanted? And if he had even the slightest doubt, he would not presume to make such an offer. He would rather forgo his intense desire to treat his guests in a royal fashion and not risk promising that which he could not deliver.

There is another incident with Avraham that seems incomprehensible. When his nephew Lot was abducted by the five Babylonian kings, Avraham took Eliezer with him and set off in pursuit. Ultimately, he had a miraculous victory and rescued Lot and his family, but when he set out he didn't know a miracle would be performed for him. Why then did he risk his life to pursue the powerful warrior kings? He knew he was likely to be killed and yet he did not hesitate. Why?

The commentators point out that when Avraham and Lot decided to go their separate ways, Avraham told him (Bereishis 13:9), "Separate yourself from me, if you go to the left, I will go to the right, and if you go to the right, I will go to the left." This is strange language. He should have referred to the compass points and said, "If you go north, I will go south" and so forth. Why did he speak about right and left?

The commentators explain that Avraham was telling Lot that although they were separating he was not abandoning him. They would always be connected like the right arm and the left arm. Avraham assured him that although there would be a physical distance between them they would always be family and he would always protect him.

At the time he made his promise, Avraham had not expected that Lot would be abducted by a powerful army from Babylon, but he had given his word, and a word is a word. Avraham was a *ne'eman*, a faithful, truthful, reliable, loyal person, and he risked his life rather than break his word.

When we speak about the Jewish home we call it a *bayis ne'eman*, a home of trustworthiness and truth. That is the foundation of a Torah home, and that is the foundation of our *chinuch*. There has to be honesty and integrity in the relationships among all the members of the family. And the children have to be taught the value and importance of being *ne'eman*. Before everything else, the home has to be a place of trustworthiness, loyalty and truthfulness, an environment of stability in which a child can grow and flourish.

✍ A Child's Fantasies

Before we discuss the importance and methods of teaching our children the value and the meaning of *emes*, truth, and the abhorrent nature of *sheker*, falsehood, it would be worthwhile to define exactly what is considered truth to a child and what is considered falsehood.

There is a world of reality and a world of imagination. A mature person knows the difference between the two. When a mature person tells you that such and such a thing happened to him, you know that it happened in the world of reality, or at least that he wants you to believe that it did. But that's not how it is with a child.

Since a young child's mind has not yet fully matured, his power of imagination is very strong, and when he imagines something, he sees it as clearly as if he was actually living through it. But because he is still immature, he cannot always distinguish between experiences he had in the real world and experiences he had in his own imaginary world.

So when a child tells you that something happened and you know that it didn't happen, it doesn't necessarily mean that the child is lying. It might very well be that he imagined it and that his imaginary experience was so vivid that in his own mind it has taken on the cloak of reality. In fact, I know a certain grownup who suffers from the same inability to distinguish between reality and fantasy. People accused him of lying, but I defended him. This man lives in a fantasy world, and whatever he says relates to his imaginary experiences. He never tells a lie. A lie is only a lie if the person telling it knows that it's a lie. If a person, child or adult, thinks something is true because he imagined it or because he somehow convinced himself it was true, then he is not lying. It may not be the truth, but this person can certainly not be considered a liar.

Children come home and tell their mothers stories about what happened to them in school. Later, the mother may go to a PTA meeting and hear from the teacher that the story is totally untrue, that it is a complete fabrication. The mother may be inclined to go home and confront the child, "The story you told me is not true. It never happened. Why did you lie to me?" But she should think twice before saying anything to the child. It's quite possible that he imagined the story on the bus coming home from school, and by the time he got home, he thought it had really happened. This child does not deserve to be reprimanded or punished.

We also have to be careful not to push a child into saying a lie. Sometimes, the child knows that when he comes home his mother will interrogate him and ask him about something or other that happened in the classroom. The child does not know the answer, but he feels backed into a corner. So what does he do? He makes up a story. The child knows perfectly well that his story is a fable, but he feels that he has no choice. We need to be careful that we do not push our children into telling lies, and if it does happen that a child tells a lie out of a feeling of self-preservation, we should not deal with it as if it were a willful lie.

◄§ The Attribute of Truth

There is a *mitzvah* of *vehalachta bidrachav*, you shall walk in His ways (Devarim 28:9). This *mitzvah* obligates us to learn from the divine attributes of the Ribono Shel Olam and to integrate them into our lives. The Ribono Shel Olam is merciful, so we should also be merciful. The Ribono Shel Olam is righteous, so we should also be righteous. But there is an attribute that takes precedence over all the rest, and that is the attribute of truth. Why? Because truth is more than just one of the Ribono Shel Olam's attributes. It is His very essence. As the Rambam writes (Yesodei Hatorah 1:4), the Ribono Shel Olam is truth. The Gemara says (Shabbos 55a), "The Ribono Shel Olam's seal is truth." Truth is His identity, and all His other attributes are included in it.

When Rabbeinu Yonah says that *"emes* is the foundation of the soul," it could very well be because it is the central attribute of the Ribono Shel Olam. A truthful person is a complete person, while a liar is deficient. There is a gaping hole in his soul.

The *Sefer Hachinuch* writes that there is nothing more repugnant than *sheker*. Furthermore, the worst calamities happen in the homes where *sheker* reigns, because the Ribono Shel Olam only blesses those who emulate His attribute of truth. Liars, however, are the opposite of the Ribono Shel Olam. If someone is not merciful, for instance, he is deficient in his emulation of the Ribono Shel Olam. But if he is a liar, he is at the opposite pole to the Ribono Shel Olam. And since the Ribono Shel Olam is totally *berachah*, liars are destined for the opposite of *berachah*.

I once heard a ruling from Rav Moshe Horowitz regarding a financial dispute. Before the Vilna Shas was published, the impending publication of the Slavita Shas generated a great deal of excitement. Printing a Shas was very expensive, and the publishers wanted to assure themselves of a minimum number of sales before they would invest in the printing. They went to many people and asked them to make a commitment that they would purchase the Slavita Shas when it came out. After they amassed a substantial list of commitments, they went ahead and printed the Shas. During this time, the Vilna Shas appeared, and it was an instant hit. Many of the people who had made the commitment to buy the Slavita Shas wanted to back out and purchase the Vilna Shas instead. So the question came before Rav Moshe Horowitz. Are they allowed to back out?

His response was very illuminating. It could be, he wrote, that according to the national laws they are not obligated. It could also be that according to Halachah they were not obligated. But when a person gives his word and backs out, there is something missing in the entire foundation of his Yiddishkeit.

Why, he asked, do we have to keep our Torah? Because we said "*naaseh venishma*, we will do and we will hear"? So why can't we say that we changed our minds? Why can't we say that at that moment, standing before Mount Sinai, we felt very inspired, and we certainly meant it at the time, but now we want to change our minds?

The answer is that even before the Torah was given, the basic humanity of a person required that he tell the truth and keep his word. From the beginning of creation, it was accepted throughout the world, even by the most violent, bloodthirsty pagans, that a word had to be kept. A promise was sacrosanct, because if it was meaningless, civilized society could not survive.

Truthfulness is the very foundation of a person, and therefore, a child has to learn from the earliest age that he must always tell the truth. If a child confuses imagination with reality, he certainly cannot be considered a liar, but he must still be taught to be more discerning in what he represents as the truth. Otherwise, he can gradually slide into dishonesty. You have to explain gently to him that what he is saying really didn't happen and that perhaps it happened some other way. You have to train him to seek the truth and speak nothing else but the truth.

One of the reasons parents sometimes find it difficult to speak to their children about *emes* is that they themselves are not always entirely truthful. They may do or say things that, even if they rationalize them to themselves, are somewhat less than truthful, and they're afraid that their children will expose their hypocrisy. If they demand truthfulness from their children, their children may remind them that they had reneged on certain promises they had made. Children have very good memories, especially about things that are important to them.

◈ Fact or Fiction

The Steipler said that *chinuch* in *emes* requires that we do not tell our children fictional stories without telling them beforehand that the stories never really happened. Today there is a great deal of fiction literature being published, and if it serves to develop the child's imagination, that is a good thing. But the child has to know that this is not a true story, that the *shofar* never spoke to Dov Dov, that it is no more than a *mashal*, a parable, meant to teach certain lessons and values.

Children are familiar with the concept of *mashal*. They've heard plenty of such stories told by the Dubno Maggid. A fictional story may be a bit more complex, but it serves the same purpose. It deals with situations and character issues, and it conveys Torah ideas, concepts and values. But it is not fact. If the child is allowed to accept it as fact, it is an exercise in *sheker*.

But no matter what, even if the child understands that the story is being told to him to convey a lesson, he must be told that the story is not true, that it is only a parable. If he is not told that it is a parable and then the child later discovers that it was not a true story, he may think that his parents told him a lie in order to teach him an important lesson. The lesson he learns will be that a lie is permitted if there is a purpose to it, and then he will tell lies when it suits him to do so.

◆§ When a Child Lies

If a child tells a lie and you know that he is not simply repeating something that he imagines to be true, the parents have to respond immediately and effectively. If you ask him if he did a certain thing and he says he didn't and you know without any doubt that he did, you have to take an unequivocal stand against *sheker*.

There is a tradition many generations old that when a child tells a lie he gets a slap. For other transgressions, it is not such a simple matter to slap a child, but telling a lie earns an immediate slap. I know that these days there are supposedly more enlightened ways of dealing with lies, such as washing out the child's mouth with soap, but there is no substitute for the clarity of a slap in these circumstances.

But before parents take a righteous stance with their children regarding truth and falsehood, and indeed regarding any other *chinuch* issue, they have to take a long hard look at themselves and decide whether or not they are being hypocritical. Children are the best judges of their parents' characters, and they know if the parents are truthful people or if they are deceitful when it suits them. The bottom line is that you cannot dare take a stance against someone else's *sheker* if you are guilty of it yourself. Your first obligation, therefore, is to work on your own truthfulness. And then, if you are meticulously careful to tell the truth, you have to show your child that you will not tolerate falsehood.

CHAPTER TWENTY-ONE

Modesty and Holiness

One of the problems in *chinuch* today is that people take direction from the latest theories in child education, and the truth is that what is known as child education has very little to do with *chinuch* in the spirit of the Torah. Many books people read, even those written by observant Jewish authors, draw material from contemporary psychological thought. We, however, seek direction from the wisdom of Chazal.

The thinking today — of course, we don't know what the thinking will be tomorrow — is that everything has to be explained to the child. If you ask your child to do something, you have to explain your reasoning to him. Laying down the law without proper explanation is considered bad parenting. This thinking is the opposite of the Torah way of *chinuch*.

In the view of *chinuch*, the child does not have to understand why he has been told to do something. It is, of course, helpful if he understands, but it is not at all necessary. The goal is to condition him with gentleness and sensitivity to do what he needs to do, but there is no need for explanations.

On the contrary, if your instructions come along with explanations, you're really inviting the child to argue and debate with you. And more often than not, the child really doesn't understand what it is all about, especially at a young age. So in essence, you are making things very difficult for him. He thinks he is expected to understand and he doesn't, so he becomes frustrated and confused. And if he can't understand, why then should he do what he was told to do? Telling the child lies or half-truths in order to try to make him understand is also a bad idea.

It is the immediate responsibility of the parents to make the decisions for the child and to condition him to behave in the proper manner according to the Torah. This serves to prepare him for the time when he is older and on his own. The *chinuch* he receives from his parents in his younger years will equip him to be successful in life and to fulfill his obligations when he is older.

There are some aspects of *chinuch* that only begin when the child is already older, and those matters usually come with explanations. But those matters that should be addressed at earlier ages need no explanation.

The Gemara discusses (Kiddushin 29a) marrying off a son at a young age "while your hand is on the neck of your son." When is the father's "hand on the neck of [his] son"? It depends on a difference of opinion regarding *chinuch*. According to one view, it's from sixteen to twenty-two, and according to the other view, it's from eighteen to twenty-four.

Rashi explains that this is the window of opportunity for a father who wants to rebuke his son about Torah and *mitzvos*. If the boy is younger than sixteen or eighteen, he will not have the sophistication to understand fully what his father is trying to tell him, and if he is older than twenty-two or twenty-four he is likely to resist and reject his father's admonitions.

We see clearly that the age of understanding is considered to be in the late teens and early twenties. Younger children are simply not expected to understand. The purpose of *chinuch* at the earlier ages is not to educate them but to train them.

Children are receptive to training if it's done with proper love and sensitivity. Children instinctively want to fit into the pattern of their family's life. They want to do what their fathers and mothers do and act as their fathers and mothers act. If parents tell a child to do something "because this is what we do in our family," that is almost always more than enough reason for the child to comply. And the younger children are the more likely they are to comply without question and to become conditioned to behave as they are expected to behave until it becomes the natural rhythm of their lives.

ᴈ§ Starting Very Young

One of the more sensitive areas of *chinuch* involves introducing children to the concepts and requirements of *tznius* and *kedushah*, modesty and holiness. We have not been given many guidelines on this topic by earlier *sefarim*. At the same time, it is a topic that must be discussed in this day and age, and it must be addressed at a very early age. It is one of the most difficult issues that parents face in the *chinuch* of their children, both boys and girls.

Parents often shy away from discussing these matters with their children, but failure to address these subjects does their children a disservice. If there is one single factor that prevents young people from reaching high spirituals levels it is their exposure to immoral influences without being properly prepared to defend themselves. If the children are left to find their own way through this mine-field, they will inevitably follow the natural impulses of the *yetzer hara* that are present in every person.

In today's society, simply walking through the street, we are bombarded from every side with harmful images and sounds. Young people often hear things they shouldn't hear from friends. It is just about impossible to shield our children completely. If we ourselves were lucky enough to be a bit sheltered, we have no right to assume that our children will be as well. It is more likely that they will be exposed to the worst of the worst. The frontal attack is so powerful that we must find within ourselves the cour-age to take responsibility for the spiritual safety of our children. We cannot, of course, sit on top of them and guard them day and night. All we can do is *daven* for them and give them a sense of direction

There are a few simple rules that we must teach them.

We have to deal with pictures and images. Looking at pic-tures or at parts of the body that should be covered leaves a deep impression on children long before they even understand what they are seeing. So it's very important to keep children away from places of immodest exposure, such as mixed bathing beaches or pools, from the youngest ages.

Furthermore, as soon as children reach a certain level of under-standing, the parents should tell them that we do not look at these kinds of things. You shouldn't make a big production out of it, because that will only pique their interest and curiosity. When you pass by an indecent billboard, you shouldn't say, "Look away! Close your eyes!" A naturally inquisitive child will only be encour-aged to take a good look. It is better to say in a calm voice, "Those are not nice things. We don't look at them."

Children accept it when you tell them we don't eat such and such things because they're not kosher. They accept that we have to have two sets of dishes and that if by mistake the wrong spoon is used you have to put it aside. If that is the way they are brought up it becomes second nature to them. By the same token, you can tell them that we don't look at such and such things because they're not kosher for viewing. There are non-kosher foods, and there are non-kosher images. That is just the way it is. Simple and direct in the best way that suits you and your children, both boys and girls. Just tell them that this is the way we live. We have a good life, and these things have no place in it. They'll accept it.

You also have to warn your children about things they may hear, and you should encourage them to tell you if they heard something of the sort from their friends. And then you have to use your common sense in dealing with the situation.

And it is far, far better to talk about these things to your children at as young an age as possible, before the *yetzer hara* has had a chance to become fully entrenched in them. Once their *yetzer hara* has been inflamed it is much more difficult to combat. But if we train our children while they are young, they'll already be conditioned to live in a certain way, and they will have an easier time dealing with the *yetzer hara* when it awakens. In a *teshuvah*, Rav Moshe Feinstein writes that boys and girls should be separated in school at an early age, even before they have any *yetzer hara*, so that they should become accustomed to the separation.

The same applies to inappropriate touching. Children should be told at a very young age, without elaboration but just as a matter of course, that there are certain parts of the body that are not to be touched. When children are very young, they can be told many things without the need for explanations. Those are the best times to establish basic rules in these areas.

The best way of dealing with these things is to present them as positives. Tell them that we are the children of Avraham, Yitzchak and Yaakov. We are different from other people, and there are certain things that we simply don't do. We do not eat non-kosher food. We do not look at non-kosher images. We do not comport ourselves in non-kosher ways. We aspire to a higher life. We aspire to purity and holiness, and we have to live a certain way to achieve these goals. And when children see their parents living by these same guidelines, the message is driven home, and this kind of comportment will come naturally to them.

Any *chinuch* in these areas that starts after the *yetzer hara* has awakened is a big struggle, and it is not likely to produce the *eidelkeit,* the fine and noble character, that we seek for our children. It may produce forced behavior, conditioned behavior, but the *eidelkeit* is difficult to achieve unless we begin at the very earliest age.

When you talk to your daughters about *tznius,* modesty, you cannot wait until their *yetzer hara* to show themselves off is inflamed. By then you will face a daunting task.

Once again, it is best not to get into explanations when you tell your daughter about *tznius.* All you have to say is that this is how a Jewish girl dresses. This is nice, this is pleasant, this is how your mother dresses. These are our standards. We are a pure and holy people, and no matter what kind of behavior and attire you see among others, that's not our way. That's the only explanation necessary, that this is not the way we live. If these ideas and attitudes are impressed on a girl at a young age, she'll be fortified to deal with the difficulties of *tznius* issues when they arise.

At the same time, you have to be careful not to give the child the impression that she can talk to a non-Jew without the proper respect and decorum. Having *derech eretz* and good *midos* is also an integral part of the *kedushah* of Klal Yisrael. The girl has to understand that she has an inner holiness and that she should take pride in it. She has to understand that this inner holiness obligates her to act in a certain way and to dress in a certain way.

Children are attuned to the *kedushah* of their *neshamos,* sometimes better than we are. If *tznius* is presented to them in this way, if they are told that they should hold their heads high because of who and what they are, they will likely respond with acceptance and pride.

As the girl grows older, however, she may begin to feel the restrictive nature of *tznius* and chafe at it. At that point, we should also introduce her to the inner concept and the beauty of *tznius*.

I once asked Rav Moshe Soloveitchik, who was a very great man, a question that was troubling me. We don't make bas mitzvah parties; even girls between themselves don't make bas mitzvah parties. Why not? What's so bad about a bas mitzvah party? The Yam Shel Shlomo says that the bar mitzvah is the greatest *seudas mitzvah* because another person in Klal Yisrael has begun doing *mitzvos*. Well, the same holds true when a girl becomes bas mitzvah. It's a time for rejoicing for the parents and the family. Why shouldn't we make a *seudah*? This was what I asked him.

"I have only one daughter," he said to me, "and I had the same question. I couldn't find a reason not to do it, but it's not in our *mesorah*, so I didn't. So on the day of her bas mitzvah I called her aside, and I said to her, 'This is a big day for you. You've become bas mitzvah. It's also a big day for your mother and me. We're all very happy, and really, we should make a *seudah* as we did for your brothers, but it seems to me that the first thing a girl has to learn when she becomes bas mitzvah is the idea of *kol kevudah bas melech penimah* (Tehillim 45:14), that a true princess remains secluded. A true princess celebrates with an inner joy and without public fanfare. But don't think, dear daughter, that our joy is any less because we are not making a public celebration.' That's what I told her. Then I brought out a bottle of liqueur and two little cups, and we drank a *lechaim*, just the two of us."

I have no doubt that this little talk made a tremendous impression on his daughter, because he conveyed to her the spirit of *tznius* rather than just a set of restrictions.

◆§ Protecting the Holiness

The Rambam divides his *sefer* into fourteen books. The one that deals with the subjects of forbidden relationships and forbidden foods is titled Kedushah. The connection between *kedushah* and these things is not that we are holy because we restrict ourselves from these forbidden things. It is rather the opposite. Since we are holy, we have to restrict ourselves, because these things diminish our holiness.

This is the innate nature of a Jewish person. We are a holy nation, and the holier a person is the more he has to restrict himself in these areas. Kohanim, we find, have more restrictions in their relationships than others do, because they have an elevated *kedushah*. And we must restrict ourselves more than the outside world does in order to protect our own *kedushah*, because it is the very essence of our being.

CHAPTER TWENTY-TWO

Neatness and Order

There's a story I once heard from Rav Eliahu Dessler, one of the few stories I was privileged to hear from him directly, about the time when he was learning in the Slobodka Yeshivah. During this time, his father, Rav Reuven Dov Dessler of the Kelm Yeshivah, one of the great *baalei mussar*, came to visit him and see how he was doing.

It was not a simple matter to travel from Kelm to Slobodka. Today, it probably would not take very long. In those days, however, it was a long and difficult journey. But Rav Reuven Dov felt it was important that he make the trip. He needed to make sure that his son was doing well.

When he arrived in Slobodka, the *rosh yeshivah* welcomed him with great honor, and they spoke in learning for a long while.

Afterward, the *rosh yeshivah* said, "You've come a long way, and I'm sure you're eager to see your son. Come, let's go into the *beis midrash* together."

Rav Reuven Dov shook his head. "Oh, no. I don't want to make a disturbance in the *beis midrash*. Take me to his room instead."

They went together to his son's room in the place of his lodging. Rav Reuven Dov opened the cupboard and saw that everything was neatly in its place. The shirts, the socks, everything.

Rav Reuven Dov turned to the *rosh yeshivah* and said, "I see that my son is learning well. Thank you. I'm going home."

And he went home straight away to Kelm.

This is the story. Rav Dessler heard it later from his father. It's not a simple story. There is much to be learned from it. But I want to bring out one particular point.

The impact of *seder*, of things being in order, extends far beyond external organization. When there is *seder*, when everything is neat and in its assigned place, it has a tremendous impact on a person's *menuchas hanefesh*, his inner serenity. The outward order of a person's life leads to the inner order of his own self, and it brings him serenity.

Neatness and order also play a crucial role in the home and in *chinuch*. It brings an atmosphere of serenity into the home, and it affects the temperament and sensibilities of a child much more than we think. Of course, parents must use common sense in training their children to be neat and orderly. They have to do it in a gentle and natural way so that the emphasis on neatness and order does not result in a stressful atmosphere, which can bring more damage than benefits.

❧ The Order of Creation

I've heard people dismiss the insistence on *seder* as compulsive behavior and perhaps also a kind of arrogance. What difference does it make, they say, if something is here or if it's there? The main thing is that you do what you have to do and accomplish what you have to accomplish. Everything else is unimportant.

But that attitude is a huge mistake. The Ribono Shel Olam created an ordered world, and Chazal make a point of mentioning it in the *tefilos*, "*Umesader es hakochavim bemishmeroseihem.* And He organizes the stars in their nightly shifts." Everything in creation is formed to work with perfect order. And in the Torah, all the times for *tefilah* and Shabbos and the Yamim Tovim, everything works with precise timing. If a person does something one minute it may be fine, but if he does it a minute later he is liable to a death sentence.

And the closer you get to *kedushah*, the greater is the role that *seder* plays. In the *avodah* of the Beis Hamikdash, we find a finely tuned *seder*. Everything must be done by a precise formula, according to precise rule and in a precise order. Even a small change can invalidate the *avodah*. There is no room for sloppiness in the Beis Hamikdash, and there should be no room for sloppiness in our lives.

Rav Simchah Zissel, the Alter of Kelm, put a very high priority on *seder*. One of his main goals in *chinuch* was teaching his *talmidim* to live with *seder*. I once heard a story about this from Rav Chaim Shmuel Lopian.

Rav Simchah Zissel once came into the room of one of his *talmidim* and saw that the slippers under the bed had been thrown down haphazardly. He immediately rushed to the *beis midrash* and gave a *shmuess* about the incredible *seder* with which the Ribono Shel Olam created the world. As he spoke, he became more and more agitated until he burst into tears.

"What about *seder*?" he cried out. "How can it be that one slipper is lying there sideways and the other is on its side?"

It's a little difficult to understand the depth of feeling that this violation of *seder* aroused in a man as great as Rav Simchah Zissel, but this story certainly highlights for us that this is no trivial matter.

⁌ Without and Within

In our day and age, the trend in society is away from *seder*. It is called being casual, which is an excuse for sloppiness. People today walk around dressed in slovenly fashion with no regard for decorum. The whole point is to be rebellious, and slovenliness is a blatant form of rebellion.

Our goal, however, is the opposite of rebellion. We work on ourselves to be *mekabel ol malchus shamayim*, to take upon ourselves the yoke of the kingdom of Heaven, and in order to accomplish this, we have to exercise discipline and self-control. Sloppiness comes from a lack of self-control. It's easier to dump things wherever they fall, so why go to the effort of putting everything in its proper place? Laziness also comes from a lack of self-control. Why disturb your rest to do what needs to be done when you can push it off to later or perhaps even entirely? But a person with self-control overcomes his inclination to sloppiness and laziness. He is in control, and he does what has to be done.

But how do you train your children to be diligent? How do you teach your children self-control? You can do it in a negative way, by denying them this, that and the other. Or you can train them to be neat and organized and impress upon them how pleasant and wonderful it is when everything is exactly where it should be, when you can find what you need because it is always in its place, when you don't have to be confronted with an unsightly mess. Developing *seder* is a much more positive approach to self-control and diligence.

Teaching children *seder* mean more then setting down rules for the children with a harsh discipline. All that will happen is that when the parents are there everything will be orderly but as soon as they turn their backs pandemonium will erupt. These children will not have learned to live with *seder*. They will have learned to be afraid of their parents. It is important for parents to inspire their children with a love and an appreciation for *seder*.

When a child learns that everything has its place, that there is an order to life, he will be transformed. The external orderliness around him will lead to an inner orderliness and reward him with *menuchas hanefesh*. And the orderliness in his life will lead to orderliness in his thought processes, and he will be much more successful in his learning.

When Rav Reuven Dov Dessler looked into his son's closet and saw that everything was exactly in its place down to the last pair of socks, he knew that all was well with him. When a person is confused, frustrated or depressed, the first thing that suffers is his *seder*; he leaves his clothing on the floor, the dishes in the sink and so on. When Rav Reuven Dov saw that his son's closet evidenced an impeccable *seder*, there was undoubtedly a *seder* in his inner being as well, and if so, there was nothing to worry about. He knew that his son was well and that he was flourishing in Torah. Everything else would take care of itself.

The Steipler said that if someone removes a *sefer* from a shelf in the *beis midrash* and doesn't put it back in its place he is a *rasha*. Strong language, but it touches on an important point. If a person doesn't return *sefarim* to their proper place, it is clear that he thinks only about himself and has a cavalier attitude toward others. Why should someone else have to put away his *sefarim*?

It also shows something more. It shows that he has no concept of *seder*. He leaves his clothes on the floor, and he doesn't put the *sefarim* he uses back in their proper place. If a person has no discipline and no sense of order, how can he expect to reach high levels in Torah and *avodah*?

In the *chinuch* of our children, we should put great emphasis on training them from a young age to be neat and orderly, to make sure that everything they take out is put back in its right place. Some people think of *seder* as an external thing of relatively little importance, but in actuality, *seder* is critical for the inner well-being of a person. It improves his *midos*, his *yiras shamayim*, his *kabalas ol malchus shamayim*, his willingness to listen and learn from others, his understanding of Torah, his relationships with other people, his ability to deal with situations, everything.

PART FIVE

On Chinuch
in Activities

CHAPTER TWENTY-THREE

Games Children Play

Adults play for recreation. Even if they get caught up in their amusements, they never lose sight of the difference between the reality of their lives and the make-believe world of play. As we have mentioned before, however, young children live in the world of imagination. They do not necessarily recognize the mark of delineation between the real world and the world they create for themselves in their imaginations. A child doesn't play in the sense that we mean it. He lives in alternate worlds.

If you ask a child coming home from kindergarten how he played that day, he'll give you an answer. And if you ask him how he worked that day, he'll give you the same answer, because to him work and play are interchangeable. When a young child plays, he is transported to the world of his creation, and he is as absorbed in it as any adult is in the world of reality. His experiences in his games and play are important to him, because at that moment, they are the reality of his life.

It follows, therefore, that the games children play can have a profound effect on their characters, their ambition, their desires, their outlook on life. We've already discussed earlier Rav Chazkel Levenstein's incisive comment that if you put a child on a rocking horse you are making him into a *baal agalah*, although it may be somewhat difficult for people living in today's world to relate to it. We also discussed games that stoke the greed of children and encourage them to aspire to wealth and power rather than Torah and *mitzvos*. It is the same with all games that children play.

People think that if it's called a game it's kosher. But it's not that simple. A game is a strong instrument of *chinuch*, and you have to make sure that you approve of the lessons it is teaching the child. Fortunately, there are plenty of Jewish games available today that can instill good *midos* in children. They may be a bit less interesting than the mainstream games, but children can still have a very good time playing them.

Games, even the most kosher, can become a serious matter. First of all, there is the risk of a child becoming caught up in *kochi ve'otzem yadi*, a sense of his own unrestrained power and ability to control his destiny. When he wins a game, he may get a heady sense of victory, which can have affect him negatively and undermine his *emunah* and *bitachon* as he grows older. But even if he plays a game of chance that uses dice over which he has no control, there is still a risk that he may learn bad *midos*.

Children get very involved in competitive games, and they get very excited when they win. Even if they had nothing to do with the victory, they still gloat and feel triumphant over the other players, who are now the losers. As for the losers, they learn to be jealous and resentful. No one wants to be a loser. So there are only bad *midos* being learned all around.

So a game should be preceded by a little orientation from the parents. This is only a game, they should tell the children, a pleasant way to spend the time. Sometimes one person wins and sometimes another. It doesn't matter who wins; the winner is no better than the loser. The main thing is that we're all going to have an enjoyable time together. All of us will have fun, no matter who wins. This is what the parents should stress. They should resist the urge to praise the winner. It will only arouse bad *midos* in everyone.

ᶜᵌ Useful Games

There are some games that serve quite a useful purpose. Chess is one game that comes immediately to mind. Some great *rabbanim* would play chess from time to time, but their motive was certainly not to gain victory over their opponents, who were probably also *rabbanim*. Chess is an exercise for the mind. It's a complex and deep game, and playing well requires strong concentration, focus and disciplined thinking. When children play chess, the skills they gain can help them later in mastering difficult and complicated *sugyos*.

Children can also gain by playing memory games. They put down cards all over the table and then they have to make matches of pairs of cards by remembering where they are. Such games sharpen the brain. They provide *chinuch* in concentration and memory, and as long as a fuss is not made over the winner, they do not have to arouse bad *midos*.

Building toys are a useful tool in the development of many skills, and they also give the child a sense of accomplishment. Puzzles are also good for the development of the mind, and in general, they are not competitive, which is a good thing.

◆§ Obsessive Involvement

The danger inherent in many games is that the children can become addicted to them. They can become obsessed with the games and play incessantly. And even when they're not playing, they think a lot about the games. Electronic games, in particular have this power of fascination for a child. You should never allow a child to play games that gain such a hold on his mind that he will not want to tear himself away from them.

Obsession with games, or with anything else, is a major obstacle to spiritual advancement. It takes the focus away from Torah and *mitzvos*, and it draws a person into an imaginary world from which it is very difficult to function in the real world. Obsessive games are the most popular on the market for that very reason. People want to escape the real world and immerse themselves in an imaginary world that they think they control. And that is exactly why these games are detrimental to *chinuch*.

Sports are another form of diversion that can be useful or harmful, depending on how they are played. A game of sports every once in a while is a good outlet for energy, it is entertaining, and it promotes the physical well-being of the child. But here again there are two caveats.

One, if there is an emphasis on winning and on being an outstanding athlete and an expert in playing the game, then it will inevitably lead to bad *midos* for both the winner and the losers. But if the game is played in good fun, and all the children have an enjoyable time simply by playing the game in the fresh air and the sunshine and getting a little exercise, it is a wholesome activity.

The second point is that it cannot be allowed to become obsessive. If the child wants to play the sport every free moment he has, it will have a negative effect on him. All his thoughts, when playing, when at home and when in school, will be on how he can improve his performance. But as he improves on the playing field, his *midos* will suffer, his learning will suffer, and his relationships will suffer.

The Gemara says (Avodah Zarah 18b) that if someone goes to stadiums and circuses and watches magicians, clowns and acrobats performing, it is considered a *moshav leitzim*, an assembly of mockers, and of that it is written (Tehillim 1:1-2), "These are the fortunes of man ... nor did he sit in an assembly of mockers. For he desires only the Ribono Shel Olam's Torah ...." From here you learn out that these things lead to *bittul Torah*, neglect of Torah. This is what the Gemara teaches.

The question that immediately arises is why the Gemara had to bring the *pesukim* in Tehillim. Why didn't the Gemara say simply that going to these events is *bittul Torah*? Obviously, when you're at the stadium and the circus you don't bring your Gemara along with you, so it's *bittul Torah*, as simple as that. Why does the Gemara need such an elaborate proof of the obvious?

The answer is that the Gemara is not just saying that the time spent in these places is *bittul Torah*. For that alone there could be excuses. Perhaps the person would not have been learning anyway at that time. Perhaps he needed a break, a little relaxation and diversion. Perhaps you could make a case that the time spent there might on occasion not be *bittul Torah*.

The problem is that going to these places causes *bittul Torah* long after the person has left and returned home. The problem is that these things captivate a person's imagination and thoughts so that his mind constantly revisits the experience and thinks about it. Months later, he can be sitting at the Gemara and his mind will float away from the *beis midrash* right into the stadiums and circuses he visited. This *bittul Torah* is inexcusable. You needed to relax, to take a break, fine. But you had no right to spend that relaxation time in such a way that your learning would be disturbed long afterward.

That is the *bittul Torah* the Gemara is addressing. That is the concept the Gemara derives from the first *pesukim* in Tehillim. If you sit in a *moshav leitzim*, you are guilty of causing *bittul Torah* at a later time.

The same applies to all games, amusements and entertainments. If you allow a child to become absorbed and excited to an inordinate degree, if you allow him to become obsessed, you are putting him at risk of *bittul Torah*, of having his learning suffer long after the amusements are over.

The problem is somewhat diminished with regard to girls, for whom *bittul Torah* is not an issue. Nonetheless, obsessive involvement with games can still be quite harmful. Even though she is not required to learn Torah, a girl has many responsibilities, both personal and for the family, and if she is completely absorbed in games or other distractions, she may very well neglect her responsibilities.

❧ Children on Computers

Then there is the question of computers. It seems to me that a computer is a very constructive instrument and a very destructive instrument. On the one hand, there are educational toys and programs available that can be very helpful to a child in language skills, mathematics, geography and many other areas. On the other hand, however, there are numerous uses of the computer that are extremely harmful.

Unless a parent has complete control over what his child is doing on the computer, he shouldn't let his child touch it. But even if a parent feels he can control the child's use of the computer, there is a significant element of risk in allowing the child to become computer literate. What happens when he gets to the age when you don't have that much control over him? If he's a computer expert — and many children have a natural affinity to becoming computer experts — there is no telling what he will do.

It seems to me, therefore, that a child should not be allowed near a computer until he is much older and the parents have complete trust in him that he will not overstep the boundaries they set for him, and even then for only a limited amount of time. Even if your computer is not connected to the Internet, there are numerous games and programs that are not for the benefit of the child, that will only cause obsessive behavior and bad *midos*. There is no one answer to this question. Every parent has to make the decision based on his knowledge of the child's inclinations and trustworthiness. And if there is any question, the safest route is caution.

It goes without saying — but I'll say it anyway — that if all the conditions are right and the child is allowed onto the computer, he should under no circumstances be allowed to play the violent computer games so popular in the outside world. Games that involve simulations of shooting and killing and other horrible behavior destroy the *midos* of a child.

If putting a child on a rocking horse puts him in the psychological frame of mind of a *baal agalah*, then what is a child being taught if he is allowed to have toy guns or to shoot and kill on a computer screen? In my day, children were not even allowed to have water pistols. Allowing children to play with guns and swords is bringing the *midos* of Eisav into the home.

Even on Purim, parents should not allow their children to use pistols that shoot caps as noisemakers when Haman's name is read in the Megilah. Nor should a child dress up as a soldier on Purim. How many children want to dress up as Haman? I would venture to say there are hardly any. There are plenty of candidates for Mordechai and Esther, but no one wants to be Haman or Vashti. So should they be taught to aspire to be gun-toting soldiers? Is that a proper ambition for a good Jewish child?

The original *minhag* of making noise while Haman's name is read is a far cry from what is has become today. They used to take two pieces of wood and write Haman's name in chalk on one of them. Every time Haman's name was read, they would bang the two pieces of wood together. Little by little, the chalk would come off, and by the end of the Megilah, Haman's name was completely obliterated. This was a symbolic fulfillment of *mechias zecher Amalek*, the obliteration of the memory of Amalek. Every child would look at his piece of wood at the end of the Megilah and see that Haman's name was gone.

Then this nice *minhag* slowly changed. Banging the two pieces of wood became stamping with the feet, and then the stamping became a *gragger*, And then the *graggers* became cap pistols. The original *minhag* was a good chinuch in the *mitzvah* of *mechias zecher Amalek*. The new version of the *minhag*, however, is a *chinuch* in bad *midos*. Hopefully, the time will come when we will put an end to the new form of the *minhag* and reinstate the *minhag* the way it used to be.

CHAPTER TWENTY-FOUR

Dangerous Books

Not every *chinuch* issue relates directly to the *chinuch* of children. Some issues relate to the parents and have an indirect effect on the children. The issue of literature in particular is troubling. I don't want to go into this subject in too much specific detail. I'm assuming that adults are responsible enough not to read improper magazines and non-Jewish books that are full of heresy and immodesty. But I would like to raise awareness about a danger from an unexpected direction.

Today, you can walk into a Judaica shop and see a man with a beard and long *peyos* behind the counter, and you think that everything sold in the shop is one hundred percent glatt kosher. There are hundreds of books, and the authors, some of whom may even be rabbis, have Jewish names. Many of the books are about psychology, and their points of view are often alien to our beliefs and values. When readers are drawn into these books, they form an entirely different outlook on family, marriage and life in general.

I've seen firsthand the damage that results from these books. A couple was having serious marital problems. They were barely talking to each other. They had been to counseling a number of times, but it wasn't going anywhere. The husband was being very cooperative, but the wife always came away dissatisfied. She claimed that no one understood her.

They came to me for advice, and I really didn't know what to suggest. So for want of anything better to say, I asked her what she did with her time since they weren't speaking to each other. She said that she read a lot. So I asked her to bring me all the books she was reading at the time.

The selections she brought were horrifying. Most were psychology books that dealt with subtle forms of spousal abuse. The books filled her head with ludicrous ideas that have nothing to do with a Torah perspective. This unfortunate woman was restless and unhappy, and therefore, she imagined abuse in everything her husband did. She wouldn't admit it to the counselors, because she would have had to support her accusations, which she knew she couldn't do. So she remained trapped in a twilight world of her own construction, making herself and everyone around her miserable.

Now, I'm not saying that spousal abuse is not a problem where it really exists. It is an extremely grave problem. But to see monsters behind every stone is not our way. It is not our way to suggest that the norm is for some spousal abuse and that the husband who is completely innocent is the exception to the rule.

This, of course, is an extreme example, but it brings to light a deep problem. There is so much nonsense out there all dressed up in fancy language and technical terminology. There is this way of thinking and that way of thinking, and each of them pronounces his views as if they were Torah from Sinai. Virtually all these views and opinions are rooted in ideologies that the Torah perspective rejects. They mold the thinking of their readers. They influence the images conjured up in their minds and the words that form on their tongues, and they're bound to confuse and confound readers and erode the foundations of their worldview and faith.

Besides the damage this causes to the individual, it can easily affect *shalom bayis* and destroy the harmonious atmosphere of the home. And even if the *shalom bayis* should somehow not be affected, the damage to the children is incalculable. If the outlook of the parents is tainted, how can they possibly provide a good Torah *chinuch* for their children? I have no doubt that this is one of the causes of the problems we are having these days with the so-called kids at risk.

⇜ Public Libraries

The books for children that Judaica shops carry generally do not have these problems. Still, parents should be careful that the books their children read have some redeeming *chinuch* value and are not just sanitized copies of non-Jewish books.

The greatest danger for children is the public library where they can come into contact with the outside world with all its lesions and warts exposed. First of all, you can assume that just about every non-Jewish story book will inevitably have indecent scenes that are unacceptable by our standards. The only books that can be deemed reasonably safe are books on history and science, and even among those, there are numerous books that are full of heresy and distortion. And parents certainly shouldn't let children spend time in public libraries by themselves, not only because of the undesirable literature found there but also because most libraries feature computers that allow the public to go online without any restrictions.

It is not impossible, of course, to find books in the public library that are not unsuitable. If the parents make a serious effort to sift through all the stacks of available books, they may indeed find something that can be safely read by their children. But there is a price to pay even for these books. First of all, it is bad *chinuch* to take children to a place where most of the products are not kosher; it's like looking for a few pieces of kosher meat in a non-kosher butcher shop. Second, it is bad *chinuch* that connects children with a non-Jewish culture that in total does not share our values and ideals.

There are certain exceptions that can be made. Sometimes, a child needs something more than is available in Judaica shops and libraries; every case is different and should be judged on its own merits. If a child for some important reason needs to go to the public library, even though it is not a place for a Jewish child, it is imperative that the parents take it very seriously. They should accompany him or at least make sure that the books he takes out will not cause him irreparable harm. It would actually be best if the parents go without the child and make the selections themselves.

CHAPTER TWENTY-FIVE

The Power of Music

Music is not a simple thing. Music plays a prominent role in every society and every culture. It touches every soul and every heart. But what exactly is music, and what is the source of its awesome power?

David Hamelech says (Tehillim 47:7-8), "Sing melodies to the Lord, sing! Sing melodies to our King, sing! For the Lord is King of all the earth, sing melodies of insight (*zamru maskil*)." The Meiri focuses on the last words, *zamru maskil*, and he observes that the songs of Klal Yisrael are more than just songs. They are expressions of intelligent thoughts.

Music is an extraordinary phenomenon that the Ribono Shel Olam created and introduced into this world. The Torah and the traditions of Klal Yisrael consider it holy and exalted. It has the ability to transport a person to the highest levels of spiritual experience and achievement, and it is quite probable that it was created for this very purpose. The Gaon wrote that music is the language of the *malachim* and that there are certain concepts that can only be understood through music.

Therefore, the *chinuch* of our children must be pointed in the direction of music as well. Our first responsibility is to ensure that the musicality of our children should not be compromised to the point that it loses its capability of bringing them to higher spiritual levels.

Some of the commentators make an interesting observation. We find that when a little baby is crying you cannot calm him down by talking to him. A song, however, can calm a baby down. If you sing to him, he is likely to stop crying. Why is that?

The source of music, they explain, is in the highest spheres of Heaven. We say that "*hasimchah bimeono*, joy is in His palace." The part of Heaven called Maon is the place where the *malachim* sing Shirah, which is the ultimate in music. Music is the language of the *malachim*, and it is also the language of the *neshamah* which is itself derived from the highest spheres of Heaven. A newborn baby's mind is not yet developed. It does not have the ability to understand the language of words. But he does understand the language of music, because he recognizes it. He heard it in the place from which he came down to this world.

Music has the ability to express thoughts and ideas with much more subtlety, nuance and depth than mere words. It speaks directly to the *neshamah* and it does so in the language it understands best. In the Beis Hamikdash, the Leviim stood on their platforms and accompanied the *avodah* with song and instrumental music. The musical accompaniment was not just some incidental ornamentation. It touched the very essence of the *avo-*

dah, which would have been immeasurably diminished without the music. It was the music that connected the *avodah* with the Ribono Shel Olam. It was the music that gave the deepest expression to the feelings inspired by the *avodah* and directed them upward to Him. That is why our tradition has always considered music to be exceedingly holy and important.

We find that many of the *perakim* in Tehillim begin with the identification of the instruments for which they were written. Some were written for the *sheminis*, the eight-stringed lyre, some for the *asor*, the ten-stringed lyre, some for the *nevel*, the *kinor*, the *ugav*. We don't know what those instruments are. We've lost that information over the years and the centuries. But apparently, David Hamelech considered it important for us to know the particular instrument for which a piece was written.

Someone once said — and I wholeheartedly agree — that if we were familiar with those instruments we would be able to understand Tehillim much better than we do now. All the pieces in Tehillim were written for the particular instruments that could best deliver their messages with the fullest precision and depth. Without those instruments, without the particular musical sound those instruments produced, it is impossible to understand the message of Tehillim to the fullest. Words cannot be substituted for those musical sounds, because they simply cannot reach the depths of feeling and devotion that can be expressed in the language of music.

The ear is the delicate receptacle that picks up the subtleties of the music. When we say something to someone, the tone of voice affects the understanding of the message. So we can well imagine how much better the message would be understood if it were delivered in a song tailor-made for the message. People think that songs inspire feelings, but it is more complex than that. Once the songs convey a deeper understanding of the message to the *neshamah*, the feelings are automatically awakened.

Rav Shlomo Alkabetz was one of the great musical composers of our history. In *Manos Halevi*, he asks an amazing question.

According to the Midrashim and all the commentators, when Achashverosh invited all the Jewish people of Shushan to his imperial feast, his intent was to corrupt and subvert them. He prepared temptations for their senses. There were lavish appointments for them to see. There was superb food and wine, all kosher, for them to taste. There were fragrances for them to smell. There were lascivious pleasures for their sense of touch. But we find no mention of music. No mention at all. It would seem that there was no music at the feast.

But how could that be? Even without the special lure of temptation for the sense of hearing of the Jewish guests, there still should have been music at the feast. Every elaborate and well-attended party has music, and the imperial party certainly should have featured bands, orchestras and strolling violinists in every corner. But there is no mention of anything of the sort. Where was the music?

The answer, says Rav Shlomo Alkabetz, is that Achashverosh wanted to corrupt the Jewish people, and for this very reason he made sure there was no music at the feast. He recognized the great spiritual power of music, and he was concerned that if he allowed music to be played, even Persian music, the Jewish people would close their eyes upon hearing it and let the music transport them to a higher spiritual existence and bring them closer to the Ribono Shel Olam. He was afraid that the music, any music, would inspire them to do *teshuvah* and leave the feast before they could be corrupted through their other senses. Therefore, he gave instructions that all the temptations of sight, taste, smell and touch should be prepared in lavish measure but that there should be no music. Having music, he knew, ran the risk of undermining his entire plan of subversion.

In our day, Achashverosh would not have had a problem. He could have hired bands to play some of the noise that passes for music in contemporary society. I don't think that kind of noise speaks to the *neshamah*. But in those days, music was melodious and genteel, and Achashverosh did not dare take the risk.

The concept that emerges from the words of Rav Shlomo Alkabetz is that all music, even music composed and played by non-Jews, has the potential power to bring us closer to the Ribono Shel Olam, as long as it is just the melodies without vulgar words. If the music expresses feelings of yearning, we can all connect with that sentiment and point in the direction where our yearning leads.

It is recorded in various *sefarim* that great people sometimes borrowed melodies and musical themes from non-Jewish sources for the holiest *niggunim*. Some Poskim say that a *niggun* composed by a non-Jew can be used for Kedushah on Yom Kippur. It is quite possible that many of the *niggunim* that we have are derived from non-Jewish sources. Music alone is holy and pure, the language of the *malachim*. Words are the problem. It would also be instructive to see what the Rambam writes regarding Arabic songs with good messages (Avos 1:17).

This then is what we know about music. Pure music without any words or music with holy words can elevate a person to the highest levels and bring him very close to the Ribono Shel Olam. But music combined with vulgar words will have the opposite effect. It will corrupt the *neshamah*. It takes the words and plunges them into the heart and the *neshamah* to a depth far greater than those selfsame words alone could penetrate. As long as the listener knows the words connected to this melody, it can do him no good, only harm. Even if he only hums the melody and doesn't sing the words, it will still have a bad effect on him, because in his mind the music will call forth the words.

In the same vein, if he knows the identity of the composer and that this composer is a vile and vulgar person, he can no longer derive any good benefit from the music, because in his mind the music and the composer are connected. You would not want to hear a *shiur* from a vile person even if it is a good *shiur*. It is the same with music. But if he knows nothing about the composer and if he does not know the words that came along with the song, then in his mind nothing exists but the pure melody itself, and pure melody is the language of the *malachim*.

With regard to *chinuch*, children should be kept away from non-Jewish melodies if they will associate these melodies with non-Jewish words or unsavory non-Jewish singers and composers.

There are also new forms of music that cannot be considered music at all. It is just a set of connected rhythmic sounds that appeals to the lowest lusts and desires of a person. Unfortunately, some of these kinds of noise are borrowed and incorporated into modern Jewish music. We hear them often at weddings, and we can immediately recognize them for what they are. No good can come out of these noises, and we should make every effort to keep them away from our homes and our children.

✤§ Music Lessons

It is quite common today to give music lessons to children. Sometimes, this can be a good thing. We must, of course, make sure that the music they learn is pure and unadulterated. But there is also something else we must consider. Music can be addictive. It can draw a child into it until he hears music in his head all day and all night, when he is at the piano and when he is sitting in the classroom in front of the Gemara. This is where music can become a problem.

It is important, therefore, that the parents maintain strict control. The child can go to lessons and have a limited time for practice, but other than that, he should be a normal child. We are not seeking to raise Mozarts and Beethovens. We want our children to be absorbed by Torah and *mitzvos*, and we must not let an obsession with music stand in the way.

The same applies to listening to recorded music. A child can become obsessed with the music, and if so, it can interfere with his learning and his development as a person. Once again, it calls for parental control and moderation. You do not want your children walking around all day with headphones. You don't want their lives to have sound tracks. It does not make for normal living. You want them to listen for a half-hour or an hour, and then it is time to get on with their responsibilities without the distraction of background music.

It used to be that a person heard music only once in a while. You went to a wedding or another *simchah*, and there was a band. There was a special occasion in the *yeshivah* or *beis midrash*, and there was a band. Maybe there were other rare occasions that a person heard music, but it was certainly rare. It was a wonderful treat, and after it was over, it was over. People did not go around with music playing in their heads. When they sat by the Gemara, they were not hearing music. When they stood for Shemoneh Esrei, they did not hear music in their heads. For a normal person, music did not become an obsession. It did not insinuate itself into every crevice of his life.

Today, we are blessed with recording devices, and they are indeed a blessing in many ways. But the downside is that we have music available to us every day, twenty-four hours a day. You walk into the house, and music is playing. You get into the car, and music is playing. The children sit down to do homework, music is playing. They go to bed, and muted music is playing. It is almost impossible to get away from it, and that is not a good thing. I know cases of many *bachurim*, good *bachurim*, who couldn't concentrate during their formative years because of the tapes they listened to all the time, and they were not successful in *yeshivah* because of it.

We have no *mesorah* on these matters, because they're so new. And they just crept into our homes and our lives without raising any alarms. What could be the problem with recordings of nice Jewish music? But there are serious problems. They can be harmful. It is up to the parents to make sure that they are played in moderation. Even the best things can be harmful if they aren't used judiciously.

CHAPTER TWENTY-SIX

Trips and Excursions

What do we do with the children on Chol Hamoed? This is a burning question in many households. The children exert a lot of pressure on the parents to provide them with the same kind of entertainment and amusements that their friends and classmates are enjoying. So what should the parents do? It is not a simple matter.

There are really two parts to this question, what you should do and what you shouldn't do. And perhaps we can use this discussion regarding Chol Hamoed to help us establish guidelines for other times of the year as well. So let's begin with what you should do.

Chol Hamoed is not meant to be a time for excitement, entertainment and amusement. It is essentially part of Yom Tov, and the same atmosphere that prevails on Yom Tov should prevail on Chol Hamoed as well. The difference is that certain activities that are forbidden on Yom Tov are permitted on Chol Hamoed within specific guidelines. Chol Hamoed is not a break in the Yom Tov when we return to regular weekday living. We still say Hallel. We still eat *matzah* and take the *arbaah minim*. It is just a less limited part of Yom Tov, and so, we have to conduct ourselves with the same exalted behavior that is expected of us on Yom Tov.

Still, there are opportunities on Chol Hamoed that are not available to us on Yom Tov. If on Yom Tov we can take a walk, on Chol Hamoed we can go for a drive. If on Yom Tov we can visit relatives that live close by, on Chol Hamoed we can visit relatives that live far away. On Chol Hamoed we can talk on the telephone and listen to music. But the general rule is that we have to preserve the Yom Tov atmosphere.

The ideal activity for Chol Hamoed is to give the children time and attention in a measure that might not be possible at other times of the year. It is excellent *chinuch* to train your children to look forward to Chol Hamoed as a time to go on outings with their parents to a park or some other place of natural beauty and spend leisurely hours talking and enjoying each other's company. It is also a good time to visit grandparents or other family members and to receive *berachos* from *tzaddikim*.

If you present this manner of spending Chol Hamoed to your children in a positive light, they can really derive tremendous pleasure from it. And when they meet their classmates after Yom Tov and compare notes about what they did on Chol Hamoed, they will speak about their experiences with pride. Others may have had wilder, more rambunctious times, a few more thrills perhaps, but your children will have spent their time in a more inspiring, fulfilling and memorable manner.

Part of the *chinuch* of children is to give them pride and confidence in the way their parents are bringing them up. If they are given to understand that everything you do is for their benefit, that you are making every effort to shape them into good and worthy people, they will take pride in your efforts.

◄§ Zoos, Museums and Amusement Parks

If you feel you must take your children on a trip that includes a special activity, there are a number of choices that are less problematic than others. As long as there are no issues with *tznius* and the like, zoos are a fairly good option. You can make a visit to the zoo educational in a Torah way. You can point out to the children which animals are kosher and which are not, just as Moshe pointed out the differences to the Jewish people in the wilderness. You can draw their attention to the rich variety of life that the Ribono Shel Olam planted on this world. If, however, the focus of your trip to the zoo is for the children to see how the monkeys jump around so that they can imitate them afterward, it would not be such a good choice.

Museums are also educational places; you are not likely to find them listed in the guidebooks under amusements or entertainment. There is much to be learned about nature, technology and history in museums. If it is possible to go to a Jewish museum that presents these subjects from a Torah perspective, that would be the best choice.

Going to an amusement park or a concert, however, is an altogether different story, even if there is nothing strictly objectionable about the entertainment itself. If the event is also being attended by non-Jews, then it is not a place for Jewish children. We always have to remember that we are a people in exile, and when we share pleasures and amusements with non-Jewish people in an atmosphere of common fun, we tend to forget that we are strangers in an alien land expelled from our ancestral home. I cannot say with certainty that it is forbidden, but it is certainly improper.

There is also another consideration. Take for example the popular theme parks that are favorite choices for many people. What does a child learn from going to such a place? It's a place where silliness is applauded. People walking around dressed up like mice and dogs and storybook characters. So you take a picture with one of these big mice? What is so uplifting about that? And let's not forget that children live in a world of their imaginations. So these mice and dogs will linger in their minds for a very long time. We struggle every day to lift our children to higher levels. We teach them Torah and *mitzvos*. We instill good *midos* in them. We train them to do acts of *chessed*. We want them to be deeply learned, elevated in their outlook on life, more spiritual, something special, and then we take them to a place of silliness? Where is the *chinuch* in that?

And how about the parents? What does it do for the image of dignity that the parents are supposed to project if the children see them taking pictures with mice or riding on roller coasters? The children may delight in seeing their parents come down to their level, but will they respect them more or less for it? And as we have discussed earlier, if the respect is diminished, the influence is diminished. So do parents come away from an amusement park with more or less influence on their children? If there is even the slightest reduction, it is too high a price to pay for a brief Chol Hamoed diversion.

So these days, there is a new plan. Organizations rent entire amusement parks or a circus for an exclusively Jewish clientele. Or they rent stadiums for Jewish concerts. In these cases, the problem of fraternization with non-Jewish people is eliminated. But there is still the issue of silliness and *kalus rosh*, frivolous behavior, and an atmosphere that is not so compatible with what we strive to cultivate in our homes and communities. Parents should think twice before selecting one of these options for their Chol Hamoed excursions.

I prefer to look at these events as *kiruv* projects. They are designed to reach out to people who might otherwise go to places that are forbidden and terribly destructive to the children. So you have to decide for yourself if you are a candidate for a *kiruv* project or if you are already close to the Ribono Shel Olam and know how to conduct yourself on a higher level. If you know that you would never take your children to a truly bad place, if you feel that your home is on a high level and that your family is close to the Ribono Shel Olam, why should you do something on Chol Hamoed that pushes your family downward instead of upward?

You can explain this to your children, and they will understand it. You should, of course, not denigrate the people who choose to go to these places. You can mention how good it is that they are going there instead of to forbidden places. You can praise them for trying to lift the level of their families. But as for your own family, you can say that this is not your tradition and this is not your custom. You seek to do things on Chol Hamoed that will give the children deep pleasure and priceless memories, things that will inspire them and make them better people, things that young *tzaddikim* should do, things they will take pride in telling their children and grandchildren that they did when they were young.

PART SIX

On Reaching for a Higher Chinuch

CHAPTER TWENTY-SEVEN

Holiness and Abstract Thought

Recently, someone asked me an interesting question about teaching *aleph beis* to children. Although this is primarily a question that relates to *chinuch* in the schools, it also has ramifications for *chinuch* in the home. This is the question.

The traditional method of teaching *aleph beis* is to show a large picture of the *aleph*, for example, to identify it by name and to drill the children until they recognize every letter. Then we show them the *nekudos*, the vowel marks, and we say "*kametz aleph uh*" over and over again until they know it. These days, new methods that use whole-word recognition, visual aids and other innovations are gaining popularity. Should we continue to use the traditional methods exclusively or is it acceptable to take advantage of the new innovations?

My first reaction was to mention the well-known passage in *Chovos Halevavos* that states that a person should not deviate from the *mesorah*; he should not suppose that he is cleverer than the *rabbanim* of earlier generations, that he can think of methods that no one before him ever conceived. But in order to take a closer look at the issues raised in the question, I decided to do some research of my own, so I collected a stack of the latest *aleph beis* books.

It is not my intention here to criticize any schools, teachers or playgroups that use these methods and materials. My purpose is only to raise awareness of some of their drawbacks.

☙ The Holiness of the Letters

All these *aleph beis* books used visual aids to teach the letters. Some of them were quite innocuous. I don't really have a problem with using a *mezuzah* to illustrate the *mem* or a *tinok* and a *teivah* to illustrate the *tav*. But when letters are blended into images of wild animals, I do have objections. The letters of the *aleph beis*, the building blocks of the Torah, are exceedingly holy, and their first associations in the mind of a child should not be with non-kosher creatures.

The frivolous spirit of the books also did not particularly appeal to me. The letters run about helter skelter. They tumble and fall and get into all kinds of trouble. But not to worry, because the Hatzalah man, Mr. *Heh*, is on the way behind the wheel of his car.

There is no question that this method catches the interest of the child, but this is not the way to teach the *aleph beis*. It may be acceptable in marginal schools where the children watch hours and hours of television and would find looking at a dignified and stately black *aleph* tedious and boring without this kind of nonsense, but otherwise, this type of teaching is far inferior to the traditional method. Our children should not play *aleph beis*. They should learn it.

The seminary in Gateshead once asked Rav Eliahu Dessler if they should promote the traditional teaching method of *kametz aleph uh* or if they should promote teaching the whole word. The question had nothing to do with pictures or stories or other silly nonsense. It was only about teaching the letters individually or teaching them in the context of simple words like *abba* and *ima*.

Rav Dessler responded that the Chazon Ish insisted on using the *kametz aleph uh* method. The letters and the *nekudos* are meant to be learned in the context of an awareness of their holiness, and any changes in the traditional method are considered an unacceptable breach. Now, if the exclusive purpose of learning the letters is only to convey the information then it would be worthwhile to seek the quickest, most efficient method. But learning the *aleph beis* is unlike any other instruction in the world. Its primary purpose is for the children to absorb the holiness of the letters and *nekudos*, to learn to love them and to draw *yiras shamayim* from them, and that is only accomplished with the time-honored *kametz aleph uh* method. It is a special *segulah* that these feelings are inspired in the children by looking at the individual letters and studying them.

This is what Rav Dessler wrote with regard to using whole words to teach the *aleph beis*. It follows, therefore, that presenting the *nun* as a ferocious tiger leaning back in a chair with his legs draped over the arm is not the way to teach the letter. It will certainly not help the child appreciate the profound holiness of the letter.

❧ The Drawback of Pictures

As for the pedagogic value of the new methods, it seems clear that they are really not effective at all. These days, there are so many children who are falling through the cracks in the *yeshivah* system, and you will find that many of them have serious reading problems. Why can't they read? Part of the problem is because they learned with the help of all these visual aids.

Integrating the letters into a story with leopards, tables and Hatzalah men doesn't make the letters stand out more distinctly. On the contrary, it is a serious distraction from the letters themselves. The letter becomes fixed in the child's mind in the context of a story, so when he sees the *heh* and the *vav* he recalls a kid with a broken leg and a Hatzalah man and when he sees a *gimmel* he recalls a pair of mismatched shoes.

The child may have learned the letters, but it is all superficial. His mind was not challenged. He did not have to exert his mental faculties. He just swallowed them whole with the story, and it created confusion in his mind. And when the images fade away, he is not left with a distinct image of the letters in his mind, only blurred outlines.

Teaching based on visual aids is quick, but it does not run deep. The more something is described and illustrated the less thinking the child has to do. This type of teaching appeals to the imagination of the child, which develops much more quickly that his ability to think in the abstract, but it does not encourage him to think hard. And as he grows up, he lags in his ability to concentrate and to have abstract thoughts. He has trouble reading, and he does not have the attention span to listen to an entire *shiur*.

In the old days, *talmidei chachamim* were able to concentrate on a difficult *sugya* for hours at a time. But in my opinion, the concentration span of an average *yeshivah bachur* is one and a half minutes. After that, he looks up from his Gemara. If you ask him what he's thinking, he may tell you that he's mulling over a difficult *kushia*, but quite often, it's not true.

And you wonder why can't he concentrate? Why does he have difficulty reading the Gemara? After all, he sang the songs so beautifully in his playgroup. He knew the whole *aleph beis* song by heart. Yes, it's true. But he wasn't taught to concentrate when he was young. He wasn't taught to think. The information was injected into his mind painlessly, but he was never asked to concentrate and to think in the abstract. Maybe he learned the songs, but he didn't learn the *aleph beis*.

When the child is shown the unadorned letter, however, and the unadorned *nekudos*, he is required to create the images in his mind and to connect the sounds with the images. That is how he will learn to concentrate. That is how he will learn abstract thought.

In the Torah, we only find pictures used to illustrate something that is beyond the experience of the learner. The Ribono Shel Olam told Moshe (11:2), "These are the animals ...." And the Gemara tells us (Chullin 42a) that He showed Moshe each and every animal. Moshe needed to know what all those animals looked like. This was not something that could be figured out by using logic. So the Ribono Shel Olam showed him the images. But otherwise, the picture engages the imagination but not the power of rational thinking. When Moshe had difficulty understanding exactly what the *menorah* was supposed to look like, the Ribono Shel Olam showed him a menorah of fire. But He did not show him images of the finished Mishkan. He gave Moshe a set of complicated instructions, and Moshe was expected to figure them out.

A child can go through school without having really used his power of thinking. Everything was made easy for him with pictures and stories. Sure, it was enjoyable and exciting, but he wasn't done any favors, because he never learned to think in the abstract. If a child has learning problems, then you might very well give him pictures. But if a child has normal learning abilities, you have to exercise and develop them. You want to challenge him to think in the abstract. You don't want to give him pictures. The easier it is, the less need there is for concentration and abstract thought, the less likely it is that the child will develop the faculties for depth of comprehension.

✍§ A Famous Gemara

The idea of using pictures to teach *aleph beis* is supposedly derived from a famous Gemara, but it is based on an erroneous reading. The Gemara tells us (Shabbos 104a) that the schoolchildren came into the *beis midrash* and presented ideas that had not even been heard in the days of Yehoshua bin Nun. They found allusions to fundamental concepts in the names of the letters and their forms.

For example, the letters *gimmel* and *daled* suggest *gomeil dalim*, kindness to the poor. Why is one leg of the *gimmel* extended toward the *daled*? Because the benefactor of the poor runs after them to help them. And why is the *daled* turned away from the *gimmel* but slightly bent in its direction? Because the poor person is embarrassed by his situation, but he still tries to make himself available to his benefactor. And the Gemara continues in this vein through the *aleph beis*.

The idea of using images to teach the letters of the *aleph beis* obviously derives from this Gemara. But it is based on the mistaken assumption that this was how the children during that period of the Gemara were taught *aleph beis*. But there is no mention of anything of the sort in the Gemara. On the contrary, the Gemara seems to be praising these children's level of accomplishment in learning Torah such that they were able to discover allusions to fundamental concepts in the names and forms of the letters.

The children were undoubtedly taught the *aleph beis* according to the hallowed traditions of *kametz aleph uh*. They were taught to concentrate on the holy forms of the letters until they achieved a deep understanding. And in this manner, the learning of the *aleph beis* serves as a springboard to a profound relationship with the Torah so that even at a very young age they were able to find their own allusions and insights in the letters of the *aleph beis*, allusions and insights that had not even been heard in the days of Yehoshua bin Nun. Had they been taught the *aleph beis* with visual aids, they never would have attained this level of comprehension.

CHAPTER TWENTY-EIGHT

An Act of Love

W here is the source for the *mitzvah* of *chinuch* with which we are all so busy? No *passuk* in the Torah specifically obligates us to be *mechanech* our young children. The only specific command is to teach them Torah (Devarim 6:7).

The *passuk* quoted most often is (Mishlei 22:6), "*Chanoch lanaar al pi darko*. Raise the child according to his way." But according to the Gemara (Kiddushin 29a), this refers to a young man either sixteen or eighteen years old. While it is true that this *passuk* is often quoted as the basis for *chinuch*, it is technically not correct.

We do find mention in the Gemara of an obligation to be *mechanech* young children in *mitzvos*. When a youngster can fast, he should fast (Yoma 82a); when he can sit in the *sukkah*, he should sit in the *sukkah* (Sukkah 28b); when he can shake a *lulav* properly, his father should buy one for him (Sukkah 42a); when he can hold his father's hand, he should accompany him to Yerushalayim for the *regel* (Chagigah 2a); and so forth. But these are all obligations that Chazal instituted to condition the young to doing *mitzvos*, to make *mitzvos* part of the very fabric of their lives so that when they grow up living a life full of *mitzvos* will be the most natural thing in the world for them, that life without *mitzvos* would be inconceivable.

But what about *chinuch* in *midos*? What about molding the character of our young children? Where do we find any source for this obligation either in the Torah or even in the words of Chazal? There doesn't seem to be any, and yet, it is generally assumed that there is such an obligation.

✺§ Reciprocal Love

The Meshech Chachmah suggests that a source can be found in the *passuk* in Parashas Vayeira. After the *malachim* left the house of Avraham and set off to destroy the city of Sodom, the Ribono Shel Olam decided that He had to reveal to Avraham what He intended to do, because (Bereishis 18:19), "I love him for instructing his descendants and his household to safeguard the way of Hashem to perform acts of righteousness and justice."

Here the Torah tells us why the Ribono Shel Olam loved Avraham. It was not because he stood up to Nimrod, which resulted in his being thrown into a fiery furnace. It was not because he abandoned his homeland and traveled to a distant land. It was not because he circumcised himself when he was one hundred years old. None of these things are mentioned. Why does the Ribono Shel Olam love Avraham? Because he was *mechanech* his children and his household to follow in the way of Hashem. Because he taught others how to live and how to act in the way that Hashem desires.

All Avraham's heroic acts were personal expressions of his devotion to the Ribono Shel Olam, but none showed his love more than his dedication to disseminating the knowledge of the Ribono Shel Olam's ways to his own family and household and to the entire world.

The Rambam says in Sefer Hamitzvos (Asei 3) that the *mitzvah* of *ahavas Hashem*, of loving the Ribono Shel Olam, is accomplished by contemplating all the wonder of His creation. But then he adds another requirement of the *mitzvah*. It is to bring other people closer to the Ribono Shel Olam, to guide them to Him, to tell them about His goodness and His greatness.

What does this have to do with love?

So the Rambam establishes an important principle here. When a person loves someone, he is so excited about it that he must tell everyone the wonderful qualities and virtues of the one he loves. This is a natural response. Therefore, if a person truly loves the Ribono Shel Olam with a complete all-encompassing love, he will be bursting with eagerness to tell the world about Him and draw everyone else into that love, and he will be perturbed if there are people who are still unaware of the Ribono Shel Olam's greatness.

All Avraham's deeds of loyalty and devotion were certainly manifestations of love, but the ultimate manifestation of his love was his reaching out to the world, and especially to his own immediate circle, to inspire everyone to serve the Ribono Shel Olam and to love him.

In response to this ultimate act of love, the Ribono Shel Olam responded by declaring His love for Avraham. Love is reciprocal, like a face reflected in water (Mishlei 27:19); if someone loves us, we are moved to love them as well. When the Ribono Shel Olam saw the extent of Avraham's love, He was likewise moved, so to speak, to declare His love for His beloved servant.

Here, says the Meshech Chachmah, is where we find the *mitzvah* of *chinuch* in the Torah. Because that is what Avraham was doing. He was instructing his family and his household "to safeguard the way of Hashem to perform acts of righteousness and justice." This act of *chinuch* expressed his love for the Ribono Shel Olam better than anything else he had ever done, and the Ribono Shel Olam praised and rewarded him for it.

If we follow this line of thought, it appears that the *mitzvah* of *chinuch* falls under the broader category of the *mitzvah* of *ahavas Hashem*. If we truly love the Ribono Shel Olam, we should express our love by drawing our children closer to Him, by telling them of His wonders and by inspiring them to love Him as well.

We should keep in mind, therefore, that the highest form of *chinuch* is reaching out to our children as an expression of our love for the Ribono Shel Olam and that the highest goal of our *chinuch* is to inspire our children to love the Ribono Shel Olam as we ourselves do. The *chinuch* cannot begin and end with you-must-do-this and you-must-not-do-that. It should rather be a beautiful experience of love, of the parents taking their children by the hand and leading them into the illuminated world of the Torah.

So what is the specific form of *chinuch* that is derived from that *passuk*? What kind of *chinuch* will bring others closer to the Ribono Shel Olam and awaken a burning love in their hearts?

The key is the phrase "to safeguard the way of Hashem." What is the *derech Hashem*, the way of Hashem? The Rambam says (Deios 1:7) that it means to emulate the *midos* of the Ribono Shel Olam. The Torah tells us (Devarim 28:9), "*Vehalachta bidrachav*, you shall walk in His ways." We have to pattern our *midos* after the *midos* of the Ribono Shel Olam — His kindness, His mercy, His forbearance, His righteousness, His justice and so many more. And when the Ribono Shel Olam gave this *mitzvah* in the Torah at Mount Sinai, the world was already familiar with the ways of the Ribono Shel Olam, because Avraham had introduced them into the world

When you teach your children about the Ribono Shel Olam's exalted *midos* and show them how to bring that divine holiness into their own lives, and you do it as an expression of your love for Him, then your children will also be inspired to love Him. And you should teach your children *midos* in that context, as part of their striving to emulate the *midos* of the Ribono Shel Olam. Don't tell them to be kind and to have respect simply because if we are not nice and sociable we cannot coexist with other people. Tell them that we must behave in the way the Ribono Shel Olam has shown us by His own actions, that we must behave in a way that will make us holier and more exalted and bring us closer to Him.

◄§ Shared Love

In Parashas Vayeira, when the *malachim* came to Avraham, the Torah tells us (Bereishis 18:7), "And Avraham ran to the cattle, and he took a young bull, tender and good, and he gave it to the youth, and he hurried to prepare it." Rashi identifies this youth as Avraham's son Yishmael. And why did Avraham give the young bull to Yishmael to prepare it? Rashi says that it was in order to be *mechanech* him in *mitzvos*.

At the end of Parashas Vayeira, as Avraham and Yitzchak are going toward the Akeidah, the Torah tells us (Bereishis 22:6), "And Avraham took the firewood and put it on his son Yitzchak, and in his hand he took the fire and the knife, and they both went together." Others say that here again Avraham's intention in having Yitzchak carry the wood was for *chinuch*. Incidentally, we see from here that *chinuch* molds a person, and even though Avraham believed that Yitzchak was about to die, he felt it was important to guide him properly even in his last moments. An interesting thought.

The Torah shows us here the ideal way of being *mechanech* our children. Avraham did not send his sons to do something in which he himself was not involved. Avraham ran to do the *mitzvah* of *hachnasas orchim*, hospitality, and he drew Yishmael into the *mitzvah* with him. And Avraham's enthusiasm was contagious. Yishmael saw his father running to do the *mitzvah*, so when his turn to participate came, he also hurried to do his part. Avraham placed the wood on Yitzchak, and he himself also had his hands full with the fire and the knife. Avraham's devotion to the *mitzvah* drew Yitzchak into the same mood and spirit.

It is not good *chinuch* to use your children to serve your needs. Children should only be asked to do things that are *mitzvos* or for their own benefit. If you need a child to do something for you, it is best to frame the request as an opportunity to fulfill the *mitzvah* of *kibud av va'eim*. If a child feels he's being used and exploited, he can become resentful.

But even when he is being told to do a *mitzvah*, the child needs to see the father doing the same thing for himself. If he thinks the father does not really care about the *mitzvah* and that he only want the child to do it, that is not good *chinuch* at all.

And even if the child knows that the father cares about his own *mitzvos*, it is still not advisable for the child to be sent to do the *mitzvah* by himself. The shared experience of doing a *mitzvah* together with his father is a tremendously important element in a successful *chinuch*. When the father and child share the effort, the enthusiasm, the passion and the excitement of doing a *mitzvah*, the spirit of love of the Ribono Shel Olam that motivates the father is transmitted to the child, and feelings of love are awakened in his own heart.

That is *chinuch* at its very best.

CHAPTER TWENTY-NINE

The Next World

We as adults know that life in this world is a fleeting dream. You come and you strive and you struggle, and then it's all over, and what was it all about? The only meaningful answer — and one of the most important tenets of our *emunah* — is that this entire life is just a preparation for the Next World, for Olam Haba.

We struggle here in this world, because we will receive our eternal reward in Olam Haba. We don't really know what Olam Haba is, but we believe with all our hearts that it is a better place than this world. And we believe with all our hearts that Olam Haba is the ultimate reality while this world is no more than an illusion.

But what about for children? If Olam Haba is a difficult concept for adults, it is certainly even more difficult for young children. So should we speak to them about Olam Haba, and if so, when?

≈§ Times of Tragedy

Unfortunately, many children first hear about Olam Haba when there is a tragedy in the family. A loved one dies, and the children want to know what happened. So the parents tell them that this person went to Olam Haba, or up to *shamayim* or however it is phrased, and that he is very happy there because he is with the Ribono Shel Olam.

Children have been known to become very upset when told something like this. "Am I going to have to go there, too?" they say. "I don't want to go to Olam Haba. I want to stay here. I like it here. I don't want to go. And if Olam Haba is such a good place, why is everyone sitting and crying?"

Clearly, this is not a good time to introduce a child to the concept of Olam Haba. The best time to tell the child about Olam Haba, if you feel he is old enough to relate to the concept, is when everything is going well and everyone is happy. And it has to be explained in the most positive way.

The same applies, of course, to explaining the concept of the Ribono Shel Olam to a child. Some parents tell the child about the Ribono Shel Olam to frighten them into doing what they don't want to do. This, of course, is a horrific mistake. I've heard of a child who was afraid to walk into a room because he thought that "Hashem was in there." How is this child ever going to have a loving relationship with the Ribono Shel Olam if he thinks of Him as some kind of bogeyman? The child has to be told that the Ribono Shel Olam is the source of all good things, that everything he enjoys in life comes to him from the Ribono Shel Olam. Only when he has come to know the Ribono Shel Olam in this way for a number of years can you tell him about reward and punishment, because then he will accept it in the right way. A difficult concept must be given over in the right way at the right time.

Regarding Olam Haba, it's best to speak to the child about it as soon as possible, first, because it's an important piece of knowledge and, second, because he should already have a positive notion of it before he encounters a tragedy. If he has already been educated about Olam Haba, he will still ask why everyone is crying if Olam Haba is such a wonderful place. Then you can tell him that we are crying because of the separation, because we will not be seeing this loved one again until we, too, come to Olam Haba. But in the meantime, we are sad, and we will miss him.

◆§ Parashas Bereishis

When you find the proper opportunity and setting for talking to your child about Olam Haba, you can begin by telling your child what Chazal say about Olam Haba, that *tzaddikim* sit there with their crowns on their heads and bask in the glow of the Shechinah.

In my opinion, the best approach to teaching your child about Olam Haba is through Chumash. When the children start to learn Parashas Bereishis, the *rebbe* usually tells them about some of the Midrashim that Rashi brings down. Right at the beginning, there is a Midrash that presents the idea of Olam Haba.

The *passuk* says that the Ribono Shel Olam created the fish of the sea and the *taninim hagedolim*, the big sea monsters (Bereishis 1:21). What are these monsters? So Rashi says they're leviathans, mammoth fish. The Ribono Shel Olam created two leviathans, a male and a female. Then he killed the female and salted her away for *tzaddikim* to enjoy in the future. If He had allowed the female leviathan to survive, the two mammoth fish would have bred many leviathans, so many that the other creatures would not have been able to survive.

These are esoteric concepts, and we don't really have any good understanding of what they mean, but on the simple level they are telling us something. The children come home having learned about the leviathan. They relate to it on their level and with their own imaginations, and they usually find it quite exciting.

So right away you can ask him a question. What happened here? First, the Ribono Shel Olam creates two leviathans, a male and a female. Then He decides that the world cannot survive with these two mammoth fish reproducing ever more leviathans, and He kills the female. So what was He thinking in the first place? Why did He create the female if He would only have to kill her right away?

The answer is Olam Haba. He created the female leviathan specifically for the purpose of preserving her flesh for *tzaddikim* to enjoy in Olam Haba. We don't really know exactly what this means. And even not exactly. What kind of reward is a piece of leviathan in Olam Haba? Whatever it is, it is. But we do see clearly that the very creation of the leviathan had nothing to do with this world but with Olam Haba. When you point this out to a child while learning the Chumash with him, he absorbs the concept of Olam Haba as a matter of course.

A little further in Parashas Bereishis, we find another place where a discussion about Olam Haba can be easily initiated. The Torah tells us (Bereishis 4:4-5) that the Ribono Shel Olam accepted Hevel's gift but that He did not accept Kayin's gift. Hevel achieved a major accomplishment. He had brought a gift to the Ribono Shel Olam, and it had been accepted. And what happened because the Ribono Shel Olam accepted Hevel's gift? Kayin killed him. So what did Hevel really achieve by the Ribono Shel Olam accepting his gift? Kayin's gift was not accepted, and he lived. Hevel's gift was accepted, and he died. How could that be?

The Daas Zekeinim says that this story cries out against those that claim that there is no Olam Haba. Hevel's gift was accepted, and he gained a wonderful share in Olam Haba, a share far better than the remaining years that Kayin managed to live in this world.

If you teach the child about Olam Haba in such a natural way and over a period of time, he will become comfortable with the idea, and it will not frighten him. Then if a tragedy occurs, he will understand that the loved one is now in a good place, and you can explain to him that we are crying for ourselves, for our own loss.

CHAPTER THIRTY

The Tefilah of a Child

We as adults know that our *tefilos* are not always answered in the form we would have liked. We are sophisticated enough to understand that when we ask for something from the Ribono Shel Olam we do not automatically receive a positive response, even if we *daven* with all our might.

But how do we introduce the concept of *tefilah* to a child without inviting disappointment and disillusionment? It is not good *chinuch* to tell a child to *daven* from a Siddur without explaining to him what he is expected to be doing.

Why should he *daven*? Because you want him to *daven*? Because all children are supposed to *daven*? These are not satisfying answers. They will not inspire a love of *tefilah* in the heart of your child.

It is also not a good idea to tell him that if you want something you have to ask the Ribono Shel Olam for it, because He is the One that provides us with everything we need. The child is likely to ask the Ribono Shel Olam for a new bike, and if by some chance he doesn't get it, he is likely to be resentful and confused.

So what are we supposed to tell the children?

ᴥᴥ Unfulfilled Expectations

Actually, before we think about what we should tell the children, we need to think about what we should tell ourselves. For all our sophistication, it is difficult to deal with unanswered *tefilos*.

A woman called me after her husband had passed away following a long and excruciating illness. "What about all the *tefilos* that I *davened*?" she asked. "What about all the Tehillim I said? What about the rivers of tears I shed? Were they all for nothing?"

This good and faithful woman was not questioning the justice of the Ribono Shel Olam. She was not complaining about the terrible fate that had befallen her family. No, she was expressing her frustration and her deep disappointment. Deep down, she had convinced herself that if she *davened* with all her might her *tefilos* would be answered and her husband would recover. But it did not happen. And now she was frustrated and confused. What happened, she wanted to know, to all her *tefilos*? Where did they go? What had she accomplished with all her tremendous emotional efforts?

Most people have similar experiences at one time or another in their lives. In times of crisis, they reach down into the depths of their souls and *daven* with extraordinary intensity and sincerity, and then, nothing happens. It seems to them as if their *tefilos* were completely futile, and they lose heart. They become frustrated and disillusioned, and they can no longer bring themselves to invest that type of intensity and concentration when they daven.

So what is the proper response to this kind of reaction? How are we to understand the meaning and purpose of *tefilah* in the proper light? How can we avoid the despair that comes from disappointment?

Chazal already recognized this problem. The Gemara tells us (Berachos 6b) that *tefilah* is "among those things that stand at the pinnacle of creation," and then they observe that "people nonetheless treat it lightly."

Rav Chaim Volozhiner, in *Nefesh Hachaim* (2:13), writes that we haven't even the faintest notion of the vast and awesome power of the *kavanos* that the Anshei Knesses Hagedolah infused into the *tefilos* they formulated for us, that every word, every letter is fraught with the most profound meaning and value. Furthermore, he writes, all the *kavanos* of the Arizal Hakadosh, which are themselves beyond the comprehension of virtually everyone, are but a drop in the ocean compared to the *kavanos* of the Anshei Knesses Hagedolah.

Most people are aware of the profound holiness and power of the *tefilos*, and yet they take them lightly. How can this be? Even if they do not understand the *tefilos* fully, shouldn't people at least stand in awe of them? Shouldn't they at least tremble when they utter the hallowed words?

Clearly, a sense of frustration is at the root of the indifferent attitude of some people toward the *tefilos*. They take the *tefilos* "lightly," in the words of Chazal, because the *tefilos* have disappointed them. They have not always delivered as expected.

The first step, therefore, is to set the parameters of why we *daven* and what we can expect from our *tefilos*. What exactly is the role of *tefilah* in our lives? It is clearly not a tool, a mechanism we use regularly to achieve our needs and wants. But if it is not a tool, what is it?

❧ The *Mitzvah* of *Tefilah*

The Mabit writes in *Sefer Beis Elokim* (15) that *tefilah* is a *mitzvah*. The Torah tell us (Devarim 11:13), "To worship Him with all your heart." And the Gemara explains (Taanis 2a), "What kind of worship is in the heart? It is *tefilah*." So *tefilah* is one of the Taryag *mitzvos* in the Torah, as are wearing *tefillin* and taking an *esrog*. When a person *davens* with *kavanah* he fulfills a *mitzvah* in the Torah. The form of the *mitzvah* of *tefilah* is to sing the Ribono Shel Olam's praises and to ask for our needs, because by doing so, we show that we recognize that the fulfillment of our needs lies in His hands alone.

Even if the Ribono Shel Olam doesn't grant our request for whatever reason, the *mitzvah* is in the asking. When a person *davens* he is rewarded just as he is rewarded when he takes an *esrog*, because he has performed one of the *mitzvos* in the Torah. And what is his reward? It's a share in Olam Haba, the Next World, just as with any other *mitzvah*.

The Mabit goes on to say, however, that *tefilah* can also bear an additional reward in this world. First of all, it is possible that the *tefilah* will be answered and the requests will be granted. And even if the *tefilos* are not granted, he may receive certain benefits and rewards that at least bear some resemblance to his original request. Moshe Rabbeinu *davened* to be allowed to enter Eretz Yisrael. The Ribono Shel Olam did not grant this request, but He did take Moshe up to the mountaintop from where He showed him the land and the important events that would shape its future. In the same way, a person who does not accomplish a reprieve from his illness through his *tefilah* may nonetheless gain a reprieve for another individual who might otherwise have fallen victim to a similar illness.

It stands to reason then that just as we embrace the *mitzvah* of esrog with the fullest enthusiasm, giving no thought to what it will accomplish for us in the here and now, so should we approach to the *mitzvah* of *tefilah*. The goal of the *mitzvah* is not to fulfill our needs but rather to express our recognition that only the Ribono Shel Olam can fulfill those needs should He choose to do so. The reward for this *mitzvah*, as with all *mitzvos*, awaits us in the Next World.

We say every day before Shacharis, "These are the things of which a person enjoys the profits in this world yet the principal remains intact for the Next World: ... concentration on *tefilah* ...." It happens sometimes that we are disappointed and our *tefilos* are not granted, but this does not diminish in the least what we have accomplished through our *tefilos*. They were not wasted, and there is really no cause for frustration and disillusionment.

Still, in a certain sense, this is small consolation. True, when we *daven* for the recovery of a sick person we are performing an important *mitzvah* by declaring that health and illness, life and death are in His hands alone. True, we are rewarded in the Next World for performing this *mitzvah* regardless of whether or not the patient recovers his health. But what about the patient himself? Is our only accomplishment that we ourselves have gained another share in the Next World? After our prodigious efforts on behalf of the patient, have we accomplished nothing for him if we have not brought about his recovery? These are questions that continue to plague us even if we understand that *tefilah* is a *mitzvah* like any other.

◈§ How *Tefilah* Works

Let us take a closer look at the effectiveness of *tefilah*. Even though we have explained that the value of *tefilah* is not dependent on the results it produces, we all know that *tefilah* very often does indeed produce quite remarkable results.

How does *tefilah* accomplish this? If there was a heavenly decree that some calamity should come to pass, is it possible for us to change the divine mind, so to speak? Can we come before Him and protest that this would not be a good thing to do? Can we convince the Ribono Shel Olam to do something other than what He, in His infinite wisdom, had planned to do? Obviously, this is completely ridiculous; it is outrageous even to suggest it. So how then can *tefilah* produce results?

The *Chovos Halevavos* (*Cheshbon Hanefesh* 18) writes that the purpose of *tefilah* is not to change the Ribono Shel Olam's mind but rather to change ourselves. It is bring us to the realization that our fate is completely dependent on His will and that we can only survive through His mercy. The very act of *tefilah* elevates, exalts and transforms us, so that we're no longer the same people we were before.

This is the secret to the effectiveness of *tefilah*. This is how a divine decree against a person, Heaven forbid, can be rescinded through *tefilah*. Since the person has been transformed through his *tefilah*, he is no longer the same person upon whom the decree was originally issued.

But a question remains. If *tefilah* works only because it transforms the one who *davens* and thereby changes his destiny, how does *tefilah* for other people work? If a divine decree is issued upon a person and he falls ill to the point that he is unable to *daven* for himself, how can the *tefilos* of his family, friends and community effect his recovery? What connection is there between the transformation of other people through their *tefilos* and the person for whom they are *davening*?

I asked this question to Rav Elya Lopian, and he gave me a very succinct answer. "When people *daven* for another person, they become like his *talmidim* in that he is the catalyst for them to gain merit."

In other words, whenever a person causes a good thing, whether consciously or unconsciously, he gains merit. Og gained merit for informing Avraham that Lot had been abducted, even though his intentions were malevolent (see Rashi, Bereishis 14:13). Balak was rewarded for his *korbanos*, even though his intentions were malevolent (see Nazir 23b). If Avraham hadn't set the example first, Bilaam would have gained merit for teaching people diligence, even though his intentions were malevolent (see Rashi, Bamidbar 22:21). It is clear that a person gains merit for causing a good thing, whether or not he intended to do so.

In the same way, when people *daven* for the recovery of a sick person and in the process draw closer to the Ribono Shel Olam, it is the sick person who has caused this transformation, and the merit goes to him. And the more people who *daven* for him and are elevated the more merit he accumulates. Ultimately, the sick person himself is transformed by all the merit he has accumulated, albeit without his knowledge, and the decree against him may be rescinded.

Moreover, if the sick person is righteous and worthy, if he is someone with fine qualities and accomplishments other people admire, then he gains an even greater measure of merit. Why? Because when people *daven* for him, they mention all the good he represents and they plead for divine mercy. And as they contemplate all the good things this person has done and accomplished, they learn from his example and become better people themselves. In this sense, he is their *rebbe* and they are his *talmidim*. He is, in effect, teaching them how to live and how to think, albeit unconsciously, and he gains merit from their elevation and transformation.

Sometimes, the merit a sick person accumulates through the *tefilos* of other people is sufficient to tip the scales in his favor and rescind the decree. Sometimes, however, the harsh decree simply cannot be rescinded. We cannot fathom the intricacies of the divine plan; we only know that the end result of the divine plan is completely good. And if the Ribono Shel Olam chooses not to rescind the decree despite the accumulation of mountains of merit through *tefilah*, we accept with full faith that this is the best way to further the divine plan for the entire world and achieve the ultimate good.

But the *tefilos* have not gone to waste. After all, for what does a faithful Jew struggle his entire lifetime in this world if not to earn a beautiful share in the Next World? And *tefilah* for a sick person accomplishes exactly that. The merits accumulated by the sick person, through his own *tefilos* and through the *tefilos* of others, belong to him for all eternity, along with the merit of all the *mitzvos* he has performed during his lifetime. These merits will raise him to the highest levels of Olam Haba and the highest degrees of illumination forever.

◆§ The Most Effective *Tefilah*

Before returning to the question of *chinuch* in *tefilah*, there is one more point we should discuss. The Rambam writes (Berachos 10:26), "A person should always cry out regarding what the future will bring and plead for mercy. And he should express gratitude over what has passed. He should thank and praise to the best of his ability. Whoever thanks the Ribono Shel Olam profusely and praises Him consistently is considered praiseworthy."

The Rambam mentions two things we have to do when we *daven* to the Ribono Shel Olam. One is to express our appreciation to Him for all the myriad blessings He has showered on us in the past. We must thank Him for our health, our sustenance, our families, our very lives, and we must acknowledge that without Him we have no existence whatsoever. Another thing we must do is cry out to Him in passionate supplication that He continue to sustain us as He has sustained us in the past and that He grant us any specific requests we have at that moment.

Our *tefilos* are constructed around these two themes — gratitude for the past and supplication for the future. In which order should they be addressed? One would think that first we should thank the Ribono Shel Olam for the past and then we can proceed to ask for more of the same in the future. But that is not what the Rambam says. First, he tells us to cry out to the Ribono Shel Olam for our future needs, and only afterward does he tell us to thank and praise Him for all He has done for us in the past. Why does the Rambam reverse the order?

Dovid Hamelech states (Tehillim 3:9), "Salvation is for Hashem, Your people must bless You forever." Rashi sees a powerful connection between the beginning and the end of this statement. "It is His obligation to save His servants and His people," writes Rashi, "and it is the obligation of His people to bless and praise Him." In other words, there is a pact, a covenant of reciprocal obligations. Why does the Ribono Shel Olam want to save His people? Because when He does, they will praise Him for it. Therefore, by being prepared to sing His praises for everything He will do for them, they merit having those things done for them. The key to everything is praising and thanking Him. That is what He wants.

Of course, anyone with the slightest bit of sophistication in the concept of the divine understands that the Ribono Shel Olam does not need our gratitude and praises in the way people desire to be thanked and praised. All the Ribono Shel Olam wants is to bring humankind, and Klal Yisrael in particular, ever closer to Him so that they will rise to ever higher levels of spirituality and holiness. When we thank and praise Him, we are propelled upward, and that is exactly what He wants.

Therefore, if we want our *tefilos* to be effective, we must resolve from the beginning that we stand ready to thank and praise Him, and by virtue of that resolve, we will merit that our *tefilos* should be answered. The Ribono Shel Olam wants to help; even more, He is committed to help. Because *al amcha birchasecha selah*, because we are obligated to thank Him. It is, in fact, quite possible that many of the difficulties people encounter in their lives come in order to lead them to *tefilah* and, thereby, to higher levels of holiness and a closer relationship with the Ribono Shel Olam.

We say in Shemoneh Esrei, "Heal us, Hashem, and we will be healed, save us, and we will be saved, because You are the object of our praise." We ask the Ribono Shel Olam to heal us. Why should He heal us? Because "You are the object of our praise."

The Tefilah of a Child ❧ 271

Because when You heal us we will praise You, and that is what You ultimately want us to do.

This is why the Rambam first tells us to cry out for our future needs and only afterward to express gratitude for the past. When a person is in distress, and he cries out to the Ribono Shel Olam to save him, he must at that very moment also thank Him for everything He did for him in the past. Even if he has already thanked the Ribono Shel Olam again and again for His past kindnesses, he must thank Him once again when he *davens* for help. Why? To demonstrate that he will thank and praise the Ribono Shel Olam when he is helped, just as he is thanking and praising Him now for His past help. Because that is what the Ribono Shel Olam wants from a person above all else — to draw him closer.

There is no question that before asking for new favors we should express our gratitude for the old favors. It is common decency. But that is not what the Rambam is discussing. This person who is coming to plead for help has already done the decent thing and thanked the Ribono Shel Olam for past favors, perhaps even many times. Now he is coming to *daven* for the future, so the Rambam adds that after he has made his requests he should thank the Ribono Shel Olam again for all the old favors to show Him that he is a grateful person and that he is prepared to thank Him again for the new favors he will be receiving.

The Rambam concludes, "Whoever thanks the Ribono Shel Olam profusely and praises Him consistently is considered praiseworthy (*meshubach*)." This language reminds us of the final lines in the Avadim Hayinu of the Haggadah, "And whoever is profuse in telling the story of the exodus from Egypt is considered praiseworthy (*meshubach*)."

Rav Elya explains that the word *meshubach* does not just mean deserving of praise for doing a good thing. Rather, he connects the word to *yayin meshubach*, fine wine, wine that has improved. By speaking at length about the exodus, says Rav Lopian, a person becomes improved. Here, too, we can say that by thanking and praising the Ribono Shel Olam profusely, we become *meshubach*, we become improved, we become better, higher, holier, worthier people, and this in itself makes our *tefilos* more effective, as we have discussed before.

There is a well-known *passuk* that we all know (I Divrei Hayamim 16:35), "And you shall say, 'Save us, O Lord of our salvation, gather us in and rescue us from the nations, so that we may give thanks to Your holy Name and glory in Your praises.'" What is this *passuk* saying?

The Mabit in *Sefer Beis Elokim* writes that this *passuk* expresses our hope that the bond of *tefilah* that existed in the dark exile, when we continuously pleaded for the Ribono Shel Olam's mercy and thanked Him for it, should not be diminished in the future when we will no longer be oppressed and persecuted. On the contrary, we *daven* that this bond will grow even stronger in the future when we will thank and praise Him endlessly for His kindness and greatness and we will see with perfect clarity that praising Him is our ultimate goal and the essence of our being.

We do not have to wait for the end of our exile and banishment to achieve this high ideal of *tefilah*. We can and should aspire to it right now. In this benighted exile, it is easy to be distracted by the difficulties and misfortunes that assail us from all sides and force us to cry out to the Ribono Shel Olam in anguish and desperation. But we should not forget the central purpose of our existence. We should not forget that above all else we have been born into this world to reach out to the Ribono Shel Olam and draw ourselves closer to Him. We should not *daven* to Him just because we need relief from our hurt. Rather, we should use our hurt as an opportunity to *daven* to the Ribono Shel Olam, to express our gratitude to Him for the past and the future and, thereby, to fulfill our purpose in life.

This is the essence of *tefilah*.

So let's summarize. First, we must recognize that *tefilah*, the astonishing phenomenon of a human being speaking directly to the Ribono Shel Olam, has the most sublime roots. It affects every person in ways that we cannot possibly imagine. Nevertheless, when we are considering *tefilah* in its most basic role, we may wonder how to deal with *tefilos* that do not bring us the desired results. The first thing we must realize is that *tefilah* is a *mitzvah* we are obligated to do regardless of whether or not it will be effective. Second, our *tefilos* may have been effective in other ways that we did not even consider. If a *tefilah* changes a divine decree, it is only because we have transformed ourselves through *tefilah*, and the decree no longer applies. If the *tefilah* helps others for whom we *davened*, it is because they earn the merit of being the cause of the transformation that occurs in those who *daven*. Finally, *tefilah* can be effective for us if we show the Ribono Shel Olam that we will express our gratitude for the blessings we are requesting.

◄§ The Greatest Gift

Most of these ideas are much too sophisticated to be conveyed to a child, but it is important that we ourselves understand the role of *tefilah* before we can consider what and how much to tell the children.

The first thing to tell the child is that *tefilah* is the way we express our gratitude to the Ribono Shel Olam. Just as we say a *berachah* to thank Him for the food we are about to eat, we also have to thank Him for all the good things He has done for our families and will continue to do in the future.

As the child grows older, you can begin to talk to him about developing a relationship with the Ribono Shel Olam. You can point out to him that, as he knows, a grandchild visits his grandparents often. That is how he stays close with them, how he expresses his love and respect for them. So how do we visit the Ribono Shel Olam? We go to *shul* and tell Him how much we love and admire Him. And we tell Him that we know that everything we are and all we have depends on Him alone, and we ask

Him for certain things to show that we understand that whatever we get comes only from Him.

This is where the ticklish part comes in. You have to point out to the child that parents don't always do what their children ask for, even though parents love their children with all their hearts. Why is that so?

If the child can't answer, you can help him. It's because the child doesn't always know what's best for everyone. Perhaps if he gets what he wants, his brothers and sisters will feel bad and the neighbor's children will be jealous. Perhaps there are other reasons why they should not give the child what he wants. The child has to know that his parents love him and that they are making a decision that's for his own good and for the good of everyone around him.

It is the same when we *daven* to the Ribono Shel Olam. He loves us and wants to make us happy. But He has to consider what is best for us, what is best for our family and what is best for other people. And we have to trust that He always makes the right decisions, even if we don't understand them.

The main thing you have to impress on the children is that the Ribono Shel Olam gave us a *mitzvah* to *daven* because He wants us to be close to Him. You have to tell them that *tefilah* is like a free pass to go in and speak with the King of the Universe at any time. And whether or not He decides to give us what we want, the *tefilah* itself is our greatest gift.

CHAPTER THIRTY-ONE

The Final Redemption

Most children have heard about Mashiach. They know that we're in *galus* and that one day Mashiach will come and bring us all back to Eretz Yisrael. They hear stories and sing songs, and they know that we are waiting for this to happen.

In the past, when the Jewish people suffered horrendous persecution in Europe and other lands, the idea of Mashiach was very meaningful to the children. They shared the fear and anxiety of the adults, and like the adults, they drew hope from the thought that one day Mashiach would come and redeem us all.

In our times, however, especially in the United States, we do not feel the same kind of oppression and persecution that were so much a part of daily life,. What then drives us to yearn for the coming of Mashiach? That is an old saying that if you hear a rich man sigh and say, "If only Mashiach would come already," you can rest assured that he is having problems in his business. Otherwise, why would he be dissatisfied with life as it is?

This is a serious question for both adults and children. For the adults at least, we can hope that they have an appreciation of the wondrous future that awaits us when Mashiach comes, a future far more exhilarating than even the most comfortable material circumstances in our present situation. But what about the children? Take a child who grows up in a free society, in a predominantly Jewish neighborhood, who lives in a large comfortable house, who has every one of his material needs fulfilled in abundant measure, who goes to camp every summer. What is he lacking? What would motivate him to yearn for the coming of Mashiach?

❧ Belief and Anticipation

One of the Rambam's Thirteen Principles of Faith is belief in the coming of Mashiach. We say, "*Ani maamin* … I believe with perfect faith in the coming of Mashiach. And even though he tarries, nonetheless I await his coming every day."

The Brisker Rav points out that this particular Principle is presented in question-and-answer format. I believe in Mashiach. But even though he is taking so long? Yes, I await his coming every day anyway. Why is it presented in this way? We don't find this language in the expression of any of the other Principles of Faith. Why is the Principle of belief in the coming of Mashiach different?

For instance, says the Brisker Rav, there is the Principle regarding reward and punishment. "*Ani maamin* … I believe with perfect faith that the Creator, blessed be His Name, rewards those who keep His *mitzvos* and punishes those who transgress His prohibitions." Here, too, we could have said, "I believe with perfect faith that the Ribono Shel Olam rewards and punishes, and even though we see that sometimes the righteous suffer and the evil prosper, I believe it anyway."

Another example is the Principle regarding the incorporeality of the Ribono Shel Olam. "*Ani maamin* … I believe with perfect faith that the Creator, blessed be His Name, has no body, that He cannot be conceived in physical terms and that nothing compares to Him." We could have said, "I believe with perfect faith that the Ribono Shel Olam has no body, and even though there are numerous references to His legs, hands, fingers, eyes and ears, these are only expressions relatinig to the divine powers."

Obviously, it was not the Rambam's intention to raise questions and give answers in his presentation of the Principles of Faith. Nevertheless, he chose to do so in the Principle of belief in Mashiach. Why is this so?

The Brisker Rav explains that the words of the Rambam are not a question and answer at all. Rather, they address the two fundamentals of the belief in the coming of Mashiach.

The Rambam writes (I Melachim 11:1), "In the future, the King Mashiach will arise and restore the Davidic Kingdom to its original state. He will build the Beis Hamikdash and gather in the exiles of Israel. All the laws of old will be reinstated in his days. Offerings will be brought. Sabbatical and Jubilee years will be observed in accordance with all the *mitzvos* stated in the Torah. Whoever does not believe in him or whoever does not await his arrival denies not only the prophecies of the Neviim but Moshe Rabbeinu and the Torah. For the Torah bears witness regarding him, as it says (Devarim 30:3-4), 'And Hashem your Lord will return your captives and have mercy on you, and He will return and gather you in from among the nations among whom He has dispersed you there. If your exiles shall be at the ends of the heavens … And Hashem your Lord will bring you to the land ….'

These explicit promises in the Torah encapsulate everything the Neviim will prophecy in later times."

The Rambam states in no uncertain terms that it's not enough to believe Mashiach will come someday. We also have to await his arrival. We have to believe in a very real sense that he may arrive at any moment. It's not just an abstract piece of knowledge, something we know but doesn't play a role in our lives, something that will happen in a vague future, a future as nebulous as the distant past. That type of knowledge and belief is not enough. We have to believe that it is something that may happen immediately, that for all we know his arrival may very well be imminent. And if a person believes that Mashiach will come but does not anticipate and await Mashiach's imminent arrival, he is also considered a heretic.

This, concludes the Brisker Rav, explains the language of the Principle of belief in Mashiach. There are two elements to this Principle. First, a person has to believe that Mashiach will one day come. Second, he has to anticipate and await his arrival every day. And if a person accepts the first element but does not accept the second element, he is considered to have rejected this fundamental principle of our faith.

The words of the Brisker Rav are clear and illuminating, but we are still left with a question. Why isn't it enough for someone to believe with all his heart that the Ribono Shel Olam has not forgotten about us, that He guards over us in our long and dark exile and that He will one day send us Mashiach to redeem us and bring us back to a glorious future in Eretz Yisrael with a rebuilt Beis Hamikdash? Why is it so critical to await his arrival every day? Why should it be that if, in the words of the Rambam, he does not await his arrival, "he denies not only the prophecies of the Neviim but Moshe Rabbeinu and the Torah"?

It is true that the Navi tells us (Chavakuk 2:3), "If he tarries, await him." But all this *passuk* is telling us is that we have an obligation to await him. There is no indication in these words that if a person does not await the coming of Mashiach he is considered to have denied the fundamental belief that Mashiach will one day come and redeem us.

Furthermore, there is no indication in any of the *pesukim* from the Torah the Rambam brings, as quoted above, that a person who does not await the imminent arrival of Mashiach with anticipation is considered to have denied that Mashiach will ever come. All the Torah tells us is that the Ribono Shel Olam will one day gather in our exiles and bring us back to Eretz Yisrael.

Perhaps we can resolve these questions with a parable. Let us imagine there is a poor man, a pauper who does not know from one moment to the next where he will find his next crust of bread. He has no friends or supporters who can help him out in his dire need, but he does have a wife and a house full of little children who are always on the verge of starvation. He has no prospects and no hope of finding a decent livelihood in the foreseeable future. He is depressed and despondent, and every day, he walks around in a cloud of darkness.

One day, a *tzaddik* who lives in the same town appears on his doorstep. Everyone knows that an untrue word never crosses the lips of this holy man and that if he makes a promise it is invariably fulfilled.

The poor man invites the *tzaddik* into his house and they sit down together.

"I had a dream about you last night," says the *tzaddik*. "In my dream, I received a message from Heaven that I was to deliver to you."

The poor man shrinks back in fright.

"No, no," said the *tzaddik*. "There is no need to be frightened. It was a good message. I am to tell you that you should not give up hope. Although your life is bleak and harsh right now, it will become much better. One day, you will wake up in the morning and right there on your kitchen table you will find a large treasure, more than enough to support you and your family in comfort for the rest of your lives. Better times are on their way."

The poor man is breathless with excitement. "When will this happen?"

"I don't know," says the *tzaddik*. "I was not told when it would be, but I was assured that it would happen."

The *tzaddik* leaves, and the poor man is beside himself with joy. Because of the reputation of the *tzaddik*, the poor man has no doubt that the message is genuine and that his fortunes will change. He just does not know when it will happen.

The next morning, the poor man wakes up and immediately runs to the kitchen table to check if the treasure has appeared. There is no treasure. He is disappointed but not discouraged, because he knows without a doubt that it will come to pass one day. He just has to be patient.

Days and months go by, and still he finds no treasure. But it does not matter. His life has been transformed, and although he is forced to live with privation and hardship, the cloud of darkness has gone. His life is now illuminated with hope.

It does not matter how long it takes for the promise of the *tzaddik* to come true. Every day without fail, when he gets up in the morning, the poor man checks to see if his treasure has arrived, because he knows beyond the shadow of a doubt that it will be there one day.

It is the same with the belief in the coming of Mashiach. It is not just that we believe Mashiach will come one day and redeem us. We also believe that the times of Mashiach will be more wonderful for Klal Yisrael than any time that existed in the history of the world. It will be as if a treasure has appeared on our table. All our worries, concerns and problems will come to an end, and we will live in utter bliss. This is what the Ribono Shel Olam has promised us, and there can be no greater assurance than the divine promise.

So if we really believe this, how is it possible that we do not wake up every morning and wonder if Mashiach has already arrived or at least if this is the day that it will finally come to pass? If we gave more than lip service to the coming of Mashiach, if it was a reality for us rooted deep in our hearts, we would surely await his imminent arrival with eager anticipation. And if it takes time, if days go by, even months, years and centuries, and Mashiach is still not here, we are disappointed but not discouraged. Because we know it will happen. The Ribono Shel Olam has promised it to us. So we live with hope and the knowledge that this long and bitter exile will one day come to an end.

This is how it must be. It can be no other way. If someone truly believes that Mashiach is coming and that the redemption will be the end to all out troubles, how is it possible that he does not think about it all the time? How is it possible that he does not await that blessed day with eager anticipation? That is why the Rambam writes that if someone does not await the arrival of Mashiach with eager anticipation he is considered to have denied the prophecies of Moshe and the Neviim.

What will it be like when Mashiach finally arrives?

The Rambam writes (Melachim 12:4-5) that the age-old yearning for the coming of Mashiach is not because Klal Yisrael wants to rule over the entire world. It is not because we want to dominate the non-Jews. It is not because we want the whole world to look up to us and honor us. And it is not because we want to eat and drink and have a good time. It is because we would have the opportunity to learn the wisdom of the Torah without any interference or distractions so that we can earn a share in Olam Haba.

According to the Rambam, we will still have the opportunity to grow in Torah and *mitzvos* once Mashiach arrives. The times of Mashiach will not only be a reward for the past but an opportunity for the future. It will be the final opportunity to carve out for ourselves a better share in Olam Haba. True, it will be a time of great material abundance, but the purpose of that abundance is to free us from the struggle to earn a livelihood. We will have everything we need with no effort or distractions.

Our time will be ours, and the choice will be ours. And what we do with that time will determine what and where we will be for all eternity. The times of Mashiach will be the final opportunity to gain the best possible share in Olam Haba.

◄§ The Lexicon of Mashiach

This is how we can tell our children about Mashiach. If we have prepared them properly about the meaning of Olam Haba, we can now explain to them that Mashiach will give us the final opportunity to secure for ourselves a good place in Olam Haba.

Even if your children have all their material needs fulfilled, even if they are lacking for nothing that their hearts desire, a successful *chinuch* will have instilled in their hearts a love for Torah and *mitzvos* and a profound yearning for Olam Haba. If they see their parents living every day with the awareness that this world is a fleeting dream that flashes by and is gone, if they see their parents striving in all sincerity to earn a share in Olam Haba, they will understand what in life is real and what is an illusion, what is important and what is trivial. And then you can explain to them that no matter how good we have it here in this world right now, the coming of Mashiach will bring us the best opportunity possible to earn a good place in Olam Haba for all eternity.

But even if parents cannot convey to the child on a rudimentary level how the times of Mashiach will be better and superior to our own times, they should still continue to speak to the child about it. For the purposes of *chinuch*, it is not critical that the child conceive of the times of Mashiach as being better in a specific way than his present life. It is enough that he simply knows that the times of Mashiach will be better, even if he cannot visualize it. Most important is that the child become accustomed to hearing the lexicon of Mashiach. It should come naturally to him to hear and speak about Mashiach, even if it will take a bit of time for him to develop a more profound understanding of the concept.

On Pesach and Tishah b'Av, he should hear his parents speaking at length about the long-awaited arrival of Mashiach. In the course of everyday conversation, he should hear his parents speak hopefully about Mashiach. He should hear his parents talking about Mashiach when they are considering purchases of great magnitude and permanence. "Why do we need such a huge house and such an expensive automobile if Mashiach is coming soon?"

Those children who hear the name of Mashiach ringing in their ears, whose parents speak with passionate hope about Mashiach, whose parents always have words of yearning for Mashiach on their lips, whose parents sense the footsteps of Mashiach coming closer and closer, those are the children who will welcome Mashiach with open arms.

May he come speedily in our days. Amein.

Appendices

APPENDIX I

A Separation Between Light and Darkness

The following article is based on an address delivered by Harav Mattisyahu Salomon to the National Convention of Agudath Israel of America in the winter of 2003. It was prepared for print by Rabbi Yaakov Yosef Reinman and appeared in the January 2004 issue of the *Jewish Observer*. Some of the thoughts and ideas presented in this Appendix also appear in the chapters.

very week, when the magnificent spiritual experience we call Shabbos comes to an end, we greet the new week with a solemn statement. We bless and express out gratitude to the Ribono Shel Olam Who "separates the holy from the secular, the light from the darkness, the Jewish people from the nations of the world." We know that to keep ourselves pure and holy we must make a clear separation between our own society and the decadent cultures of the gentile nations.

The Beis Halevi draws a comparison among these three separations. We can see plainly that the separation between light and darkness is demarcated by twilight, which is the closest light and darkness can ever come to each other. There are also similar lines of demarcation between the holy and the secular, between the Jewish people and the nations of the world. Just as it is impossible for light and darkness to be fully together, so too is it impossible for the holy and the secular, the Jewish people and the secular world, to be fully together. There is a line, a margin that simply cannot be crossed. That is how the Ribono Shel Olam designed the world.

Should anyone attempt to cross these lines of demarcation, the Beis Halevi concludes, and try to come close to the gentile nations and participate fully in their culture, the gentiles themselves will push him away. The space of separation is unbridgeable.

From painful knowledge, we know that this is true. Our history has shown very clearly that the separation between light and darkness, between the Jewish people and the gentile culture is always there, whether we establish it for ourselves or whether the gentiles force it upon us. It is inescapable.

The challenge of our generation is to enjoy the blessings the Ribono Shel Olam has granted us without losing sight of that critical line of separation. It is far better that we establish it ourselves on our own terms than to have the gentiles do it for us, not so gently.

The Chovos Halevavos says that just as it is impossible for water and fire to coexist in one vessel so too is it impossible for the love of Olam Hazeh, this world, and the love of Olam Haba, the Next World, to coexist in the heart of a faithful person. You put water and fire together in one vessel, and one of them will displace the other. Either the water will extinguish the fire or the fire will boil out the water. But they cannot remain together in peaceful coexistence. In the same way, a person cannot have a passionate love for both this world and the next. Of course, he can love and enjoy many aspects and experiences in this world and use its benefits to help him prepare for the next. But to love this world with a fierce passion? To yearn for it for its own sake? That is impossible for a person who passionately cares about, loves and yearns for Olam Haba.

So how do we know where we are? What litmus test can we apply to determine our true attitudes?

There is a beautiful piece in the *Sefer Chareidim* that provides an answer. "Shuls and *batei midrash* are like an orchard for the *tzaddik* and a prison for the *rasha*." Two people go into the same *beis midrash*. For one of them, it is like an orchard, a wonderfully pleasant spot to spend a morning. For another, it's like a prison, a place from which to escape. One of them is *davening* with concentration and intensity and savoring every minute as he draws closer to the Ribono Shel Olam; he feels he's in a fragrant orchard. The other is looking at his watch impatiently, thinking, So when do we finish already?

So this is our litmus test. When do we look at our watches in the *beis midrash*? When do we feel that time is dragging on interminably? Is it when we are waiting for a *chavrusa* to arrive or for the *shiur* to begin? Or is it when we have had enough and cannot wait to escape?

Some people may become impatient and look at their watches simply because they do not have the ability to concentrate so hard for such a long period of time. They go strong for perhaps half an hour and then they grow tired and restless. I am not talking about these people. Everyone has to find a subject he enjoys, a *chavrusa* he likes and a *shiur* he finds stimulating. That takes some doing, but the effort is eventually rewarded. I am talking about the people who don't want to be there in the first place, who are looking at their watches from the first minute and cannot wait to escape.

To where are these people escaping? What awaits them outside the *beis midrash*? Is it Olam Hazeh or Olam Haba? Which do they love with all their hearts? Which is their source of true pleasure? It has to be one or the other. It cannot be both.

These are the critical questions we have to ask ourselves, especially when we consider our responsibilities to the next generation. How concerned are we about the future of our children? What messages are we sending to them? How have we used the great blessings of prosperity and opportunity the Ribono Shel Olam has given us? Have we used these blessing to encourage the love of our children for the timeless rewards of Olam Haba? Or we have perhaps allowed indulgences and temptations to enter our homes that can only inspire love for Olam Hazeh?

Have we clearly delineated for our children the *havdalah bein kodesh lechol,* the boundaries between the holy and the secular?

Let me mention just a few somewhat unusual examples to highlight the almost unconscious blurring of the boundaries.

Recently I saw a child with a balloon tied in her hair. A little child.

So I asked her, "Why is there a balloon in your hair?"

"Today I learned *beis*," she told me proudly. "*Beis* is for balloon."

The *aleph beis* is much more than an alphabet that enables one to read. It is part of the very Torah itself. For many children, learning the *aleph beis* is their first introduction to learning Torah. So why can't we connect the letter *beis* to *bayis*, as the Gemara does, and speak about the concept of a Jewish home and Jewish hospitality. Why connect this holy letter to a balloon? Is that the way to educate children by the standards of *kedushah*? I didn't ask whether *gimmel* was for girl, or whether *daled* was for jellybeans. But something is askew. Why are we mixing the holy with the secular?

Someone showed me an advertisement in the Charedi papers that states in large, bold type, "This Pesach inspire your soul — and the rest of your senses as well." What does that mean? Is this what the holy Yom Tov has come to mean to us? I understand that some people need to go to a hotel for Pesach, and I'm not taking them to task for it. But how about the rest of us? Because we can afford to go to hotels, we should use the Yom Tov as an opportunity to indulge "the rest of our senses"? Where is the focus on *vehigadeta levincha*, passing on our traditions and memories to the children? Where is the focus on family time? Where is the focus on the purity and holiness of the Jewish *neshamah*? All right, the hotel has two swimming pools, but is that what has become of Pesach?

Not long ago, someone told me, with quite a bit of pride, that he took his family to Orlando on Chol Hamoed Sukkos. "We had a *sukkah*. There were *minyanim* and even a Daf Yomi *shiur*. There were hundreds of *frum* Jews there — many of them *bnei Torah!*"

Many *bnei Torah*? If that is so, then I *must* be mistaken in my definition of *bnei Torah*! While it is certainly important to make Chol Hamoed an enjoyable and memorable experience for the children, is it necessary to make faraway amusement parks the focus of this experience? Will a Chol Hamoed spent in this fashion enhance the children's overall appreciation for the Yamim Tovim? And I'm not even talking about all the questionable aspects of going to such places. What happened to the time-honored traditions of sharing the Yom Tov joys with grandparents and other family, perhaps even visiting *gedolim* — and taking the children to a park for a few hours? Why shouldn't the children come away from a Chol Hamoed with a little inspiration?

What have we come to? Where have we lost the separation between the holy and the secular, between the Jewish people and the rest of the world?

Think of this. Every single new food that is developed for the market immediately sparks a competition for who gets to give the *hechsher* and who gets to package and distribute it for the kosher market. Has it ever occurred to anyone that there is no *mitzvah* to experience every possible taste and texture, that on the contrary, there is a *mitzvah* of *kedoshim tihyu*, of keeping our pleasurable indulgences under control?

A *dayan* in England asked me about a certain new food made from ingredients that exactly simulate the taste of pork; that's how it's advertised in the mainstream press. Someone in the community had approached this *dayan* and asked him to give the *hechsher* on this product for the kosher market. He wanted to know if he should do it.

I don't understand. Should a Jewish person go out and buy a product whose advertised selling point is that it tastes exactly like pork? Is this the level we've reached? Should we be so intent to share the experiences and the pleasures of the gentiles? Is this how to establish a separation?

Where is the sensitivity to *kedushah*? And without that sensitivity, how are we to protect out children from the terrible scourge of the Internet, videos and the images that confront them on every street corner?

If we don't tell the children about *kedushah* when they are young, if we don't impress on them that we live a different life, that there is a separation between our world and the outside world, what chance do they have for a life of *kedushah*?

We are not making the proper *havdalah*, and the results are evident all around the world. Why are the gentiles turning against us today more than they have just a few short years ago? It is because we have come too close. Since we do not keep our distance, the gentiles make the *havdalah* for us.

There is an old Yiddish saying that *"ven a Yid macht nisht Kiddush, macht der goy Havdalah."* Roughly translated, it means that when the Jewish people do not make Kiddush, when they do not have *kedushah* in their lives, then the gentiles make Havdalah; they erect the separation that we have failed to construct. That's it in a nutshell. If we don't set our own boundaries, if we are not conscious of what it means to be Jewish, there are other, more painful ways for the separation to be effected.

This has been part of our national experience for thousands of years, ever since we came too close to the Egyptians and they reacted. Do we have to wait for them to make the separation for us? Isn't it time to wake up and make the *havdalah* ourselves? And above all, isn't it time we fulfilled our responsibilities to our children?

The Chafetz Chaim writes in Mishnah Berurah (47:10), "It is the duty of fathers and mothers to be accustomed to *davening* that their children be *lomdei Torah*, *tzaddikim* and *baalei midos tovos*. They should especially concentrate on this plea in Ahavah Rabbah and in Birchos Hatorah when they say, 'May we and our offspring and the offspring of Your people, the House of Yisrael, know Your Name and learn Your Torah for its own sake.' And also in Uva Letzion, when they say, 'So that we should not struggle in vain nor give birth in confusion.'"

The Chafetz Chaim writes this in Mishnah Berurah; it is a *halachah*. It is our responsibility to *daven* for our children constantly, and any parent who doesn't do so is irresponsible. It's pure negligence, and I dare say, to use today's language, we could call it abuse.

What can you expect if you don't *daven* for them? You don't know with whom they converse. You don't know whom they meet. You don't know what they see. You really can't control them totally once they're out the door. The only thing you can do is shed a tear for them when you *daven*, and do so every day.

For what precisely do we *daven*? The Chafetz Chaim tells us to *daven* in Birchas Hatorah, which beseeches, "*Vehaarev na* … Please make the Torah sweet to our taste." That is what we want. Give our children a *geshmak*. If we would be asked to institute a *tefilah* for Torah, what would we recommend? We would be clever, no doubt, and ask for wisdom, insight and understanding.

But that is not what Chazal tell us to request. If we want to guarantee a durable attachment to the Torah, it has to be sweet. It has to be *geshmak*. And they also instituted that we should ask this for all other Jews as well, for the entire House of Yisrael. Why? Because every Jew needs millions of *tefilos* to support him and help him acquire a *geshmak* in learning.

We need each other, and the children need us most of all. Ask any of the unfortunate children who have not been successful, and they will tell you that they had no *geshmak*. That is why they went astray. And why didn't they have a *geshmak*? Because their friends and families did not *daven* for them sufficiently.

"Arise and sing in the night," says the Navi at the end of Eichah, "at the beginning of the watch. Pour out your heart like water before Hashem. Lift up your hands to Him for the souls of your children on every street corner."

Our *galus* today is a *galus* of the street corner. The children are swooning, fainting away on the street corners. That is where their *kedushah* drains away. That is where they get lost.

And what is the Navi's solution?

Tefilah.

Tefilah will give us and our children a *geshmak* in Torah and *mitzvos*. *Tefilah* will enlighten us and lead us to love Olam Haba rather than Olam Hazeh. *Tefilah* will give us the wisdom and the insight to establish clearly the boundaries between the holy and the secular, between the Jewish people and the gentile nations of the world. And only through *tefilah* will the Ribono Shel Olam send us Mashiach and lead us out of this *galus*, speedily and in our days.

APPENDIX II

Save Our Children

The following article is based on an address delivered to the Lakewood community by the Mashgiach at a mass rally during Asseres Yemei Teshuvah of 2005. Reportedly, over three thousand people were in attendance. It was prepared for print by Rabbi Yaakov Yosef Reinman and appeared in the *Jewish Observer* (January-February 2006).

As I look out at this large and crowded hall, with the knowledge that there are at least twice as many listening over speakers right outside the doors, my heart fills with pride for this holy community. *"Kesser yitnu Lecha malachim hamonei maalah im amcha Yisrael kevutzei mattah.* The *malachim,* the hosts of the upper world, along with Your nation Yisrael assembled below, are presenting You with a crown." That is what we are doing here today. We have come together — in our thousands! — to present the Ribono Shel Olam with a crown. We have come together here today to look for ways and means to preserve the holiness and purity of our homes. Above all, we have come together to protect our children from the appalling influences that threaten to erect barriers between them and their Father in Heaven.

When Chazal describe their pain and frustration with the endless spiritual ordeals of Klal Yisrael, they say, "*Hasatan adayin meraked beineinu.* The Soton still dances amongst us." That same Soton, who caused the destruction of the Beis Hamikdash, is still dancing among us.

What do they mean with these words? They should have said that the Soton is still present amongst us, that he is still enticing us to do *aveiros,* that he is still subverting us. But dancing? Why do they describe him as dancing? What does dancing have to do with anything? What is the significance of the Soton's dance?

Rav Eliezer Gordon *zatzal,* the Telshe *rosh yeshivah,* explains that the answer lies in the cadence and rhythm of a dance. It starts slowly and softly to the introductory strains of the music. Then the tempo of the music increases, and the dance gathers force. Soon the dancers are cavorting about the floor. The music goes faster and faster, and even faster, until the dancers go wild. That is the process by which the Soton draws us into his web. He starts off so slowly that we hardly sense any peril, but once he has induced us to dance with him, he speeds up the tempo of the dance until he forces us to go wild.

We are living in a period of our history when the Soton is going wild. His dance has reached a stage of absolute frenzy, and he has grabbed hold of us and is pulling us into the dance with him. We are faced with a terrible crisis and a terrible choice. The Soton has pulled us into the dance perhaps as never before in our history. He has grabbed hold of us — yes, even of some of our best and most outstanding people — and he is spinning us around and around, faster and faster. The danger is overwhelming. The questions cry out to us in desperation. What are we going to do? What choices will we make? Will we allow the Soton to draw us so far into his dance that we will never again be able to break away from him? Or will we rip ourselves away from his grip and save our holy *neshamos* from contamination and destruction?

I venture to add that if we do manage to rip ourselves away from the Soton while he is in the height of his frenzied dance, if he suddenly finds himself in a dizzying spin all by himself, he may lose his balance, so to speak, and collapse onto the ground. Then we may be rid of him once and for all, and Mashiach will finally come.

It is difficult to assess the ordeals that past generations faced, but it is beyond imagination that Klal Yisrael was ever confronted with a more insidious spiritual threat than the Internet, which threatens to destroy us today. Almost daily, we hear new heart-breaking stories of families torn apart, broken marriages and ruined lives, all because of the Internet.

The Soton has come up with a new tool, a new invention that has invaded the sanctuaries of our homes. You can lock your doors and shutter your windows against the outside world, but the Soton has found a new way to get in. He comes in through the wires or through the wireless airwaves. You think you are safe, but he is right there with you, drawing you into his dance.

For a faithful Jew, one who strives to live in holiness and purity, the outside world has always presented an endless parade of challenges, even more so in recent times when society has been increasingly characterized by a high level of technology, instant communication and moral laxity. We are no longer bound by the old restrictions; for instance, it used to be that a journey of any distance was a major undertaking, but today, we can be on the other side of the world in a few hours. We can go anywhere we please and do anything we choose, and that is why we are in such great danger.

The opportunities for *aveiros* are there as they never have been before. The temptations are right before us, easily in our grasp. And it is so easy to think that perhaps we can just touch it gingerly with our toes just to get an idea of what it is all about. But it never stops there. A mere glance can ultimately lead us down the road to destruction.

That is the world in which we live, but bad as it is, the Internet has made it infinitely worse. It used to be that a person at least had to make an effort to venture out into the forbidden reaches of the outside world. Today, the Internet has brought the farthest, most illicit corner of the outside world right into the heart of our homes. What is the Internet? It is the entire world condensed and reduced to digital code and piped into every online computer. Today, through the invention of the Internet, there are innumerable places where we should not be that can now be accessed with just the push of a button.

It used to be that a person who wanted to see what he shouldn't see or meet people he shouldn't meet had to make nerve-wracking preparations and endure heart-pounding anxiety. Today, the Internet allows him to do so in the privacy and comfort of his home where, with the push of a button, he can see images that will contaminate his mind or enter chat rooms where he can be exposed to the most alarming enticements. Today, the Internet allows him to do whatever he wants with impunity, without controls, with no fear of discovery, with the illusion that there are no consequences, no repercussions.

ᴥᔓ Why Eyes Shed Tears

There is a *sefer* titled *Machzeh Einayim*, written more than one hundred years ago by one of the *maggidim* of Bialystok. He asks a very interesting question. Why is it that the Creator constructed people in such a way that no matter what part of the body is injured it is the eyes that cry? If your hand hurts, your hand should cry. If your foot hurts, your foot should cry. Why is it that when any part of the body hurts it is the eyes that cry?

The answer, he says, is that the eyes are the magnets to *aveiros*. The eyes see and the heart covets, as Rashi writes at the end of Parashas Shelach, and the person is drawn down the path of the Soton. For the most part, when a person suffers physical pain it is as a result of the *aveiros* he has committed. Therefore, the eyes, which are responsible for those *aveiros*, are the ones that shed the tears.

Everything starts with the eyes, those wonderful organs that can do so many valuable things but can also do so much dreadful damage. David Hamelech says (Tehillim 119:136), "*Palgei mayim yardu eini al lo shamru torasecha*. My eyes have shed tears because they did not keep Your Torah." Rabbeinu Yonah points out that he doesn't say "because I didn't keep Your Torah" but rather "because they didn't keep Your Torah." He is talking about the eyes! The root of tragedy is that the eyes didn't keep the Torah.

So how can we protect ourselves from the Soton's dance? How can we preserve our innate holiness and purity as descendants of Avraham, Yitzchak and Yaakov? How can we screen our eyes from exposure to the images of sin? Only by erecting walls around ourselves and our homes, walls that shut out the pernicious influences of the outside world, by creating sheltered islands in the turbulent seas of iniquity through which we navigate. The ideal would be to remain within the *koslei beis hamidrash*, to seek refuge within the walls of our centers of Torah. But that is not always feasible for everyone.

For most of us, there are times when we have to step into the outside world, whether it is to earn a livelihood or for some other purpose. We must realize that when we go into the cities, the offices, the airports or wherever else it may be, we are exposing ourselves to images, messages and influences that are corrosive to who we are and to what we should be. In those cases, we must, as much as possible, carry our walls with us. Instead of looking about with wide-eyed wonder, we must walk with downcast eyes, deaf ears and minds focused inward. "*Al tevieinu lidei nisayon*," we *daven*. "Don't put us to the test." But before we have the right to beseech the Ribono Shel Olam, we must make our own efforts to avoid the tests. We must seek out the avenues of least exposure and stay within the invisible walls we create for ourselves. Otherwise, we take the risk of joining in the Soton's dance.

If we want to stay pure, if we want to stay away from falling into the net of *aveiros*, we have to do everything in our power to protect our eyes, and what greater risk to our eyes is there than the Internet? We have to be afraid to come close to it, to let it into our homes. And we have to realize that any *heter* we receive for accessing the Internet is only a *bedieved sheb'dieved*, a last resort.

I do realize that in today's day and age, many businesses depend, in one form or another, on access to the Internet. The first choice for faithful Jews is to seek employment and careers that are not dependent on the Internet. That is far and away the best option. But if for some reason — and after consulting with *rabbanim* — they consider this impossible, the next line of defense is to keep it out of the home. Let it remain in the office, in full view, so that everyone can see which sites are being accessed. As for those people that do their work, or a substantial part of it, out of offices in their homes, the need for safeguards and controls is that much greater. They should get the best filters available, and they should set up a system of accountability. As one example, I would suggest that husband and wife should make an agreement never to clear the History on their Internet browser and to make random checks of each other's History. In this way, there will always be a readily accessed record of all the sites they have visited, and there will be accountability.

But most important of all, safeguards have to be put in place to protect the children. We cannot control the behavior of adults. All that we can do is warn and advise them and hope they will act with the prudence and responsibility expected of adults. But we cannot demand of children that they act with maturity and responsibility. We cannot expect them to suppress their natural curiosity and act with a high degree of self-control. We have to keep them a million miles away from the Internet.

✍ Motorcars and the Internet

A while ago, someone who was aware of my opposition to the Internet came up to me and said, "Rabbi, you're not keeping up with the times. We live in the Internet age. You cannot reject the Internet, just as you could not have rejected the motorcar in the motorcar age."

Listening to this fellow, I realized how apt a comparison he had made. Everyone understands that there have to be rules governing the operation of a motorcar — speed limits, stoplights, traffic laws, automotive regulations, seat belts, fines for reckless drivers. Everyone understands that it has to be this way. Everyone understands that a motorcar is lethal, that if it is handled improperly and irresponsibly it can kill other people or the driver himself. No one complains that the rules and regulations governing the use of motorcars are intrusive or an infringement of privacy.

Well, the Internet is equally lethal, perhaps not as much to our physical well-being — although the danger of predators is real and frightening — but certainly to our spiritual well-being. A person's eyes take one look at an improper image, and it can stick in his mind. Can these selfsame eyes then say to the Ribono Shel Olam in all sincerity, "*Veha'eir eineinu besorasecha*, illuminate our eyes with Your Torah"? Even one look can be devastating, let alone many. How can anyone then deny that the Internet needs regulation — at least as much as a motorcar?

But most of all, it needs regulation for the children. Would any parents be so irresponsible as to give their young children the keys to their motorcar? Certainly not. Then how can parents even begin to consider exposing their children to the Internet?

Having an accessible computer with Internet capability in the home is like keeping a loaded pistol in a drawer in the kitchen. It would be almost impossible to keep the children away from the Internet. Installing passwords and even removing modems will not stop the curious child, especially because today's children are much more technologically knowledgeable than most parents. The only option for people that must have Internet-enabled computers in their home offices is to keep them securely locked up and out of reach of the children. If someone complains that even these minimal safeguards are too difficult, I would advise him to quit his job and go begging from door to door rather than jeopardize the Olam Hazeh and Olam Haba of his children. In any case, I think that anyone who can afford a computer can afford the simple safeguards to protect his children.

⇜ Guidelines and Safeguards

Recently, a group of Lakewood principals, in consultation with *rabbanim*, drew up a list of *takanos*, guidelines for the parent bodies. It was agreed by all that a child exposed to the Internet would be a negative influence and could conceivably bring down an entire class. Therefore, the schools would not accept a child whose parents had Internet in the home. If the parents insisted that they absolutely needed it, they would be required to produce a letter to that effect from one of the Lakewood *rabbanim*. They would also have to agree to keep the computer under lock and key whenever it was not being used for business.

It is to the great credit of the Lakewood community that the idea of the guidelines was well-received, as evidenced by this great gathering, which is truly a *kiddush Hashem*. The parents understand that these *takanos* are necessary to safeguard the well-being of their own children and to maintain the overall level of holiness and purity in the community. It is my hope and *tefilah* that this courageous step will serve as a shining example to other communities across the United States and around the world.

The Navi cries out (Eichah 2:19), "Arise, cry out in the night, at the beginning of the watches, pour out your heart like water in the presence of the Lord, lift up your hands to Him for the lives of your children who are swooning from hunger at the corner of every street." Our children swoon and faint away at the street corners, where they are exposed to the perils and temptations of the outside world. We know full well that no matter what we do, we cannot guarantee that our children will not be influenced and contaminated. The only choice is ceaseless *tefilah* for the physical and spiritual safety of our children, to say Tehillim for them and shed hot tears over them ever single day. But before we come to the Ribono Shel Olam with our pleas and entreaties, we must do everything in our own power to protect our children. Only then can we ask the Ribono Shel Olam to do the rest.

When Children Stray

The following article is based on an address delivered by Harav Mattisyahu Salomon to the National Convention of Agudath Israel of America in the winter of 2008. It was prepared for print by Rabbi Yaakov Yosef Reinman. Some of the thoughts and ideas presented in this Appendix also appear in the chapters.

When children go astray, the pain of the parents is very deep. Children are the continuity of what their parents represent. Everything parents struggle all their lives to achieve is preserved and perpetuated through their children. And when children turn away from the lives their parents have constructed, when they reject the values and ideals that form the foundations of the homes in which they were raised, parents cannot help but feel the profound anguish of abject failure.

When a child goes astray, it's a tragedy for his parents and family, but when large numbers of children go astray, it's a tragedy of much greater proportions. It's a danger and a tragedy for all of Klal Yisrael. At different times in our history, we've suffered epidemics of children going astray. During each of these times, different identifiable factors have come into play. Sometimes, these epidemics were caused by the assaults of relentless *kefirah*, sometimes by the materialistic attractions of the outside world, sometimes by problems within our own society, sometimes by a combination of many factors.

In our times, we are again suffering through such a terrible epidemic. Children are going astray in the thousands. It is, of course, our obligation to try and identify the causes and do whatever we can to remedy the situation. But my purpose here is to view this dreadful situation from a different perspective, to take the long view of history and consider why the Ribono Shel Olam is periodically allowing these factors to emerge and threaten the very existence of Klal Yisrael and uncover the message that He is sending us.

ᏉᏮ Divine Pain

Chazal tell us that when Klal Yisrael is in *galus* the Shechinah is in *galus* with us, that the Shechinah is suffering, so to speak, along with us. We cannot even begin to understand the concept of divine pain, because the Ribono Shel Olam is perfect and certainly feels no pain. The pain metaphor is used to represent the unfulfilled will of the Ribono Shel Olam and to impress upon us the extreme gravity of this lack of fulfillment. And it is our responsibility to care about the *tzaar* of the Shechinah and to include it in our *tefilos*.

The Ribono Shel Olam sent Yeshayahu to cry out in anguish before the First Beis Hamikdash was destroyed, *"Banim gidalti veromamti ...* I brought up children and elevated them, but they betrayed me." It was a powerful expression of the divine pain, so to speak. Klal Yisrael should have felt that pain and should have responded immediately, "Father, dear Father, we are sorry. We want to return and be loyal to You."

Unfortunately, Klal Yisrael did not hear the message and were driven into *galus*. And still they did not hear the message. So the Ribono Shel Olam decided to raise our sensitivity to the pain of wayward children, and from time to time, he subjected us epidemics of children going astray. What does it mean that children rebel? How does it feel when all our efforts to reconcile are in vain? Today again, we are hearing the Ribono Shel Olam's message of *banim gidalti*. Once again, we feel the Ribono Shel Olam's pain on our own backs.

We need to stop and ask ourselves a few questions. Are we doing all we should to fulfill the Ribono Shel Olam's objectives? Are we responding to His goodness and kindness? Are we acknowledging His love for us or are we complaining because we still lack certain comforts? Do we begin to understand what the Ribono Shel Olam wants from us?

Every period in *galus* has its trials and tribulations and has been labeled accordingly. There were eras of pogroms, of the Inquisition, of persecution, of expulsion, of slaughter. What is the classification of our own period of *galus*? We need only note that Yirmiyahu prophesied about a *galus* situation and gave it a name: The street corner. He said (Eichah 4:1), "Holy stones are poured out on the street corners." Our children's precious, holy *neshamos* now find themselves on the street corners, helpless and exposed. The Navi exhorts us (Eichah 2:19), "Rise up, *daven* to the Ribono Shel Olam in the middle of the night. Pour out your hearts like water toward the Ribono Shel Olam." Let us cry out to the Ribono Shel Olam, because our children are swooning from spiritual hunger. They are falling away at every street corner."

Who is at fault here? Some blame parents for not understanding their children. Some blame the schools. But we cannot underestimate the influence of the street, for that is where the *yetzer hara* is to be found. That is where the mockery of all that is holy and precious begins. That is where children take up the challenges and ask themselves, "Why should we listen to our parents?" That is where they get the impudence to reject their heritage. On the street corners.

✑ *Tefilah* with Tears

The Ribono Shel Olam is talking to us. The Navi's prophecy has come true. Too many of our children are on the street corners. And we must rise up in the middle of the night and pour out our hearts to the Ribono Shel Olam. We must *daven* for our children who are suffering a spiritual starvation. No matter what else we are doing to bring the children back from the street corners, it all begins with *tefilah*, which is the underpinning of our *chinuch*.

We have to beg the Ribono Shel Olam, as we say every day in Maariv, "*Vesakneinu be'eitzah tovah milfnecha.* Set us right with good counsel from before You." We have to beg the Ribono Shel Olam to give us the wisdom to deal with these problems and to direct us to effective sources of counsel and guidance. Parents have to cry out to the Ribono Shel Olam, "This is my future, and this is what we're here for. Nothing else matters. Help us!"

Rav Yechezkel Abramsky *zatzal*, the great gaon and *tzaddik*, once walked into the apartment of the Brisker Rav in Yerushalayim and saw him and his children were sitting around the table. The Rav was saying a *dvar Torah*, and his children were listening intently, their faces shining.

Later, Rav Abramsky asked the Brisker Rav, "What is the secret of your *chinuch*? How you were *zocheh* that every single child walks faithfully in your footsteps?"

"My secret in *chinuch*?" said the Rav. "*Tehillim mit treren.*"

Tehillim with tears.

That is the way to bring up our children. Tehillim with tears. This potent combination gives us an awareness of how to protect our children from harmful influences. From this, we gains the sensitivity to understand how to speak to them, when to rebuke and when not to rebuke. From this, we gain the *siyata dishmaya* to inspire them to want to walk in the footsteps of their parents. And from this, the Ribono shel Olam directly inspires them with *yiras shamayim*.

❧ Approaching the End of *Galus*

The Ribono shel Olam is talking to us, telling us that we're coming to the end of the *galus*. And the *tzaar* of the Shechinah has not yet been addressed. We have wasted a lot of valuable time pursuing wordly pleasures and distractions. If we had been more sensitive to the divine pain, the *tzaar* of the Shechinah, so to speak, we would have invested our *mitzvos* with much greater *geshmak* and enthusiasm. We would be different people, and we would set better examples for our children, and the curse of the street corners would disappear.

Rabbi Paysach Krohn tells a story about a certain playgroup in Antwerp that has a Shabbos play every Erev Shabbos. There's a Shabbos Mommy, a Shabbos Tatty and a beautifully set table. The Mommy lights candles, and the Tatty makes Kiddush. From week to week, the children take turns in the leading roles, and they enjoy it immensely. The play generates a *ruach* of Shabbos, which the children bring home with them.

One week it was Yankele's turn to be the Shabbos Tatty. The Shabbos Mommy lit the candle, and it came the time for Yankele to make Kiddush. The teacher poured the grape juice for him and said, "Now, Yankele, say Kiddush."

Yankele squeezed his eyes shut and rocked back and forth. "Oy," he cried out. "What a hard week I had. Such a hard week." He sighed and then began the Kiddush, "*Yom hashishi* ...."

If this is what the child sees in his home, if the weekly Kiddush begins with a groan, how is the child supposed to have a love for Shabbos? If the father welcomes Shabbos by saying Kiddush in a joyous *niggun*, if his face is aglow with happiness and excitement, those feelings will be transmitted directly into the hearts of his children and they will love Shabbos for the rest of their lives. But if the father starts off on the wrong note, all is lost.

The *passuk* says (Tehillim 112:1), "*Ashrei ish yerei Hashem*. Fortunate is the man who fears Hashem." The Gemara comments (Avodah Zarah 19a), "A man and not a woman? Rav Amram said in the name of Rav, 'Fortunate is the one who does *teshuvah* while he is still a man [i.e. in full youthful vigor].'"

The Beis Halevi wonders about the special fortune of one who does *teshuvah* when young since *teshuvah* in old age also wipes the slate clean. The answer, he says, lies in the next *passuk* (Tehillim 119:2), "His offspring shall be the mighty of the earth, a virtuous generation that shall be blessed." It is true that whenever a person does *teshuvah* it will be accepted. But what happens to his children if he only does *teshuvah* late in life when they are grown and gone? The earlier a person does *teshuvah*, the earlier he resolves to improve and perfect himself and focus on what is truly important in life, the more successful he will be with his children.

The Ribono Shel Olam wants us to draw close to Him. He wants our *tefilah*. But we have not yet responded as we should. Children are still swooning at the street corners. We do whatever we can to bring them back from those street corners, and if we want to be successful, we must turn to *tefilah*.

Rabbi Chaim Brim told me that he was once by the Chazon Ish, and a young man came and asked, "Rebbe, I'm trying so hard for so many years to learn, and I can't get a *geshmak* in learning. It's an ordeal for me just to sit by the Gemara."

The Chazon Ish gave him a *berachah* and told him, "Learn more, and it will be good."

When the young man left, the Chazon Ish turned to Rabbi Chaim Brim and said, "This young man is missing the tears of his mother by candle lighting."

Why wasn't he successful in learning? Because there was not enough *tefilah* to support him.

When I was Mashgiach in Gateshead, there was a certain *bachur* who was a less than average student, yet he always managed to get one of the best *bachurim* in the *yeshivah* to learn with him *b'chavrusa*. They never lasted more than one *zman*. At the end of the *zman*, they separated. To the amazement of everyone in the *hanhalah*, the next *zman* he would again succeed in finding a *chavrusa* from among the best *bachurim*. We all marveled at his success, even if it was short-lived.

One day, Rabbi Moshe Schwab, the senior Mashgiach, came bursting into the staff room and said, "I've learned the secret! I was walking up the stairs to the *beis midrash*, and I heard him speaking on the hallway telephone. He was speaking to his mother, "Mamme, you can stop saying Tehillim. I found my *chavrusa* for next *zman*."

How incredible is the *tefilah* of a parent, especially a mother!

Let us rise up to *daven* in the middle of the night. Let us pour out our hearts like water to the Ribono Shel Olam. Let us feel the *tzaar* of the Shechinah. Let us say to the Ribono Shel Olam, "We heard the message. We won't betray You any more. And we're coming closer."

Then the Ribono Shel Olam will say to us, "As you come back to Me, so will your children come back to you." Then we will see the fulfillment of the prophecy (Malachi 3:24), "*Veheishiv lev avos al banim veleiv banim al avosam.* He will reconcile the hearts of fathers with the children, and the hearts of children with their fathers."

Glossary

Note: All words listed in the Glossary are Hebrew unless otherwise indicated.

abba: father

Acharon: later Talmudic scholar

adam hashalem: complete person

aleph beis: Hebrew alphabet

aleph: first letter of the Hebrew alphabet

Amora(im): sage(s) of the Talmud

arbaah minim: the four species taken in hand on Sukkos

asor: ten-stringed lyre

Asseres Hadibros: the Ten Commandments

aveir(ah)(os): transgression(s)

avodah zarah: idolatry

avodah: divine service

azus panim: brazenness, audacity

baal agalah: wagon driver

baal gaavah: arrogant person

bachur(im): boy(s)

baruch Hashem: bless God

bein adam la'Makom: a person's relationship with the Ribono Shel Olam

bein adam lechaveiro: a person's relationship with other people

beis din: court

Beis Hamikdash: Holy Temple

beis: second letter of the Hebrew alphabet

ben sorer umoreh: a rebellious son

ben Torah: a Torah scholar

bincha (bneichem): your son(s)

bitachon: trust

bittul Torah: neglect of Torah

chassan: groom

chavalah: hitting

chavrusa: study partner

Chazal: our Sages

cheder (chadarim): elementary school(s)

chessed: kindness

chillul Hashem: desecration of the Name

chinuch: education, upbringing

chupah: wedding canopy

daled: fourth letter of the Hebrew alphabet

daven: pray

David Hamelech: King David

dayan: judge

derech eretz: respect

derash(ah)(os): lecture(es)

Devarim: Deuteronomy

Din Torah: lawsuit

divrei harav vedivrei hatalmid divrei mi shom'im: if there is a conflict between a teacher and his student, whose words do we heed?

divrei Torah: Torah thoughts

dmus diukno shel aviv: the image of his father's face

Derush: homiletics

dor: generation

ehrlich: sincere [Yiddish]

ehrlichkeit: integrity, sincerity [Yiddish]

eidelkeit: refinement [Yiddish]

emes: truth

emunah: faith

frum: observant [Yiddish]

gaavah: arrogance, haughtiness

galus: exile

gedolei Yisrael: great Jewish people

geshmak: enjoyment, gusto

gimmel: third letter of the Hebrew alphabet

gomeil dalim: kind to the poor

hachnasas orchim: hospitality

hakaras hatov: gratitude

Halach(ah)(os): law, laws

harbatzas Torah: dissemination of Torah

Hashem: God

hashgachah pratis: divine providence

heh: fifth letter of the Hebrew alphabet

im yirtzeh Hashem: God willing

ima: mother

Ir Miklat: City of Refuge

kabalah: license

kallah: bride

kalus rosh: lightheadedness, frivolous behavior, hilarity

kavanah: concentration, intent

kavod: respect

kedushah: holiness; (cap.) part of the Shemoneh Esrei liturgy

kefirah: heresy

Kesuvim: Hagiographa, Writings

kibud av va'eim: honoring parents

Kiddush: sanctification over

wine of Shabbos or Yom Tov

kinor: harp

kiruv: outreach

Klal Yisrael: the Jewish people

klei haseichel: instruments of intelligence

kochi ve'otzem yadi: my own power and strength

kollel: Torah school for married scholars

Krias Yam Suf: the Splitting of the Reed Sea

kushia: question

lamdan: creative Talmudic scholar

lashon hara: gossip, slander

Lashon Kodesh: the Holy Language; Hebrew

lechaim: toast

lesheim shamayim: for the sake of Heaven

lo saaseh: prohibition

maamar(im): articles(s)

maasim tovim: good deeds

malach(im): angel(s)

mashal: parable

Mashgiach: spiritual guide of a *yeshivah*; supervisor

Mashiach: the Messiah

matzah: unleavened bread

mechalel Shabbos: to desecrate the Shabbath

mechanech: educate, train

mechias zecher Amalek: the obliteration of the memory of Amalek

mekabel ol malchus shamayim: to accept the yoke of the kingdom of Heaven

menuchas hanefesh: inner serenity

mesorah: tradition

mevater: to forfeit or step aside

mid(ah)(os): character trait(s)

minhag: custom

minus: heresy

minyan: prayer group

mispallelim: members of a prayer group

mitzv(ah)(os): commandment(s)

mizbeyach: altar

mocheil: to forfeit, to forgive

moshav leitzim: an assembly of mockers

mussar sefarim: books of ethical instruction

naaseh adam: let us make a person

naaseh venishma: we will do and we will hear

nachas: parental pride

nachash: snake

namar: leopard

Navi (Neviim): Prophet(s)

ne'eman: faithful, trustworthy

nekudos: the vowel marks

nesham(ah)(os): soul(s)

nevuah: prophecy

niggun(im): song(s)
nirdaf: persecuted one
nivul peh: vulgar language
Olam Haba: the Next World
onaah: persecution
parashah: weekly Torah reading
passuk (pesukim): verse(s)
perek (perakim): chapter(s)
peyos: earlocks
prikas ol: insubordination
rachmanus: mercy, compassion
rasha(resha'im): villain(s), evil person (people)
rav (rabbanim): rabbi(s)
rebbe: Torah teacher
rechilus: gossip
regel: festival
Ribono Shel Olam: Master of the Universe
Rishon: early Talmudic scholar
rosh yeshivah: dean
rotzeiach beshogeg: inadvertent murderer
ruach hakodesh: divine inspiration
ruach: spirit
s'char va'onesh: reward and punishment
schmuess(en): talk(s)
sef(er)(arim): book(s)
segulah: mystical remedy, charm; treasured possession
seudas mitzvah: a feast in honor of a *mitzvah*

Shabbos: the Sabbath
shaliach: agent
shalom bayis: domestic harmony
shanah rishonah: giving special attention to the wife during the first year of married life
Shechinah: Divine Presence
shechitah: ritual slaughter
sheker: falsehood
sheminis: eight-stringed lyre
shemiras halashon: the avoidance of gossip and slander
Shirah: song of praise
shiur(im): lecture(s)
shlita: may he live long
shmuess: talk [Yiddish]
shochet: ritual slaughterer
shofar: ram's horn
shuckle: shake back and forth [Yiddish]
shulchan aruch: code of rules and regulations
Siddur(im): prayer book(s)
simchah shel mitzvah: the joy of a *mitzvah*
simchah: joy, pleasure
siyata dishmaya: divine assistance
taam: taste, rationale
tachanun(im): entreaty(ies)
takanah: enactment, guideline
tallis: prayer shawl
talmid chacham: Torah scholar
talmid(im): student(s)

tefil(ah)(os): prayer(s)
tefillin: phylacteries
Tehillim: Psalms
Teivah: box, Noah's Ark
teshuvah: repentance, return
teshuvah: responsum
treren: tears [Yiddish]
tzaar: pain
tzaddik(im): righteous one(s)
tzelem Elokim: [people, who are made in] the Image of the Lord
tzitzis: fringes
tznius: modesty

vaad(im): talk(s)
vav: Hebrew letter
yarmulke: skullcap
yasom: orphan
yeshivah: religious school
yetzer hara: evil inclination
Yiddishkeit: Jewishness [Yiddish]
yiras shamayim: fear of Heaven
Yom Tov (Yamim Tovim): festival(s)
zechus (zechuyos): privilege(s), merit(s)
zemiros: songs
zman: semester

This volume is part of
THE ARTSCROLL SERIES®
an ongoing project of
translations, commentaries and expositions
on Scripture, Mishnah, Talmud, Halachah,
liturgy, history, the classic Rabbinic writings,
biographies and thought.

For a brochure of current publications
visit your local Hebrew bookseller
or contact the publisher:

Mesorah Publications, ltd.

4401 Second Avenue
Brooklyn, New York 11232
(718) 921-9000
www.artscroll.com